I0729691

An Apothecary of Art

First published in the United Kingdom in 2023 by
Batsford
43 Great Ormond Street
London WC1N 3HZ

An imprint of B.T. Batsford Holdings Ltd

ISBN 9781849948142

A CIP catalogue record for this book is available from the
British Library.

10 9 8 7 6 5 4 3

Reproduction by Mission Productions Ltd.
Printed by Dream Colour Printing Ltd, China

This book can be ordered direct from www.batsfordbooks.com
and www.ravenousbutterflies.com, or try your local bookshop.

An Apothecary of Art

To soothe your soul

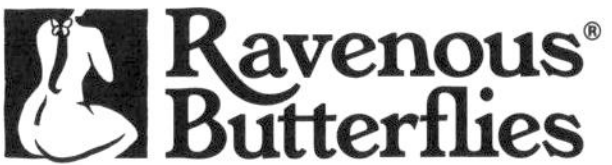

Ravenous® Butterflies

BATSFORD

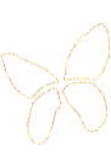

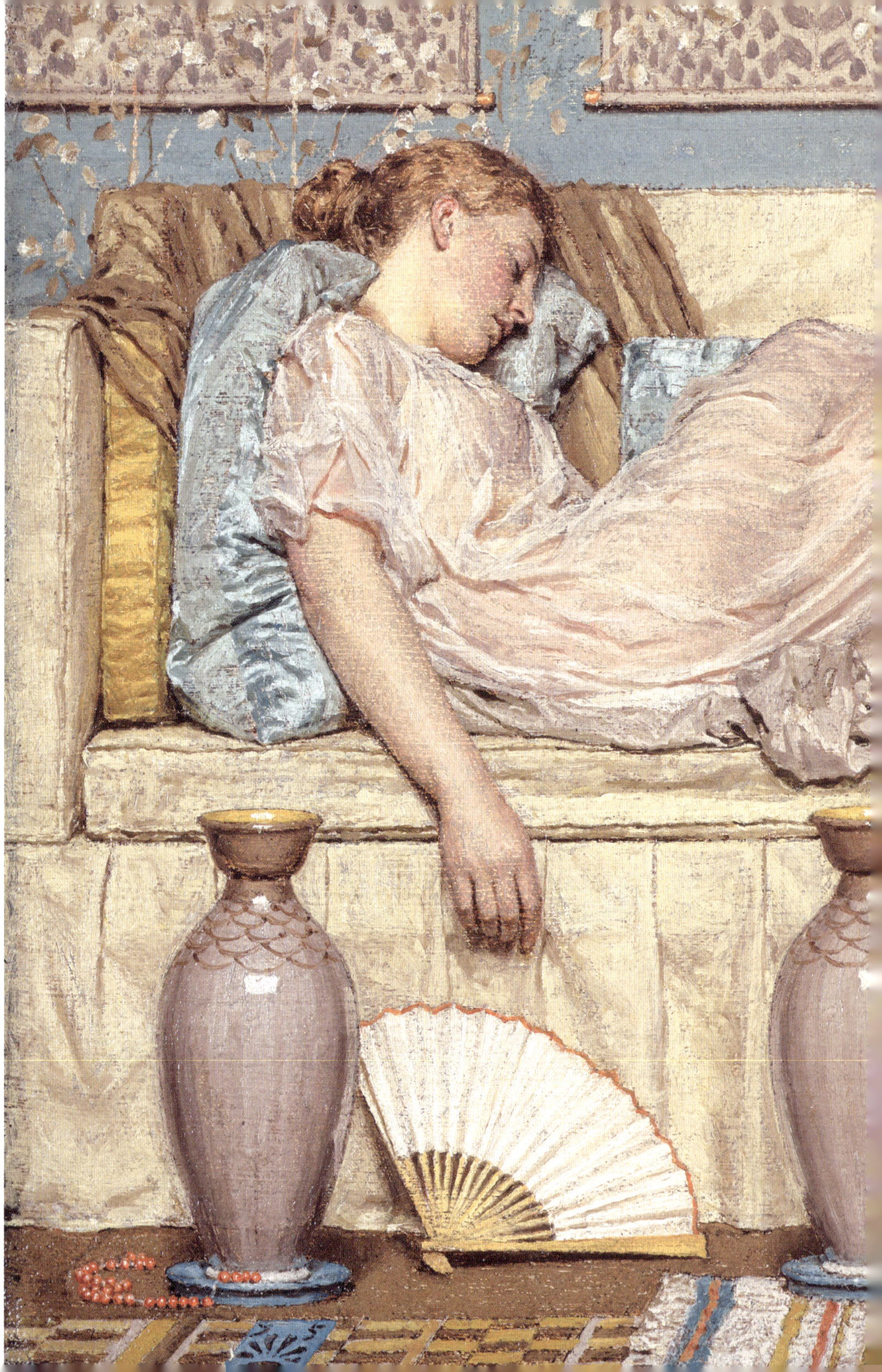

Joseph Albert Moore,
Beads, 1880

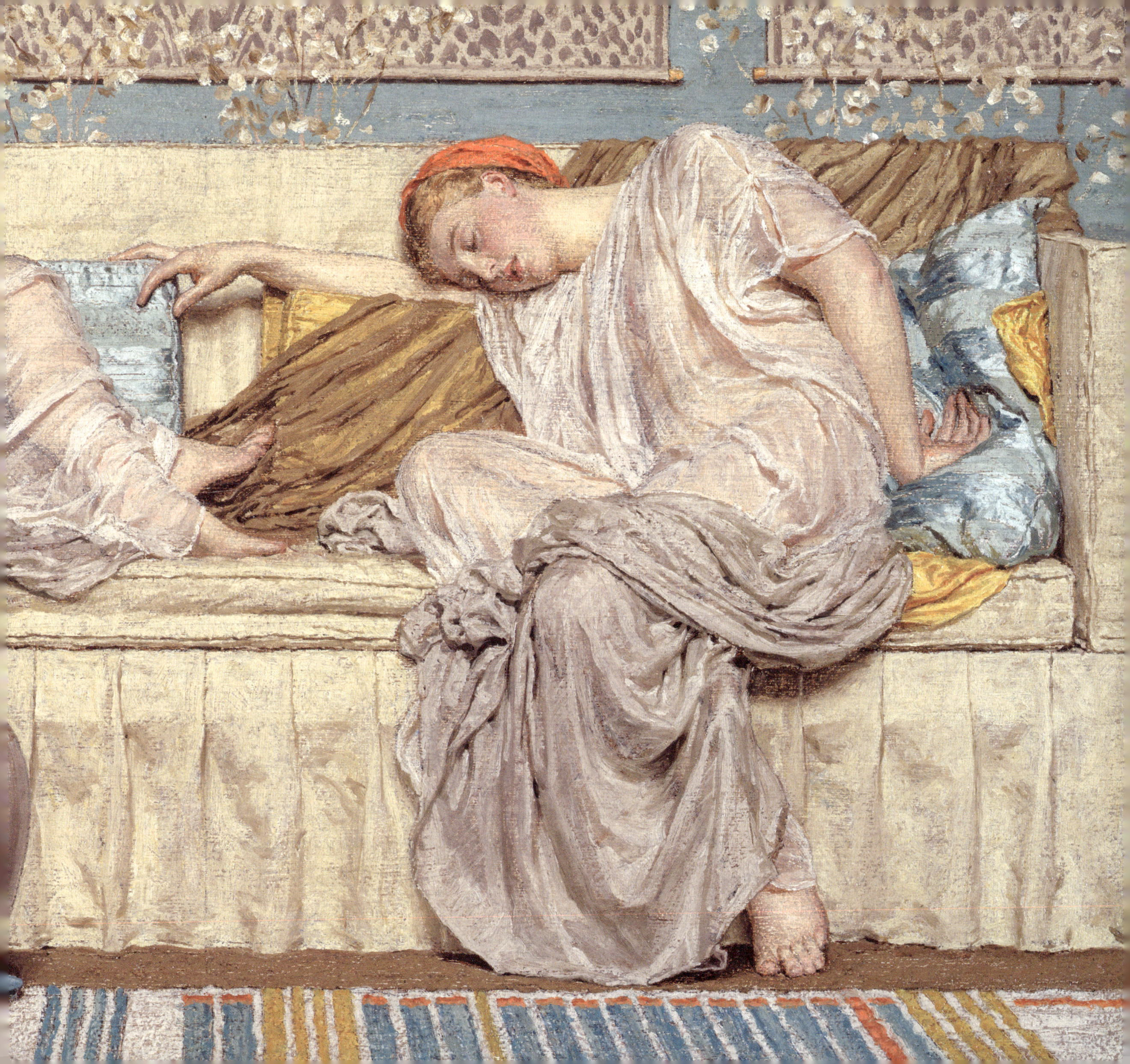

The journey finder

Travel through your emotional inner-scape; explore places and feelings along the way using this useful 'journey finder.' Simply match the emotion to the page number. You never know where you might land, or what you'll discover along the way.

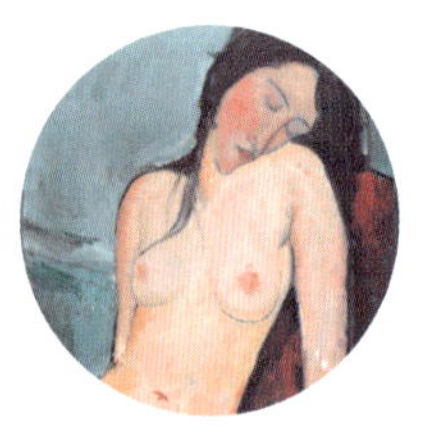

ACCEPTANCE

32–33, 58–59, 84–85, 110–111

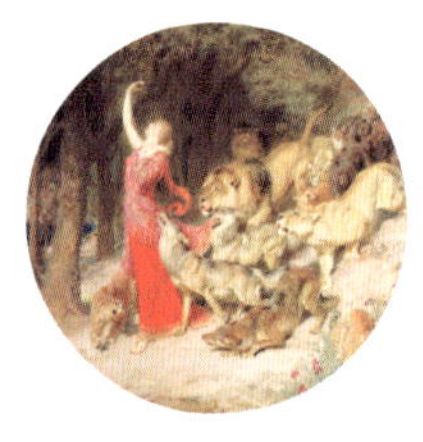

ANIMALS

56–57, 12–13, 118–119

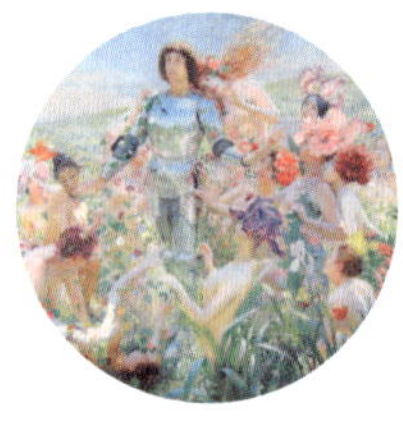

BEAUTY

28–29, 12–13, 18–19, 134–135

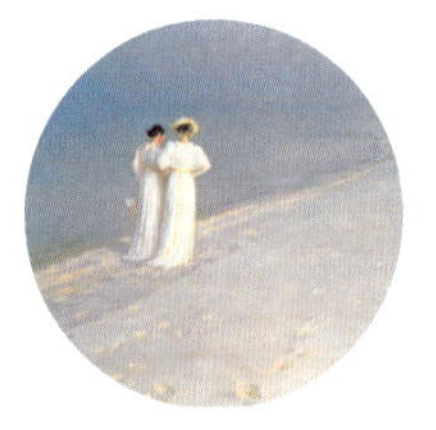

FRIENDSHIP

94–95, 116–117, 126–127, 136–137

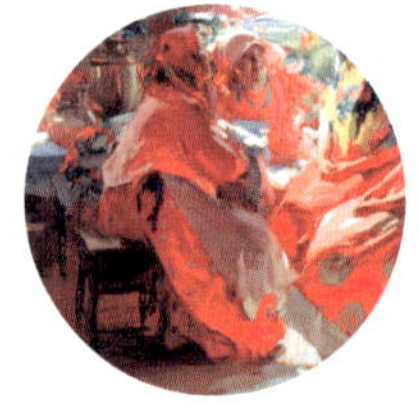

GRATITUDE

70–71, 74–75, 138–139

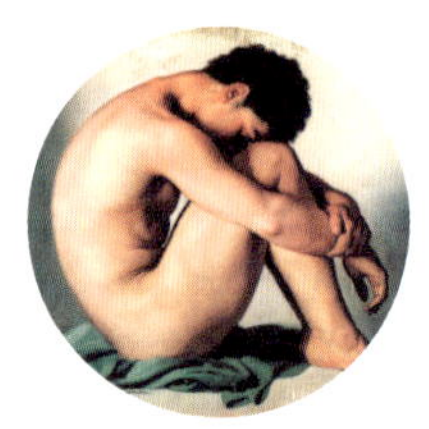

GRIEF

40–41, 92–93, 142–143, 170–171

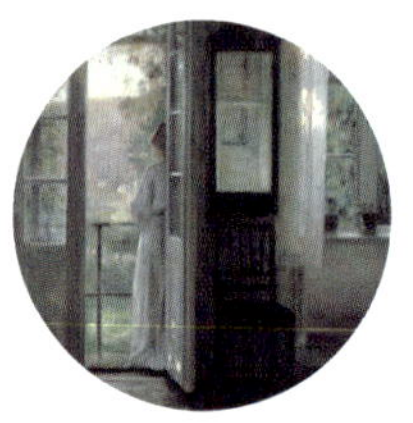

LOSS

82–83, 90–91, 112–113

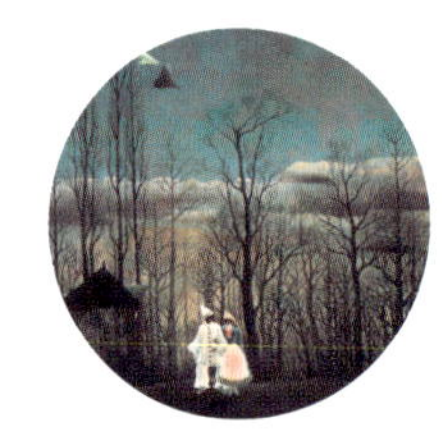

LOVE

30–31, 12–13, 42–43, 140–141, 52–53, 80–81, 164–165

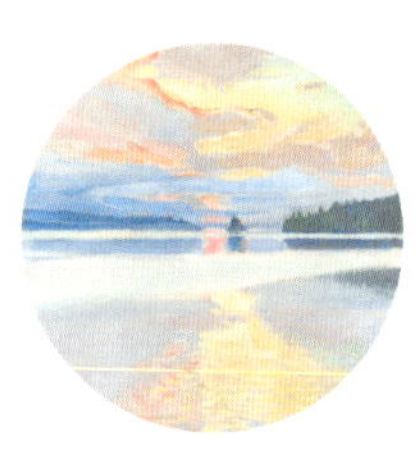

OPTIMISM

16–17, 54–55, 60–61, 122–123, 156–157

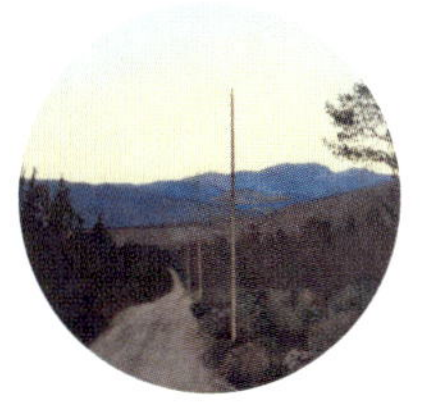

BECOMING

22—23, 72—73, 114—115,
130—131

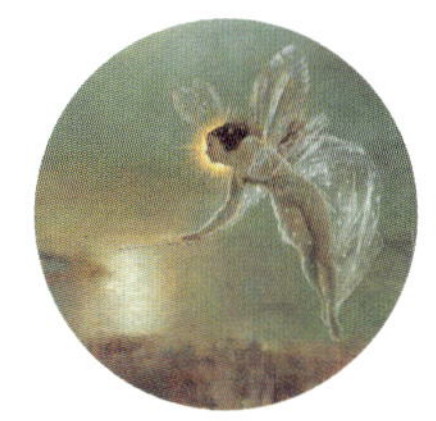

CHILDHOOD

38—39, 46—47, 64—65

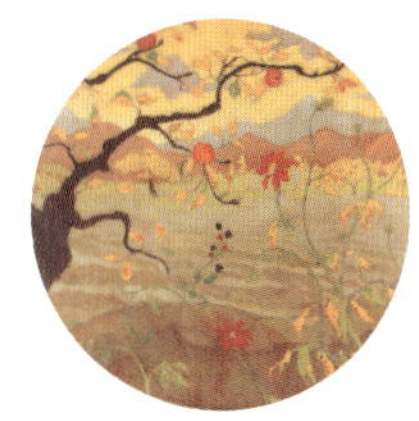

COURAGE

62—63, 14—15, 20—21,
96—97

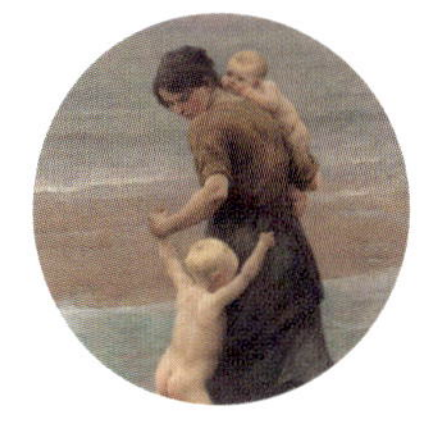

FAMILY

104—105, 154—155, 158—159

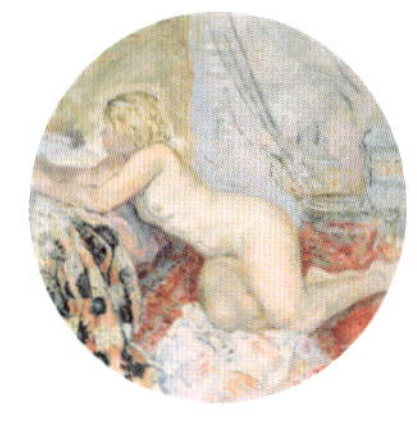

FREEDOM

66—67, 22—23, 100—101,
120—121

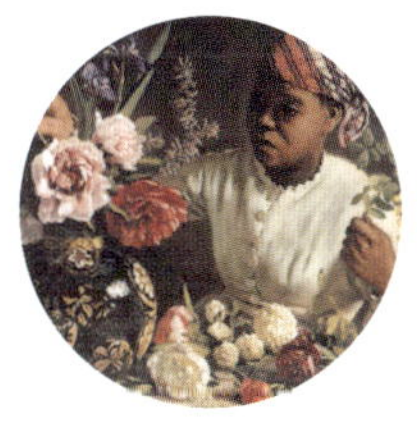

HOPE

36—37, 98—99, 128—129,
162—163

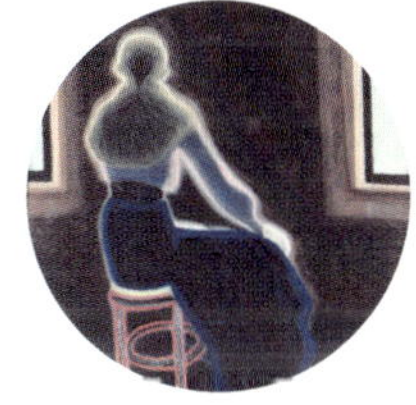

INSPIRATION

76—77, 16—17, 76—77,
146—147, 150—151, 168—169

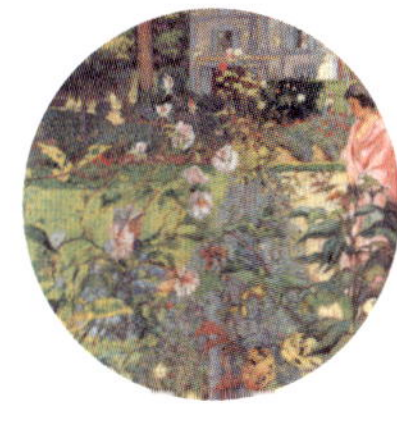

JOY

68—69, 12—13, 86—87,
144—145

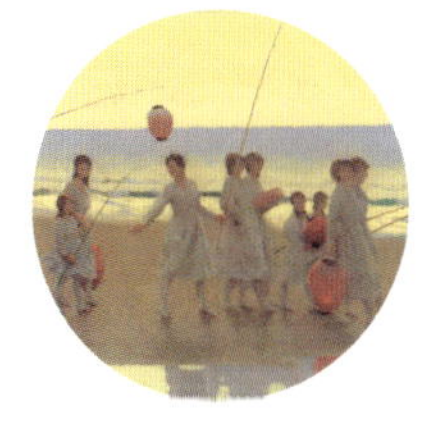

KINDNESS

20—21, 132—133

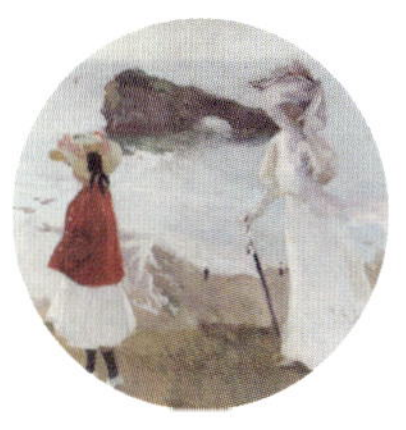

LEADERSHIP

14—15, 124—125

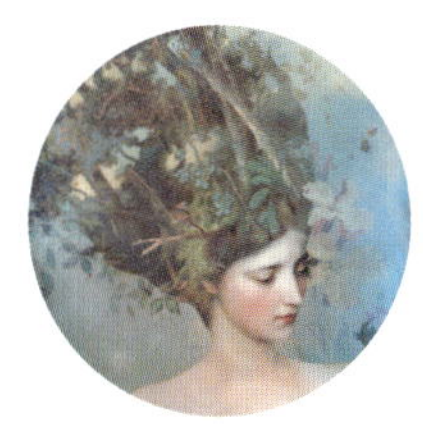

PEACE

34—35, 50—51, 102—103

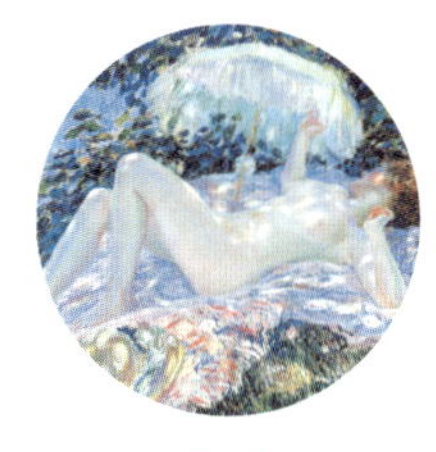

PLEASURE

24—25, 78—79, 148—149

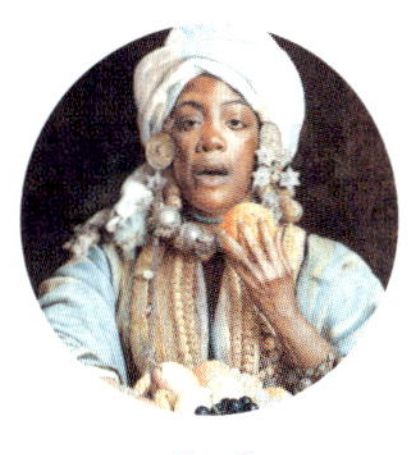

SELF LOVE

48—49, 44—45, 88—89,
106—107, 160—161

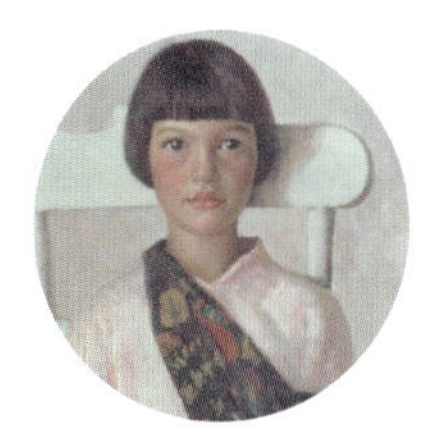

STRENGTH

60—61, 36—37, 58—59

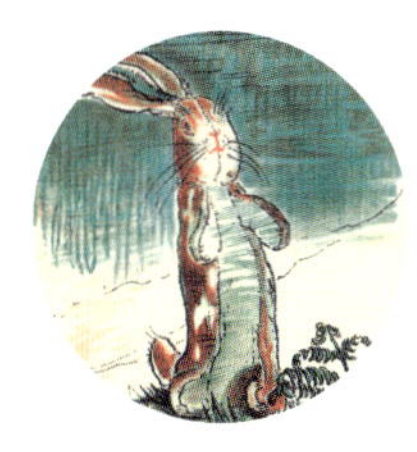

WISDOM

26—27, 108—109, 152—153,
166—167

Welcome to *An Apothecary of Art* by Ravenous Butterflies. Wrap yourself inside these pages, find a quiet place where nobody wants anything, nobody needs anything, and enjoy. Take some time, commune with the profound beauty found here, and breathe. Breathe in each work of art, its colour, light and texture, and speak the accompanying words gently in your head, repeat them, soak up their sound and essence. There's no right or wrong; this is a balm for the senses.

We all have our own phenomenology, and each one of us is unique. We have all led entirely different lives from each other, with varied experiences, but there are common threads shared by many. Birth, love, passion, success, failure, courage, fear, hope, loss and, eventually, death. The final stanza of Robert Frost's poem 'The Road Not Taken' expertly conveys these shared emotions and the choices we face in life.

'I shall be telling this with a sigh
Somewhere ages and ages hence:
Two roads diverged in a wood, and I—
I took the one less travelled by,
And that has made all the difference.'

How we respond to life's journeys, with each marvellous twist and unexpected turn, depends upon individual circumstances and the decisions we make. Ravenous Butterflies was born out of a desire to make a positive impact, to help make sense of the roads we travel, and to offer a companion in the darkest of times.

I've had my fair share of twists and turns, some of my own making and others a result of youth, stubbornness, and naivety. I've learned that with age comes knowledge, and with knowledge comes responsibility. Responsibility to grow, change, love oneself and live authentically.

The combination of authenticity and self-love are a powerhouse, and once I realised this, there was no turning back. Ultimately, Ravenous Butterflies helped me heal in anticipation of a bright future — through the awe-inspiring power of art and literature.

Let's rewind to the beginning. I was born in Sri Lanka, and my formative years were steeped in the tropics' humidity, sounds, smells and tastes. My father was a tea taster, and my mother his supportive wife. I don't remember my parents being around much, but Dad would read Oscar Wilde's short stories to me at bedtime, kindling my imagination. I was wild and free, a barefoot Indian Ocean girl who spent afternoons playing in the garden and swimming. At weekends, we would sometimes run away to the hills and tea plantations to escape the heat.

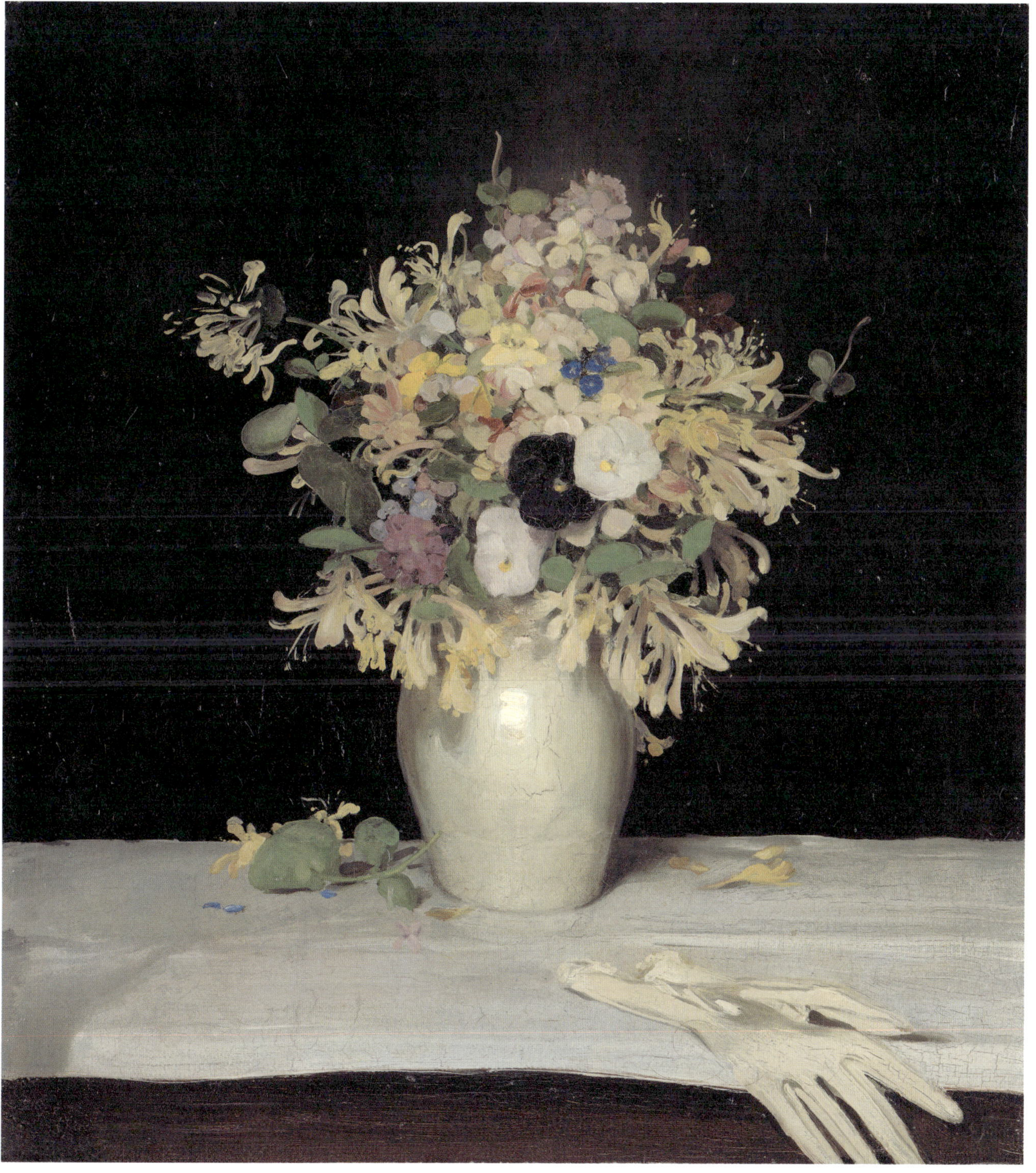

I was almost three when my brother was born and five when we moved back to the UK after a short stay in Malawi.

When we arrived in the UK, snow was on the ground, a frozen blanket of white. England was a strange and lonely land; apples replaced mangos, and cornflakes replaced curried eggs for breakfast. There was black and white television, something I'd never seen before, and the days were cold and dark. I didn't like it. I suppose I've been searching all my life to replicate those first five years of bliss, but time moves forward and, as my father rightly says, 'you can't trade backwards.'

At the age of seventeen, I met and later married my husband. We moved to London; he graduated in quantum physics, and I in fine art. The world was our oyster; we thought we knew it all! Unfortunately, mine was a lonely marriage, and rather than confront our differences, I ate to compensate for the emptiness I felt.

I painted, taught art and design, and worked in media before moving to New York for my husband's career, where I continued to eat.

It was a miracle when I became pregnant with our first child. By this point, I was morbidly obese and unable to walk unaided.

I shed half my body weight after undergoing weight loss surgery. Finally, I felt free. It was as if I was a butterfly emerging from the cocoon. I spread my wings and began to feel vital and beautiful; it was time to catch up with the decade or so that I'd lost. After becoming pregnant with our second child, we moved back to London and, not long after, had our third.

Unfortunately, our marriage deteriorated, so I sought help and began analytical psychotherapy, which was a revelation. I was given the tools to understand why I made certain decisions and how to take responsibility for my actions. The work I was doing allowed me to take control of my future, and with that, sadly, I decided to divorce. Although agonising for all concerned, it was the only way to free myself and give ourselves a chance to be happy.

During this traumatic transition, I decided to make something for myself that was wilfully optimistic and bursting with beauty. And so, my lifelong passion for the arts culminated in a little blog, Ravenous Butterflies. It was a virtual self-help diary, a space to post images and text that resonated with me. I posted what I found inspiring or uplifting daily, and it made me feel better. I'm a self-confessed technophobe and had no idea about social media's potential global reach and impact, but one post soon led to another. Everything was trial and error, there was never a grand plan and no commercial strategy to speak of. I remember the excitement I felt when I reached my first hundred followers, then my first thousand, a hundred thousand — and so it grew organically and continues to do so.

With every post comes a flurry of comments offering endless support and wisdom for fellow followers. People respond not only to the art or words but also to the effect that their combination has on the psyche. I've been repeatedly humbled by the discussions raised within the post threads, and the kindness and compassion shared so freely. Ravenous Butterflies quickly developed its own ecosystem, an open forum where everyone is welcome without judgement. I'm sure, like me, many friendships have been forged over the years. There's been laughter and tears, debates about love, loss, pets, relationships, freedom and hope. Everything and anything supportive has a place.

One thing is certain: the sum of the whole is far greater than its parts. Alchemy occurs when the images and text combine, resulting in a wellbeing balm for the senses.

Over the years, our audience has expanded, and so has my curiosity for the arts. I've learned more while sourcing images and texts for Ravenous Butterflies than I ever learned at school. I've also delved into aspects of art and literature that I previously knew little about, which is a constant source of pleasure and excitement. I recall the words of my favourite tutor: 'The trick is to find what you're passionate about, then it won't feel like work.' I'm fortunate to have achieved this.

There was one constant through all the roads less travelled: I never went backwards; I kept up my stamina and strength and continued forward, unburdened by regret. Through years of drama and heartache, Ravenous Butterflies became my compass, my one true star, keeping me moving on. It's not always easy to continue when you have no idea where you're heading or why, but I was sure to persist and keep going, through thick and thin.

This book is the culmination of all of these life experiences and a reflection of my time curating and growing Ravenous Butterflies. At last, something tangible that can be passed from hand to hand, human to human, soul to soul.

I made this for you, with love and gratitude always,

Curated by Lisa Azarmi,
founder of Ravenous Butterflies

'For myself I know not how to express my devotion to so fair a form: I want a brighter word than bright, a fairer word than fair. I almost wish we were butterflies and liv'd but three summer days — three such days with you I could fill with more delight than fifty common years could ever contain.'

John Keats, from a letter to Fanny Brawne (1819)

Martin Johnson Heade,
Blue Morpho Butterfly, 1865

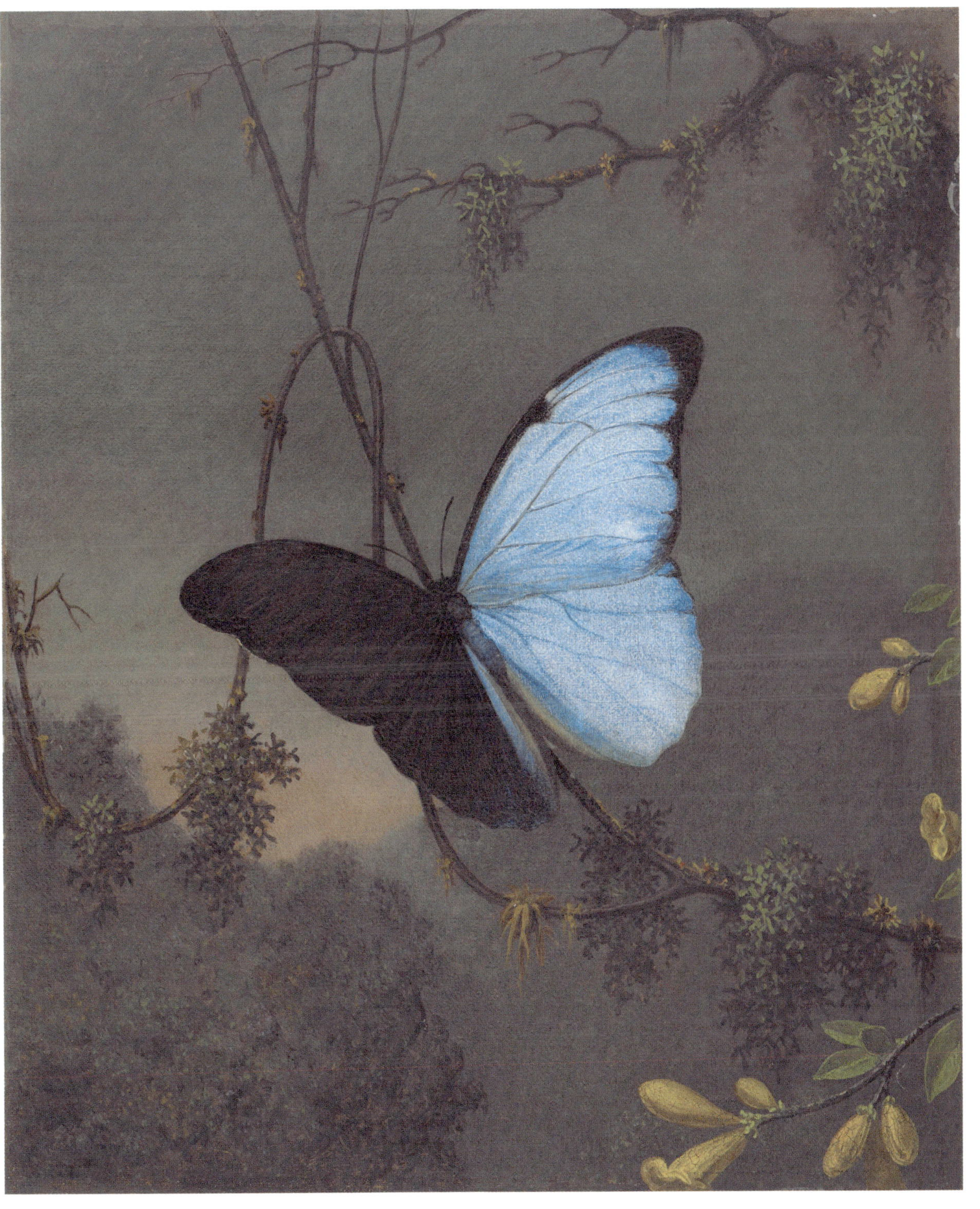

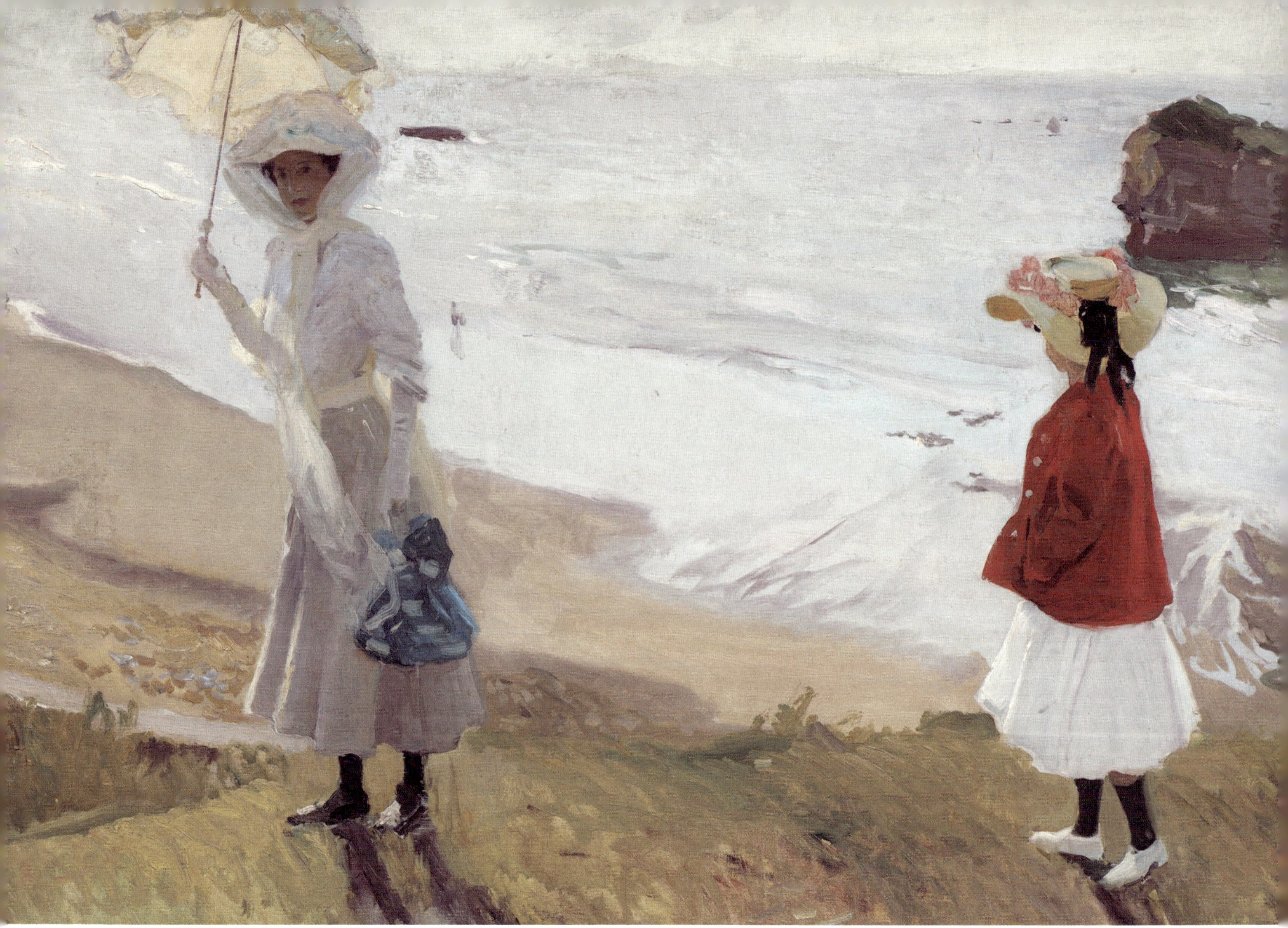

Joaquin Sorolla y Bastida,
Lighthouse Walk at Biarritz, 1906

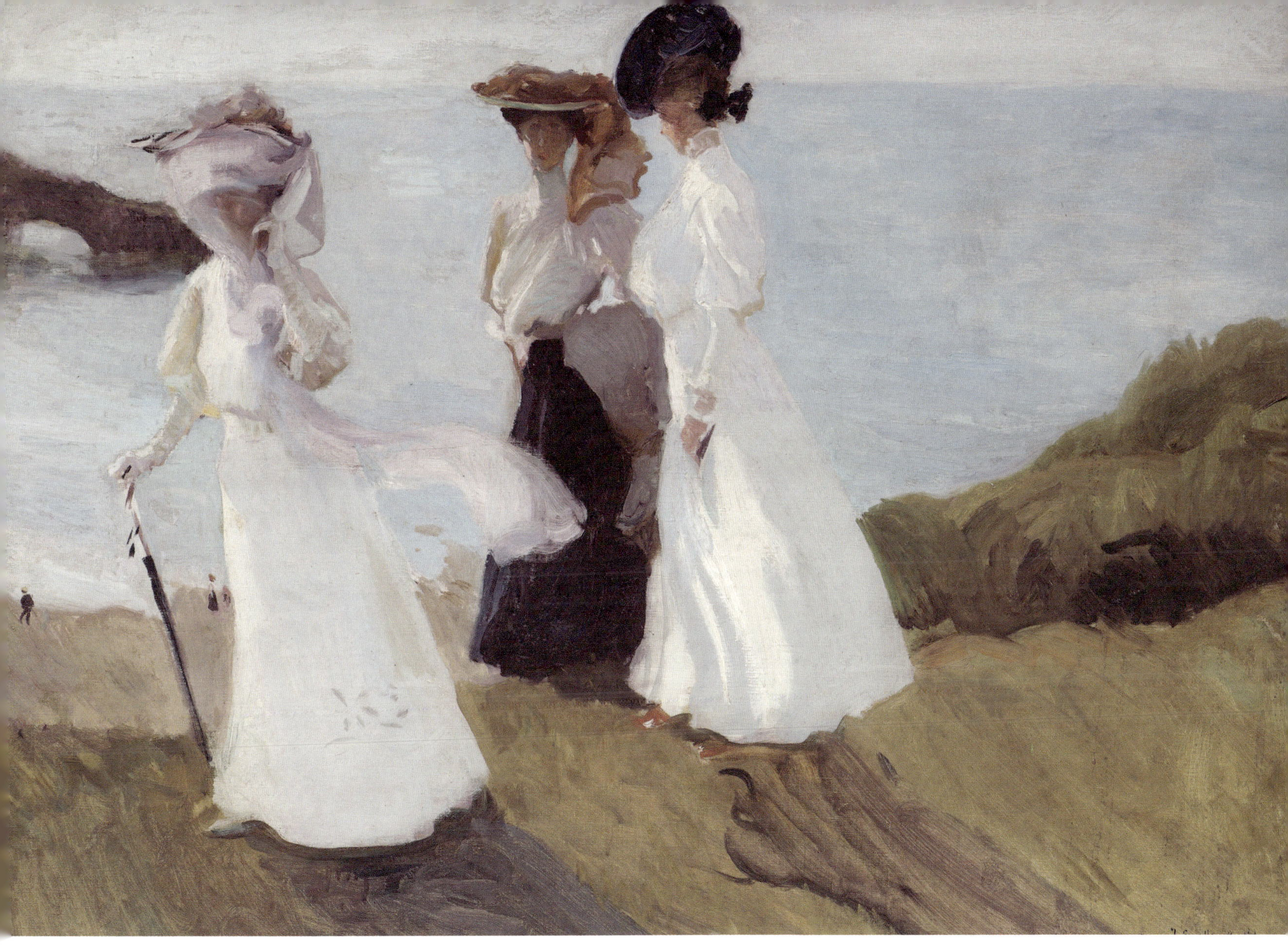

'A good leader inspires people to have confidence in the leader,
a great leader inspires people to have confidence in themselves.'

Eleanor Roosevelt (1884–1962)

'Shine on, majestic one!
Shine on, O glorious sun!
And never fail to cheer
My life so dark and drear.
Whene'er thou shinest bright,
And show thy brilliant light,
The cares I know each day
Silently steal away.'

Akseli Valdemar Gallen-Kallela,
Sunset over Lake Ruovesi, 1915–1916

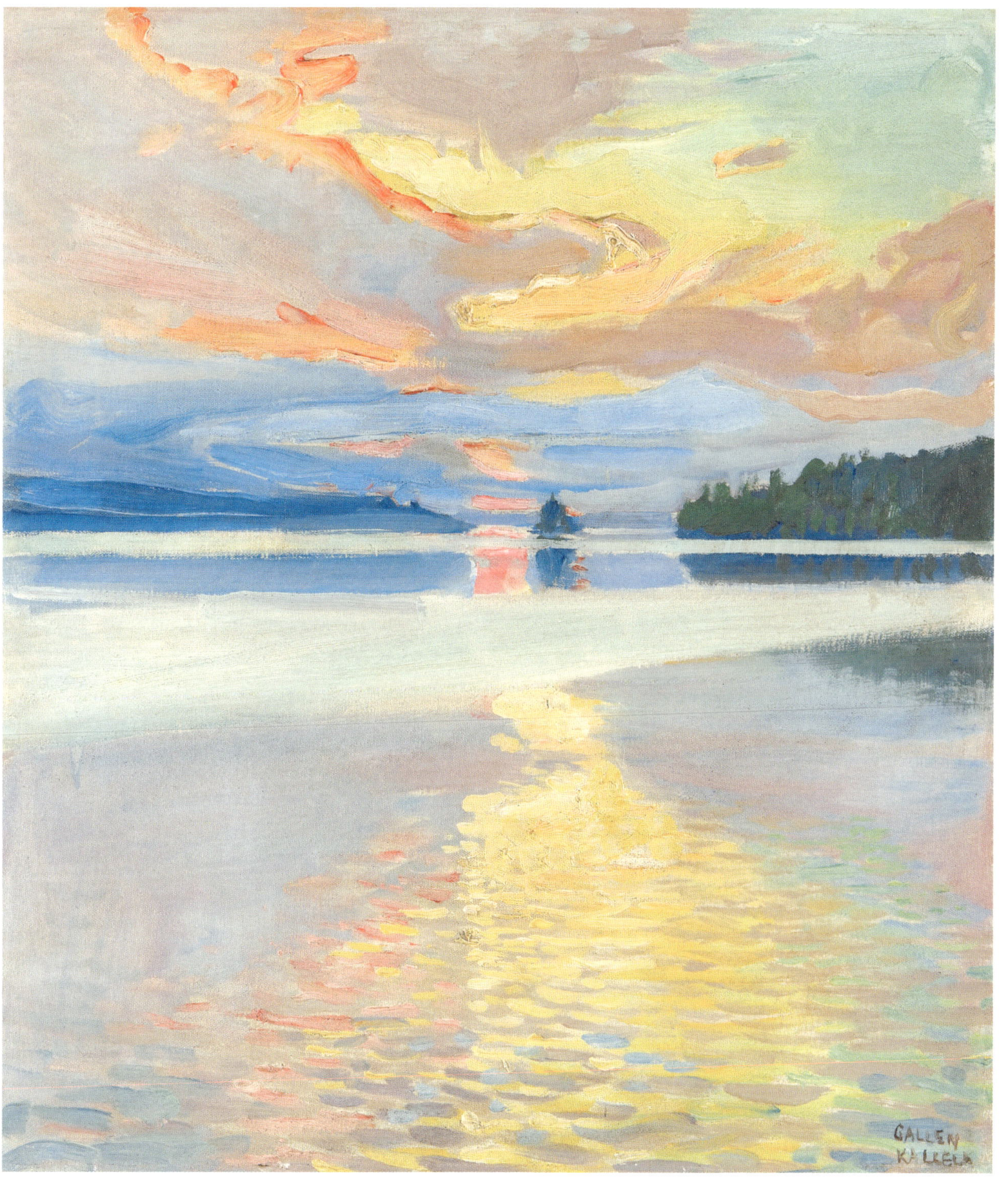

GALLEN
KALLELA

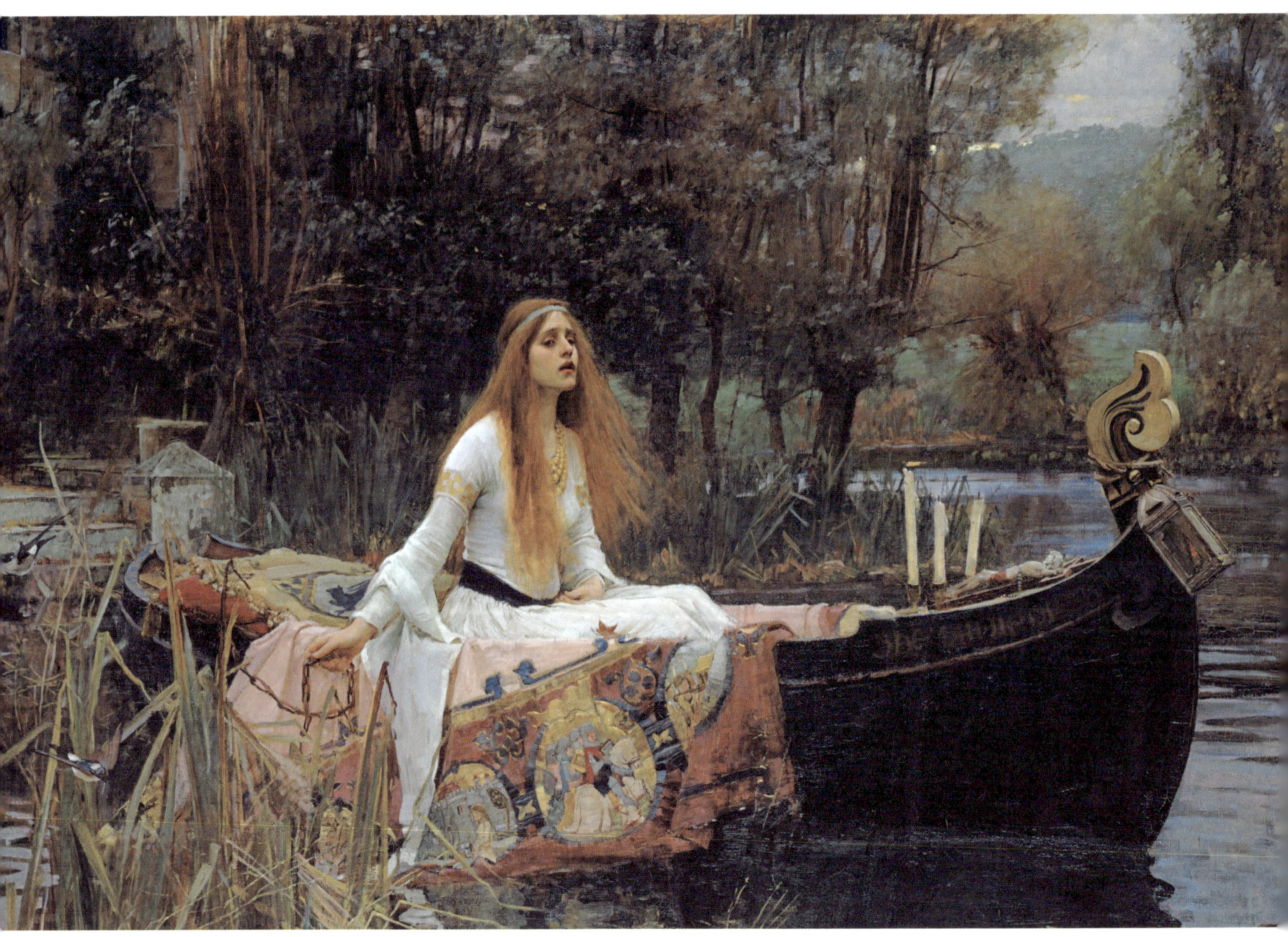

'Underneath the bearded barley,
The reaper, reaping late and early,
Hears her ever chanting cheerly,
Like an angel, singing clearly,
O'er the stream of Camelot.
Piling the sheaves in furrows airy,
Beneath the moon, the reaper weary
Listening whispers, "Tis the fairy Lady of Shalott."'

Alfred, Lord Tennyson, from *The Lady of Shalott*, 1832

John William Waterhouse,
The Lady of Shalott, 1888

'It's dark because you are trying too hard.
Lightly child, lightly. Learn to do everything
lightly. Yes, feel lightly even though you're
feeling deeply. Just lightly let things
happen and lightly cope with them. I was
so preposterously serious in those days …
Lightly, lightly — it's the best advice ever given
me … to throw away your baggage and go
forward. There are quicksands all about you,
sucking at your feet, trying to suck you down
into fear and self-pity and despair. That's why
you must walk so lightly. Lightly my darling …'

Aldous Huxley, from *Island* (1962)

Thomas Cooper Gotch,
The Sand Bar

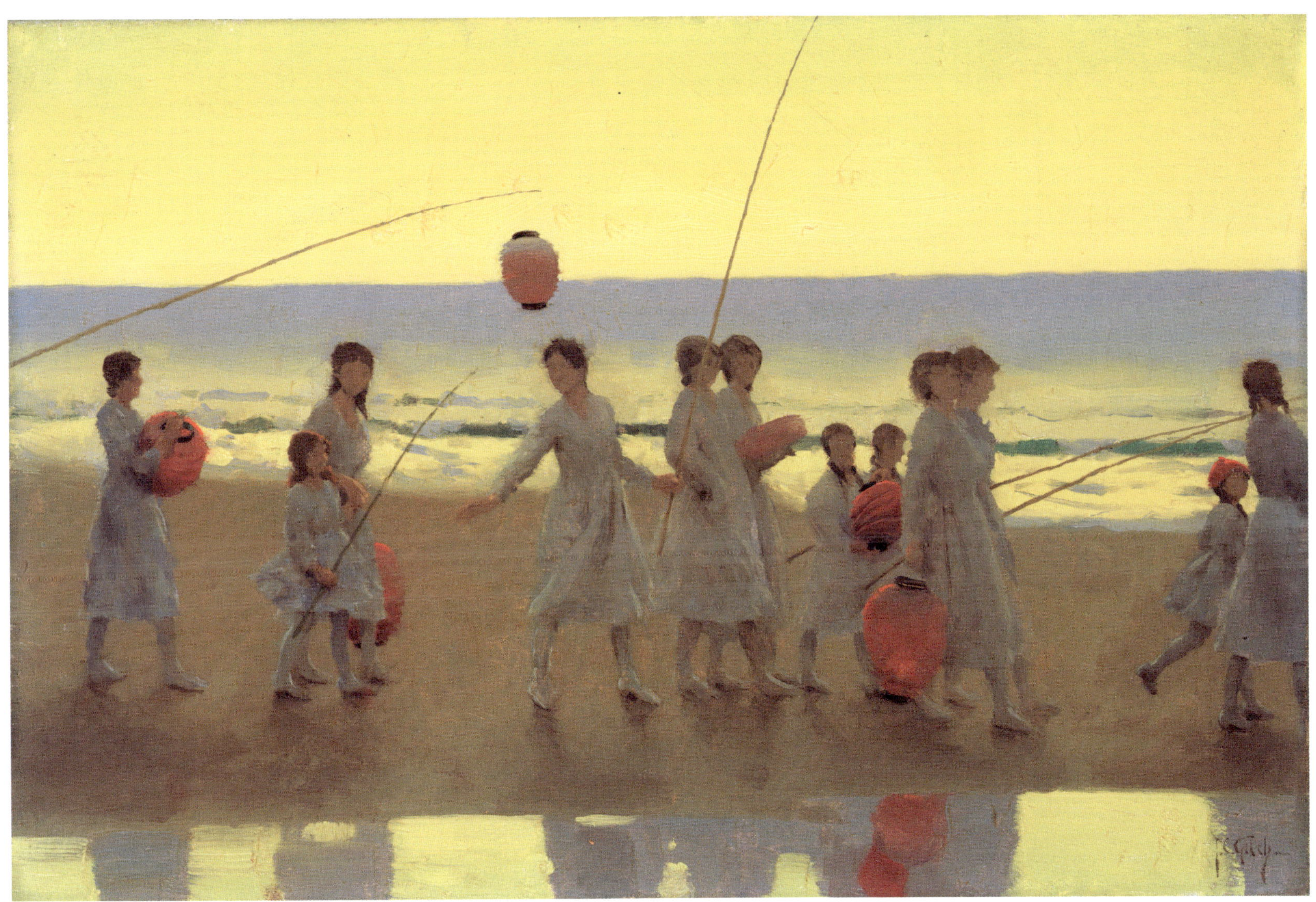

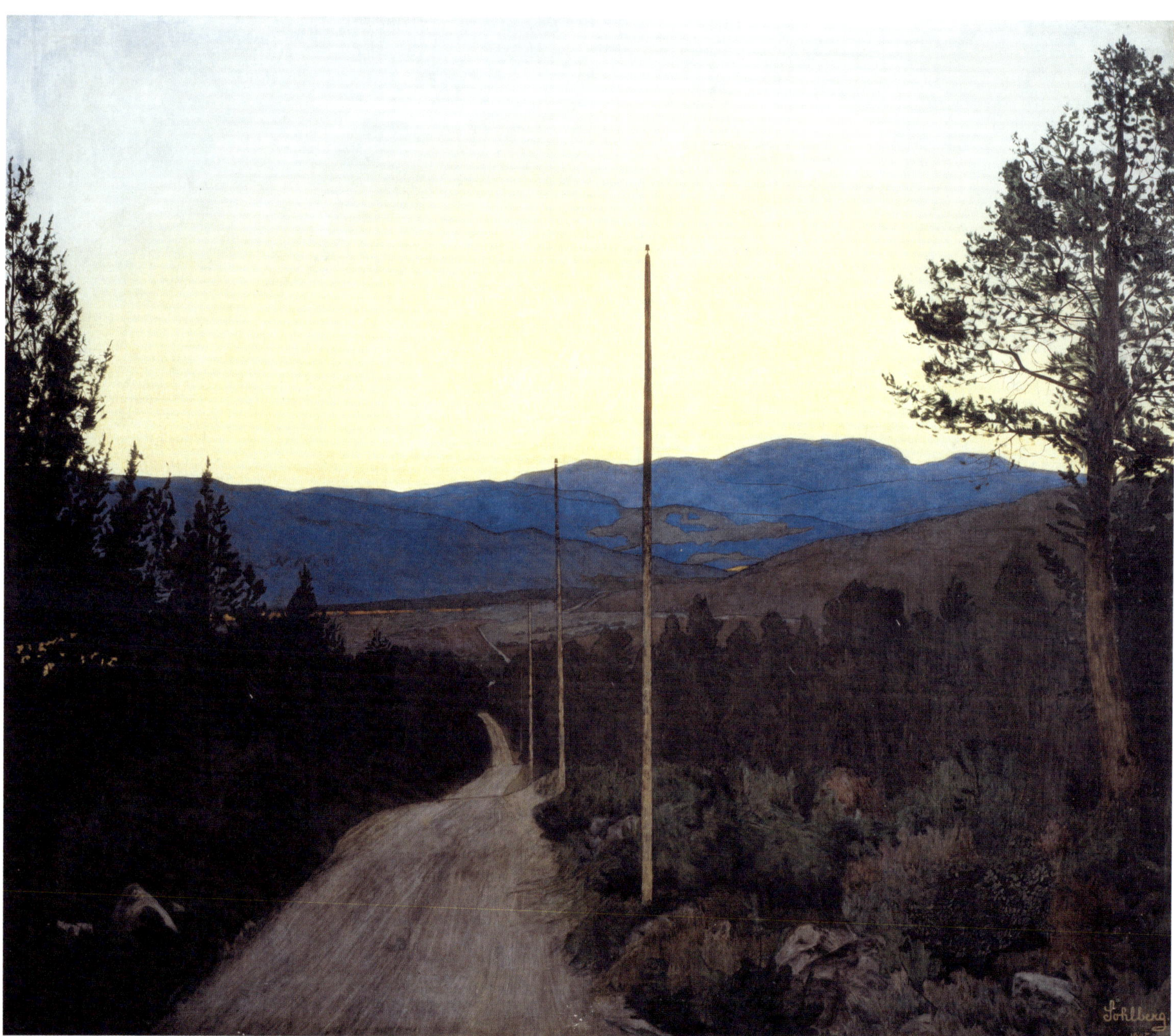

'Not I, nor anyone else can travel that road for you.
You must travel it for yourself.

It is not far, it is within reach,
Perhaps you have been on it since you were born and did not know,
Perhaps it is everywhere on water and on land.'

Walt Whitman, from *Song of Myself*, verse 46

Harald Oskar Sohlberg,
Country Head, Landevei, 1905

'And so with the sunshine and the great bursts of leaves growing on the trees, just as things grow in fast movies, I had that familiar conviction that life was beginning over again with the summer.'

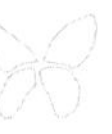

Frederick Carl Frieseke,
Sunbathing, 1913

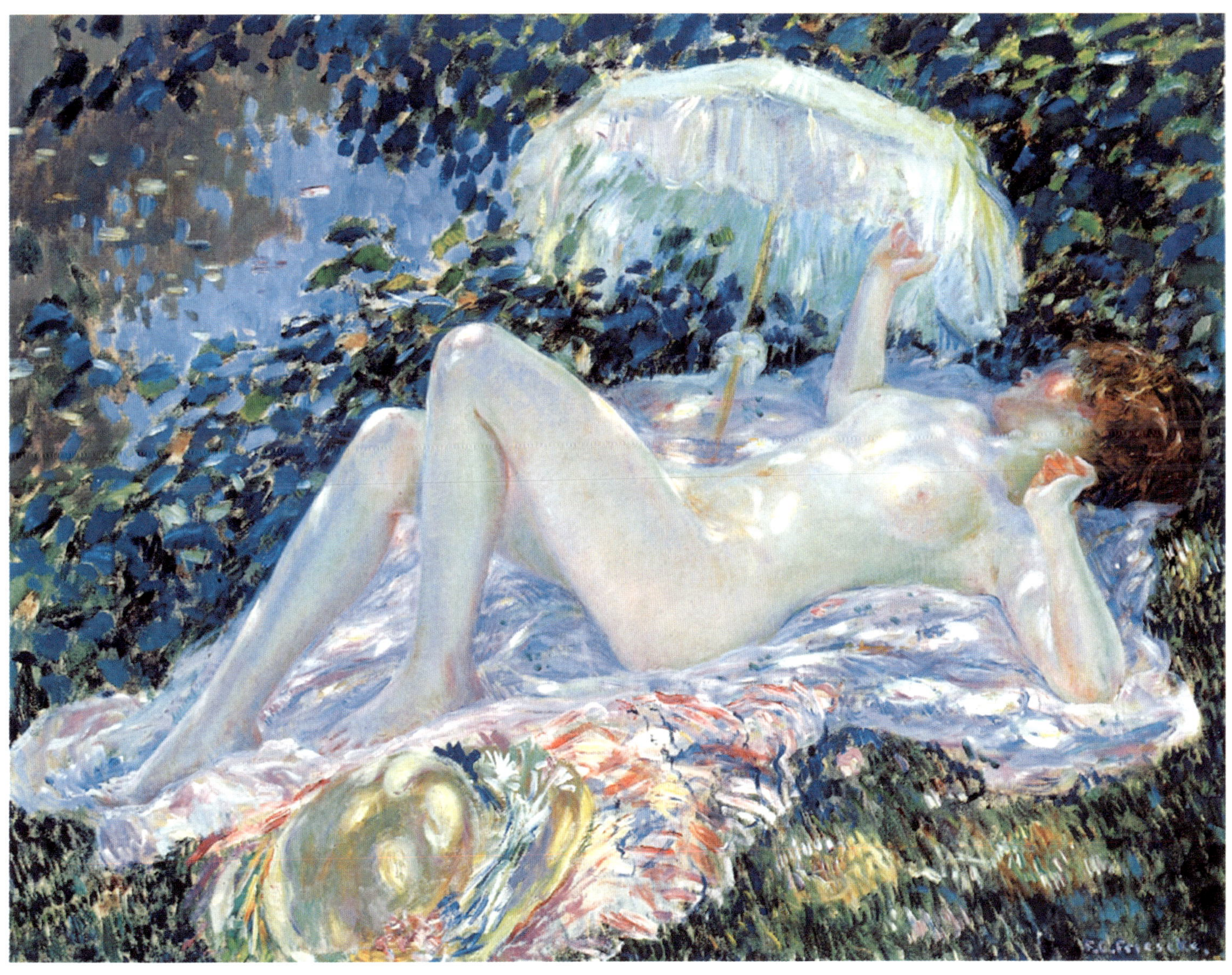

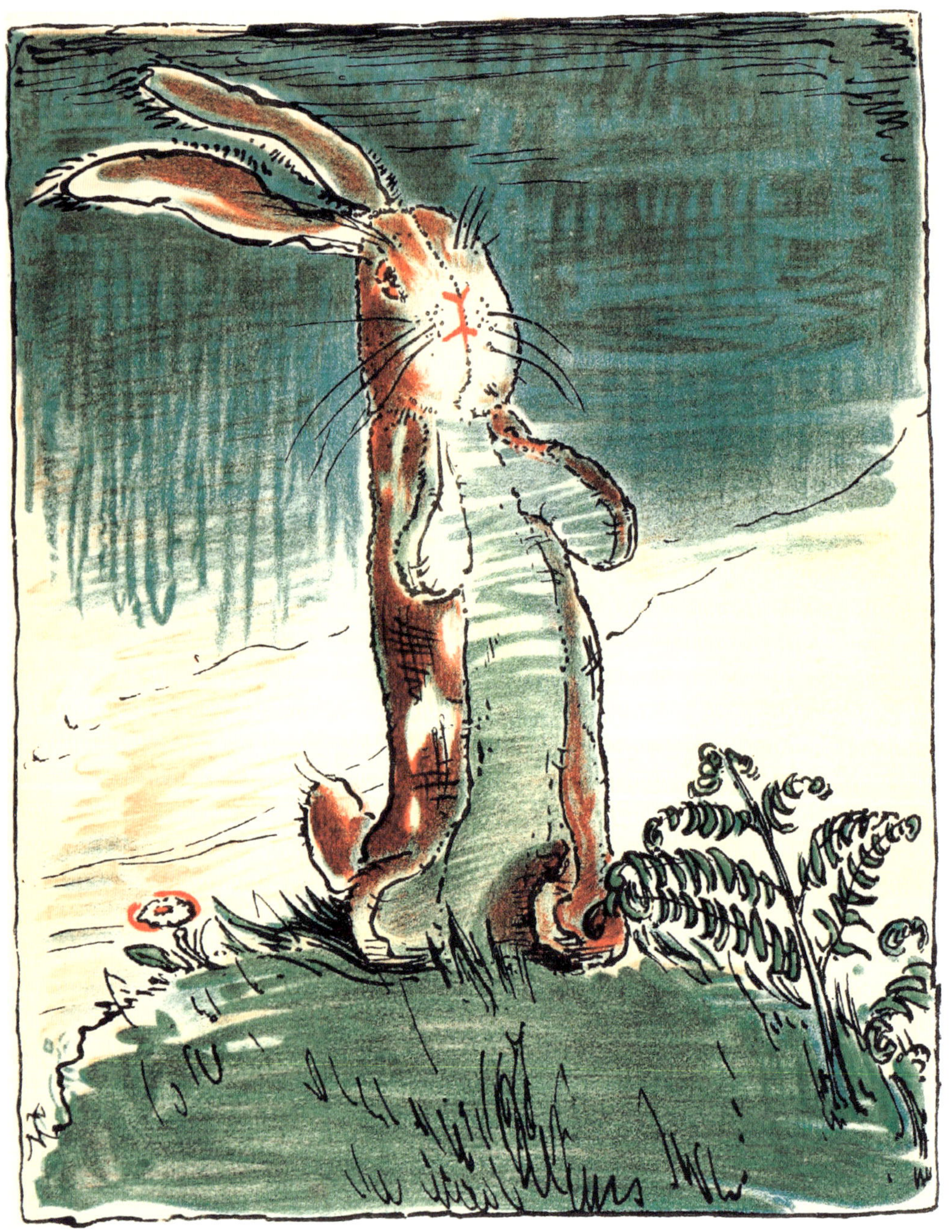

'You become. It takes a long time. That's why
it doesn't happen often to people who break
easily, or have sharp edges, or who have to
be carefully kept. Generally, by the time you
are Real, most of your hair has been loved
off, and your eyes drop out and you get loose
in the joints and very shabby. But these
things don't matter at all, because once you
are Real you can't be ugly, except to people
who don't understand.'

Margery Williams Bianco, from *The Velveteen Rabbit* (1922)

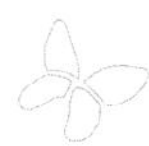

William Nicholson,
The Velveteen Rabbit, Spring Time, 1922

'You will have memories
Because of what we did back then
When we were new at this,
Yes, we did many things, then — all
Beautiful ...'

Sappho, from *Come Close* (c.610 – c.570BCE)

Georges Rochegrosse,
Le Chevalier aux Fleurs, 1894

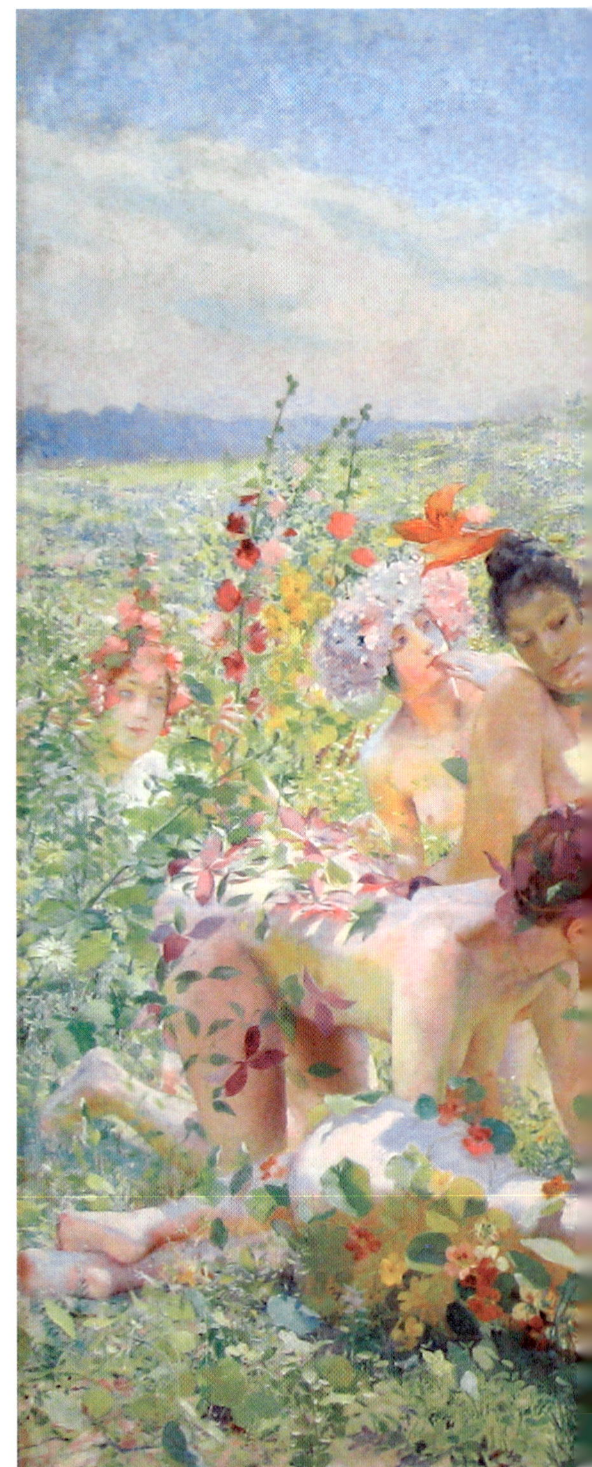

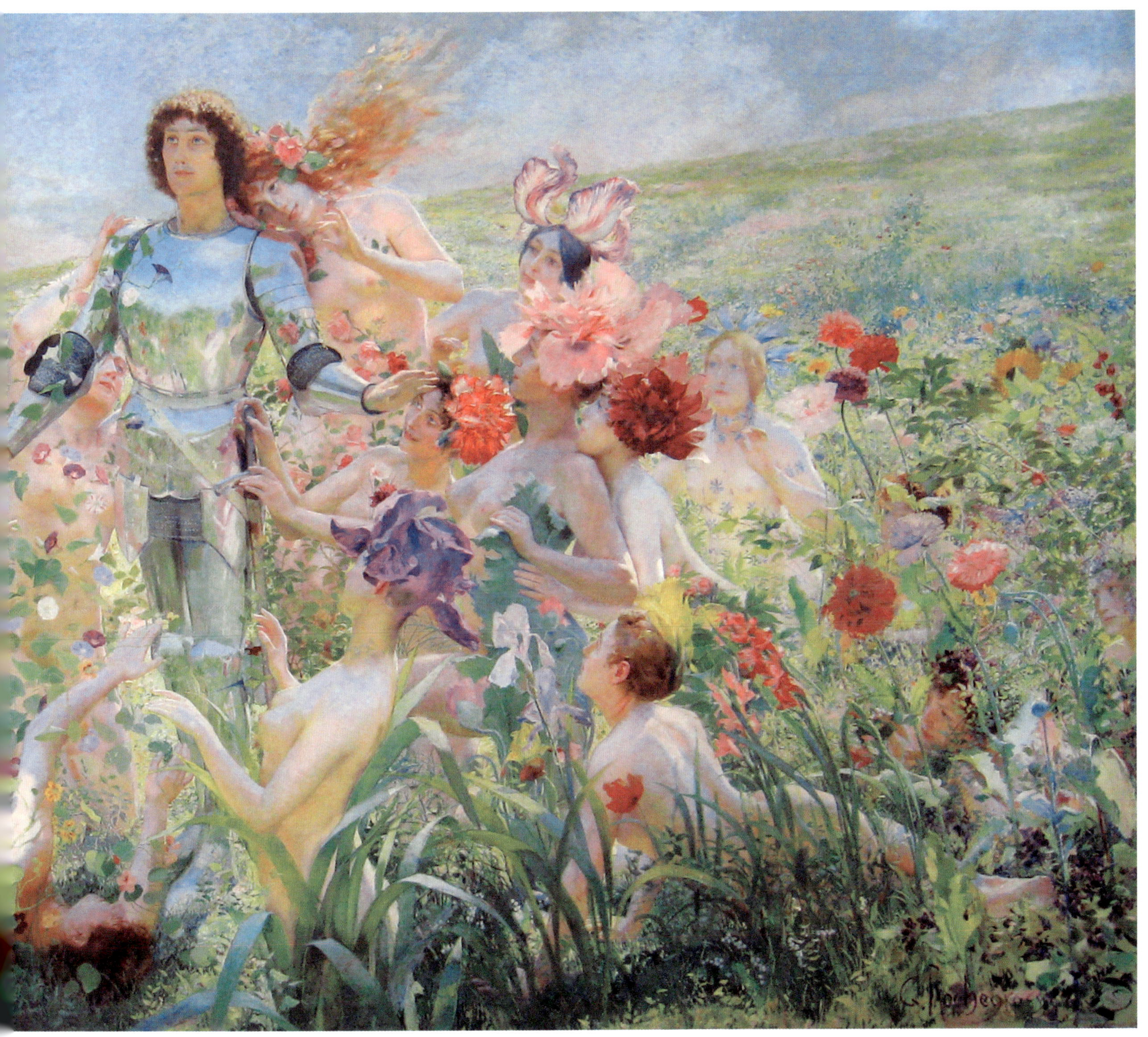

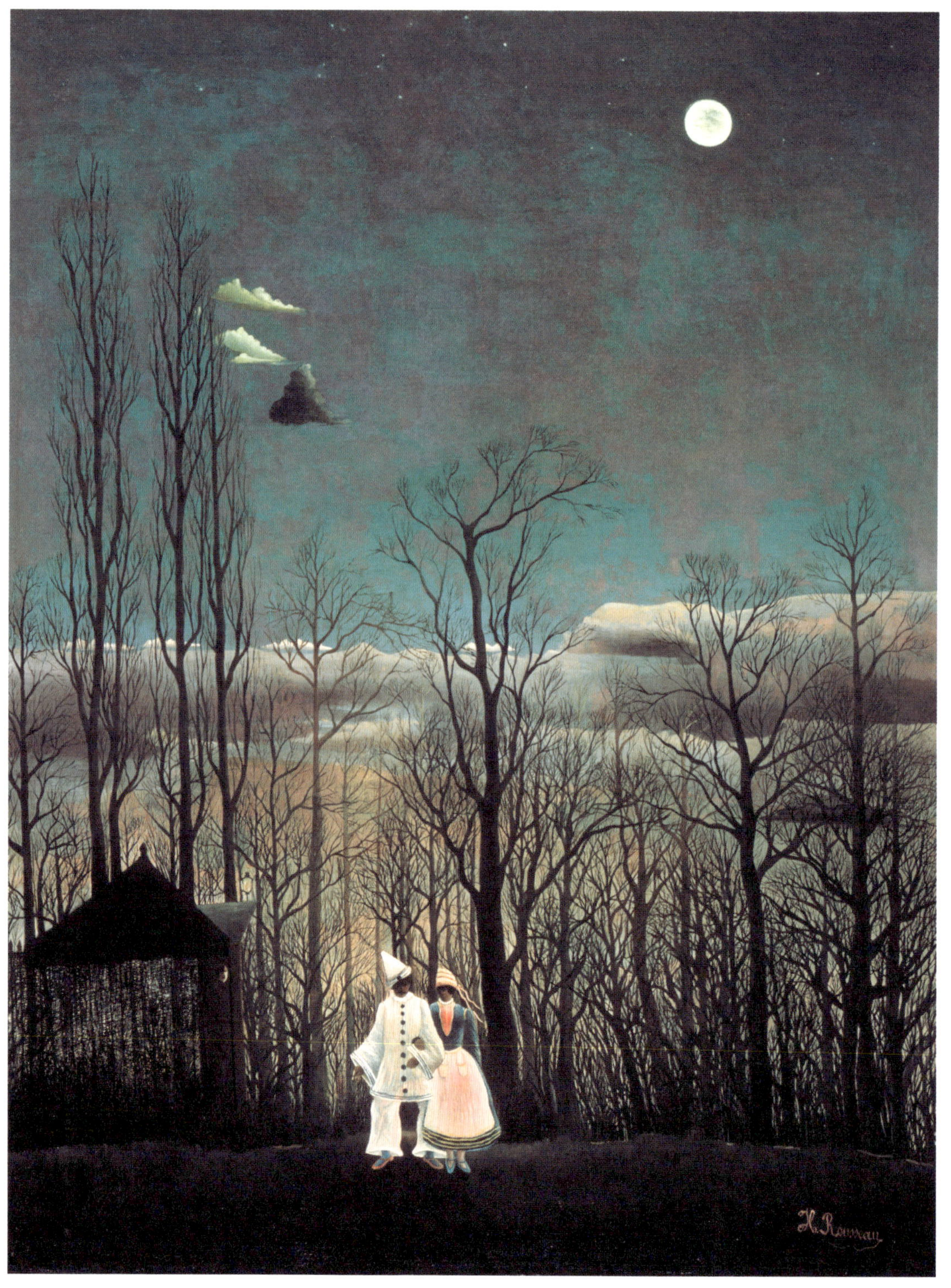

'He feeds upon her face by day and night,
And she with true kind eyes looks back on him,
Fair as the moon and joyful as the light.'

Christina Rossetti, from *In an Artist's Studio* (1856)

Henri Rousseau,
Carnival Evening, 1886

'I have been and still am a seeker, but I have
ceased to question stars and books; I have
begun to listen to the teaching my blood
whispers to me.'

Hermann Hesse, from *Demian: The Story of Emil Sinclair's Youth* (1919)

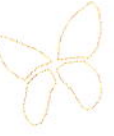

Amedeo Modigliani,
Female Nude, 1916

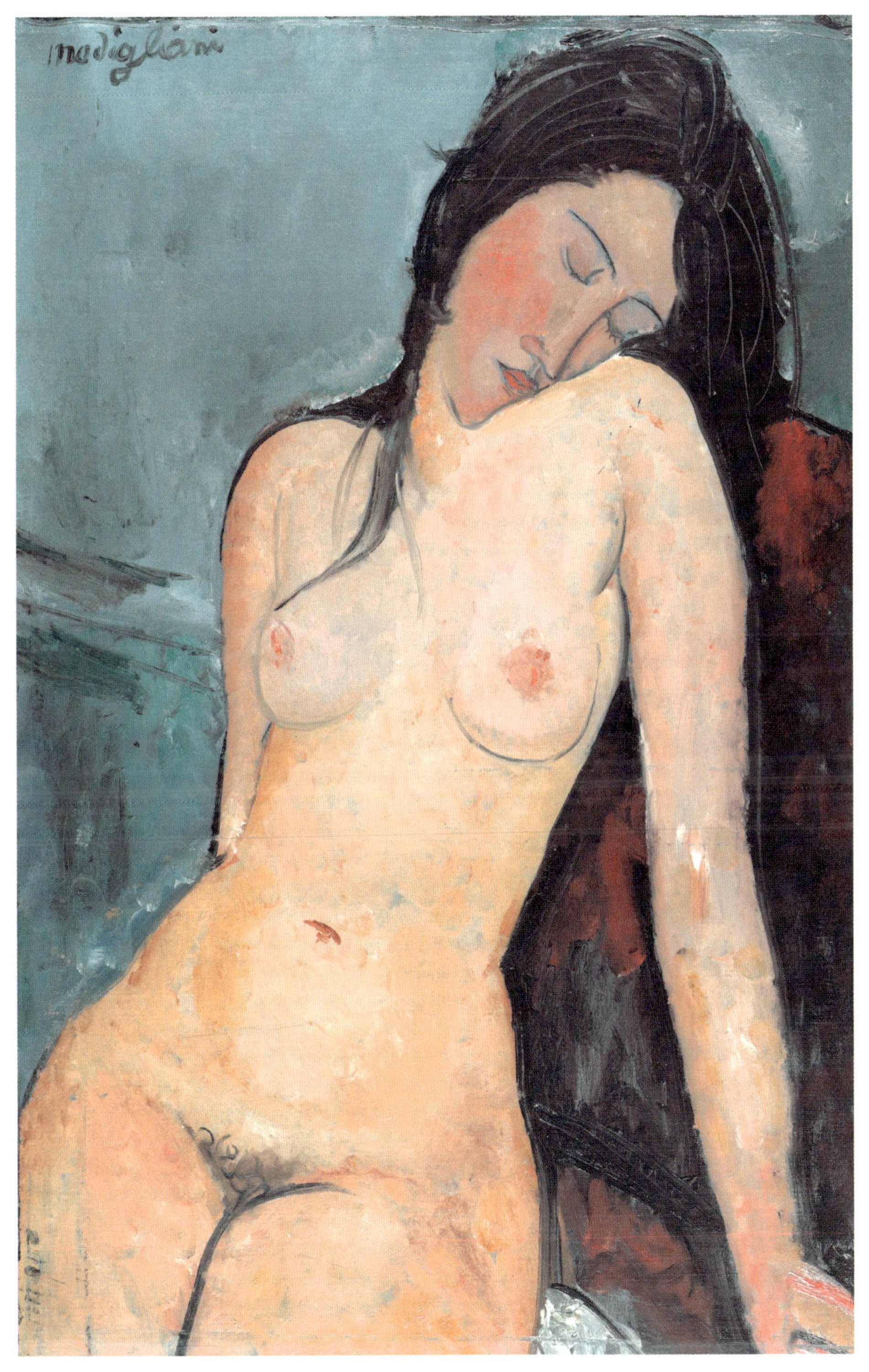
modigliani

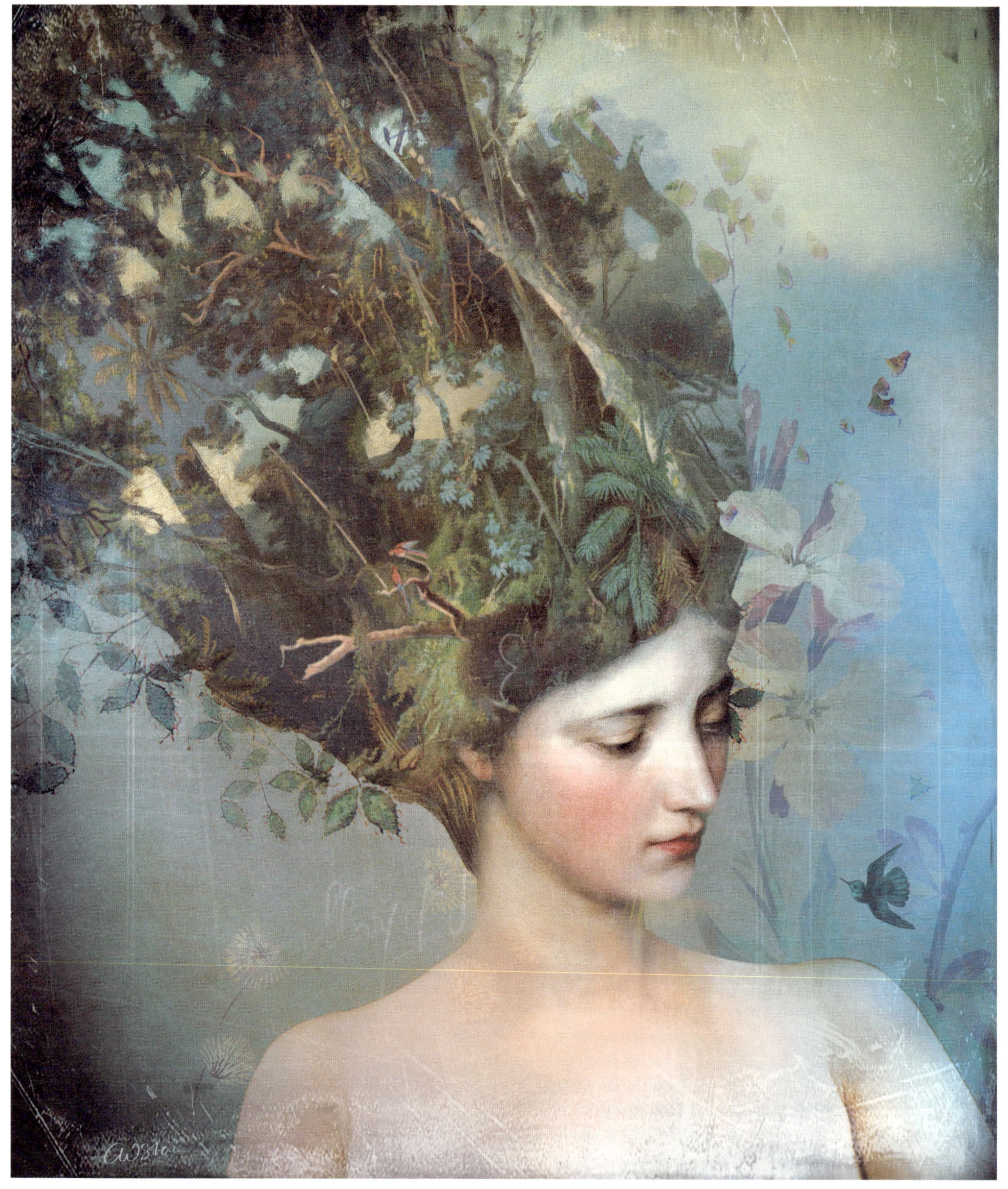

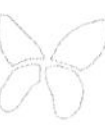

'Her voice is like clear water
That drips upon a stone
In forests far and silent
Where Quiet plays alone.

Her thoughts are like the lotus
Abloom by sacred streams
Beneath the temple arches
Where Quiet sits and dreams.

Her kisses are the roses
That glow while dusk is deep
In Persian garden closes
Where Quiet falls asleep.'

Sara Teasdale, *A Fantasy* (1911)

Catrin Welz-Stein,
Portrait 17, 2020

'Do not be dismayed by the brokenness of the world.
All things break. And all things can be mended.
Not with time, as they say, but with intention.
So go. Love intentionally, extravagantly, unconditionally.
The broken world waits in darkness for the light that is you.'

L.R. Knost

Jean Frédéric Bazille,
Black Woman with Peonies, 1870

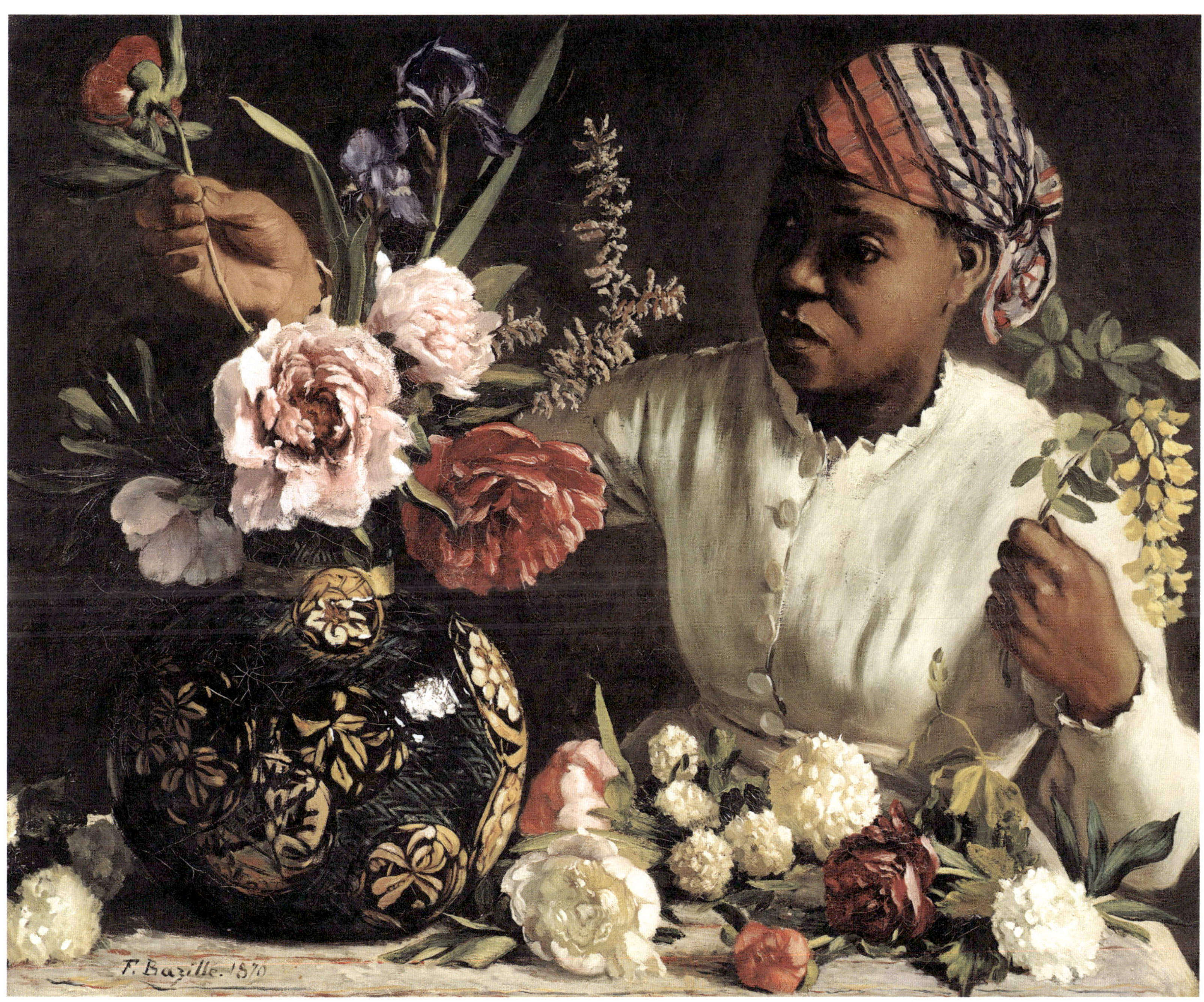

F. Bazille. 1870

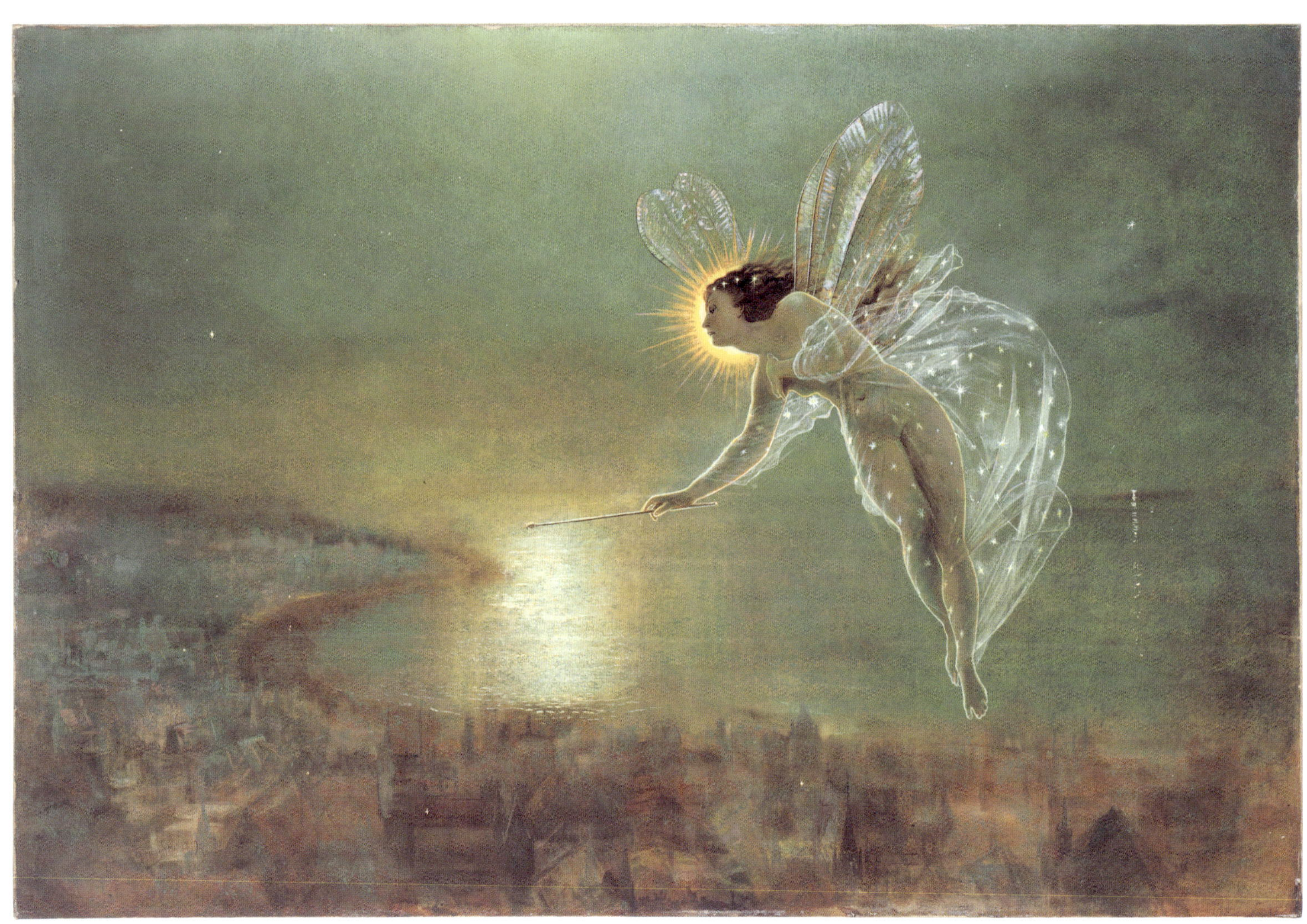

'I remember I used to half believe and wholly play with fairies
when I was a child. What heaven can be more real than to
retain the spirit-world of childhood, tempered and balanced
by knowledge and common-sense.'

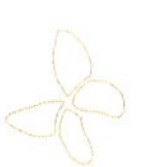

John Atkinson Grimshaw,
Spirit of Night, 1879

'Every man has his secret sorrows which
the world knows not; and often times we
call a man cold when he is only sad.'

Jean-Hippolyte Flandrin,
Study of a Nude Young Man, 1836

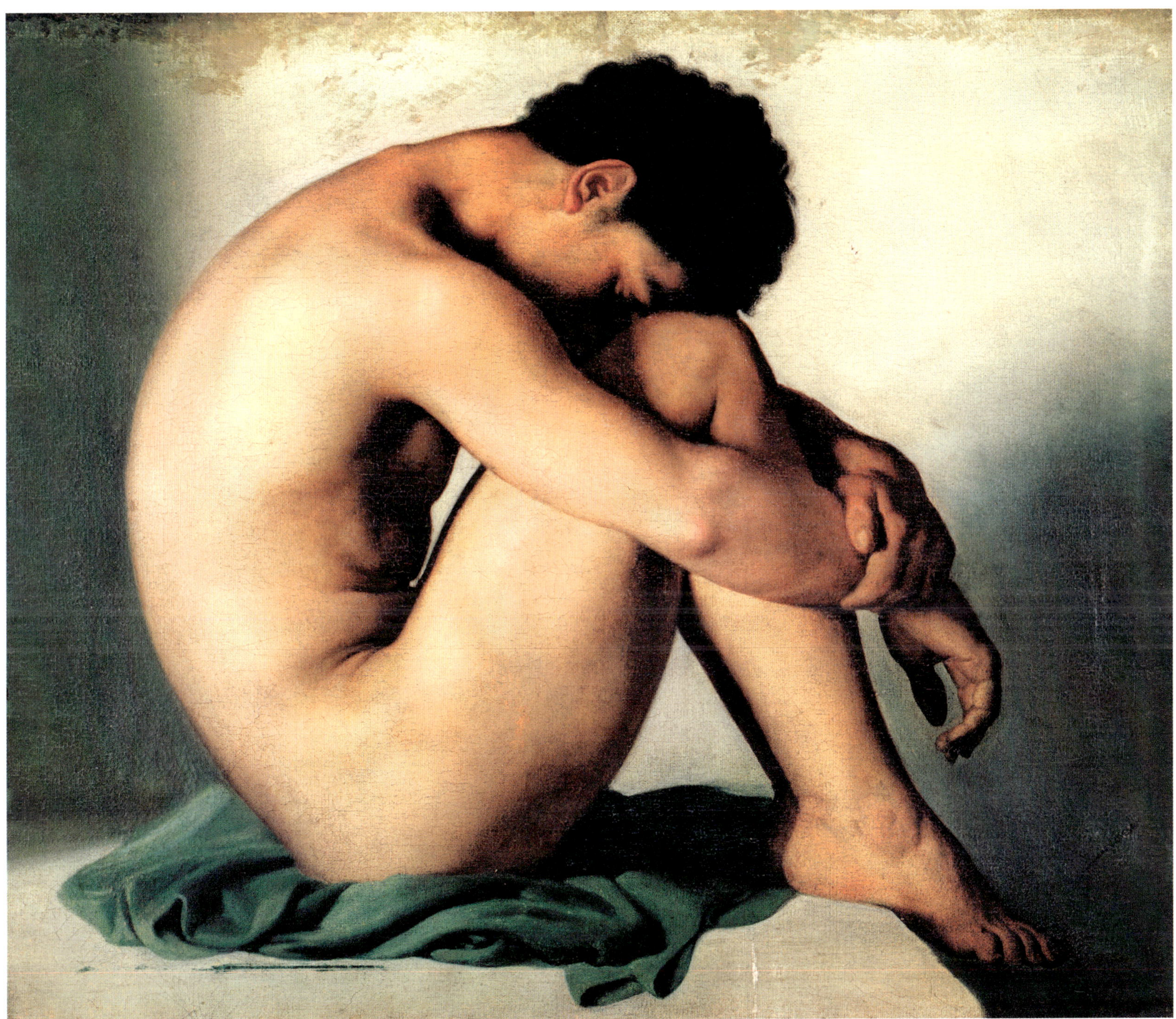

'People discuss my art and
pretend to understand as if it were
necessary to understand, when
it's simply necessary to love.'

Claude Monet (1840–1926)

Claude Monet,
The Artist's Garden at Giverny, 1900

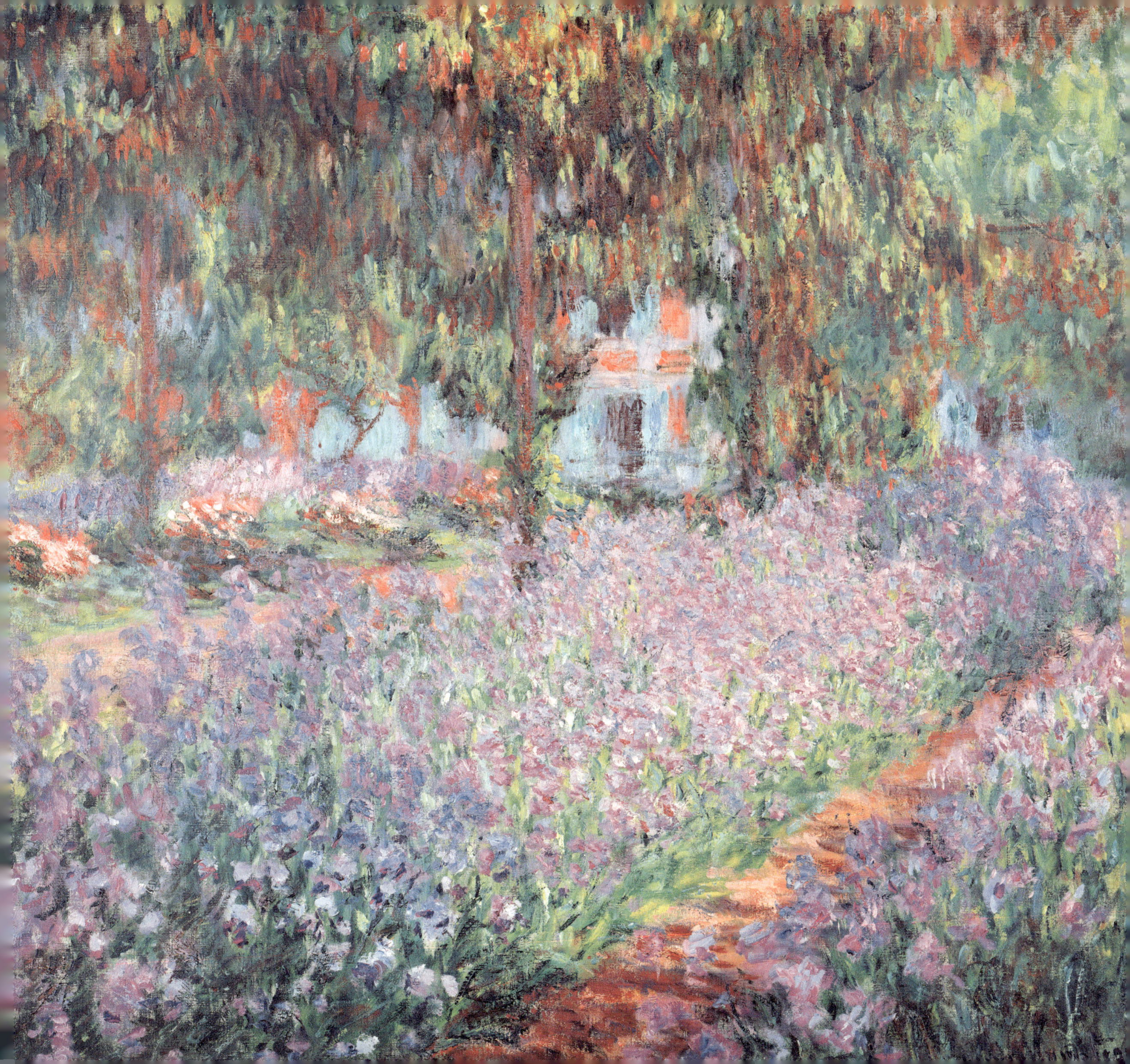

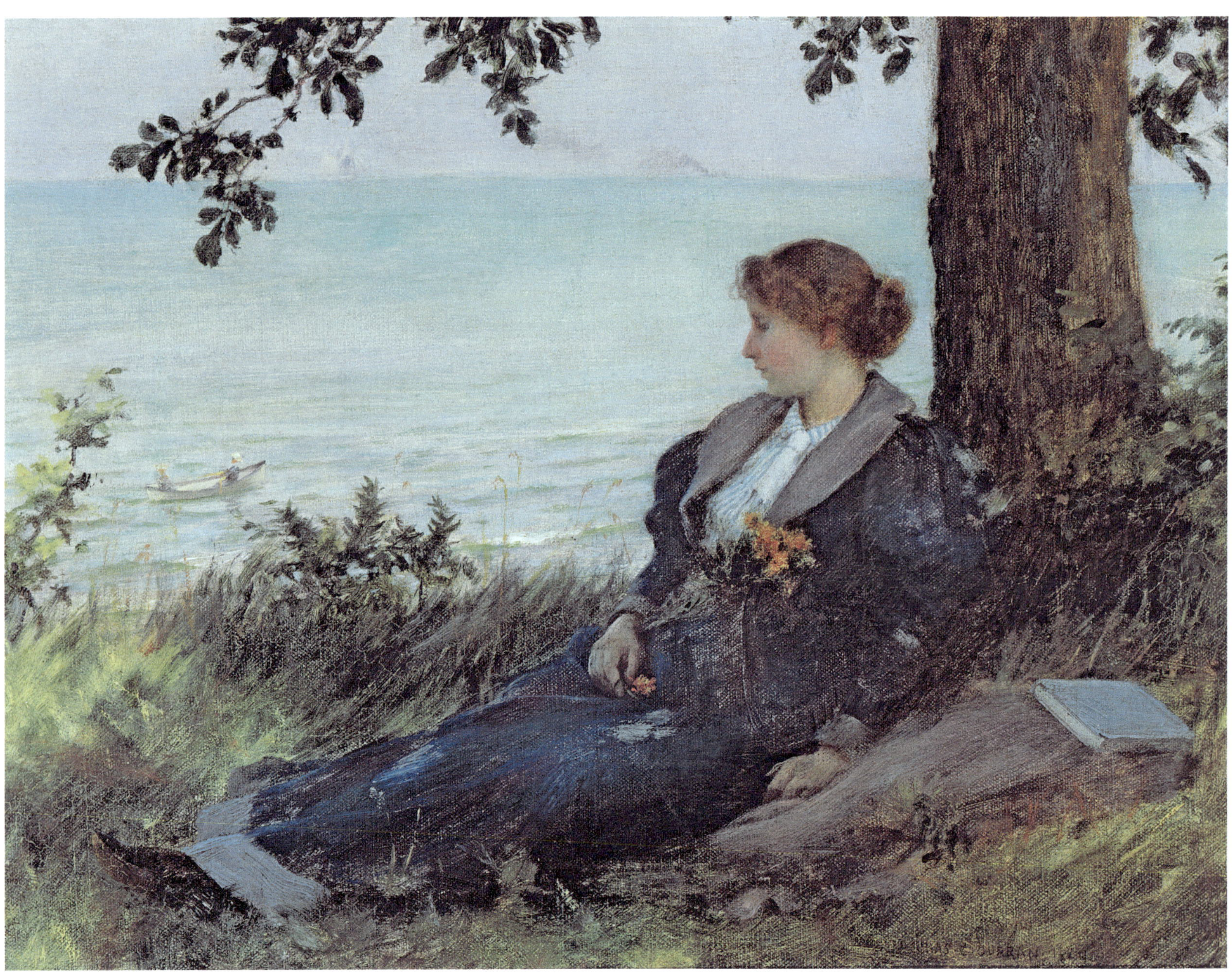

'No need to hurry. No need to sparkle. No need to be anybody but oneself.'

Virginia Woolf, from *A Room of One's Own* (1929)

Charles Courtney Curran,
Daydreams

'I felt it was for this I had come: to wake at dawn on a hillside and look out on a world for which I had no words, to start at the beginning, speechless and without plan, in a place that still had no memories for me.'

Laurie Lee, from *As I Walked Out One Midsummer Morning* (1969)

Dorothea Sharp,
An Afternoon Walk

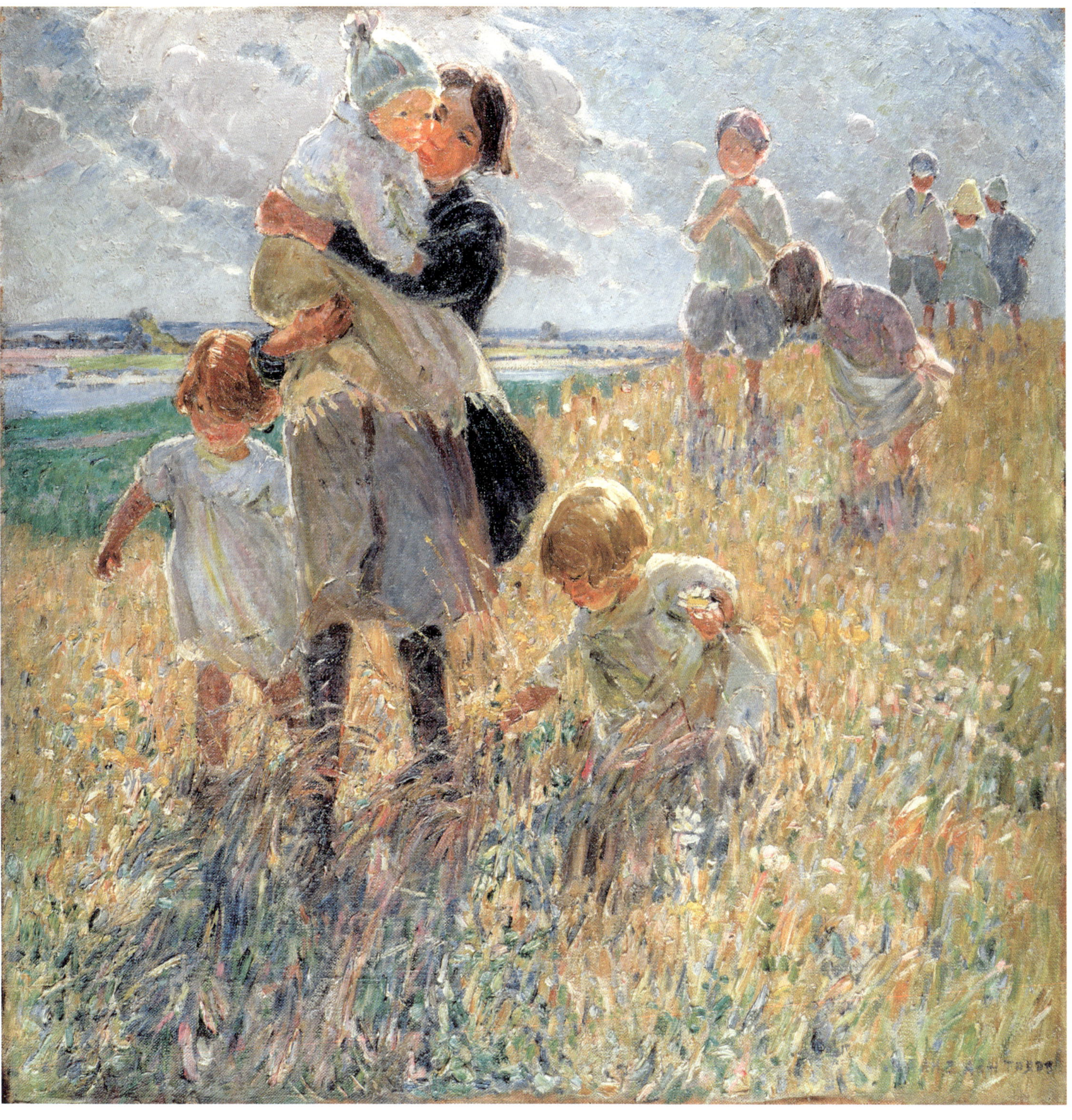

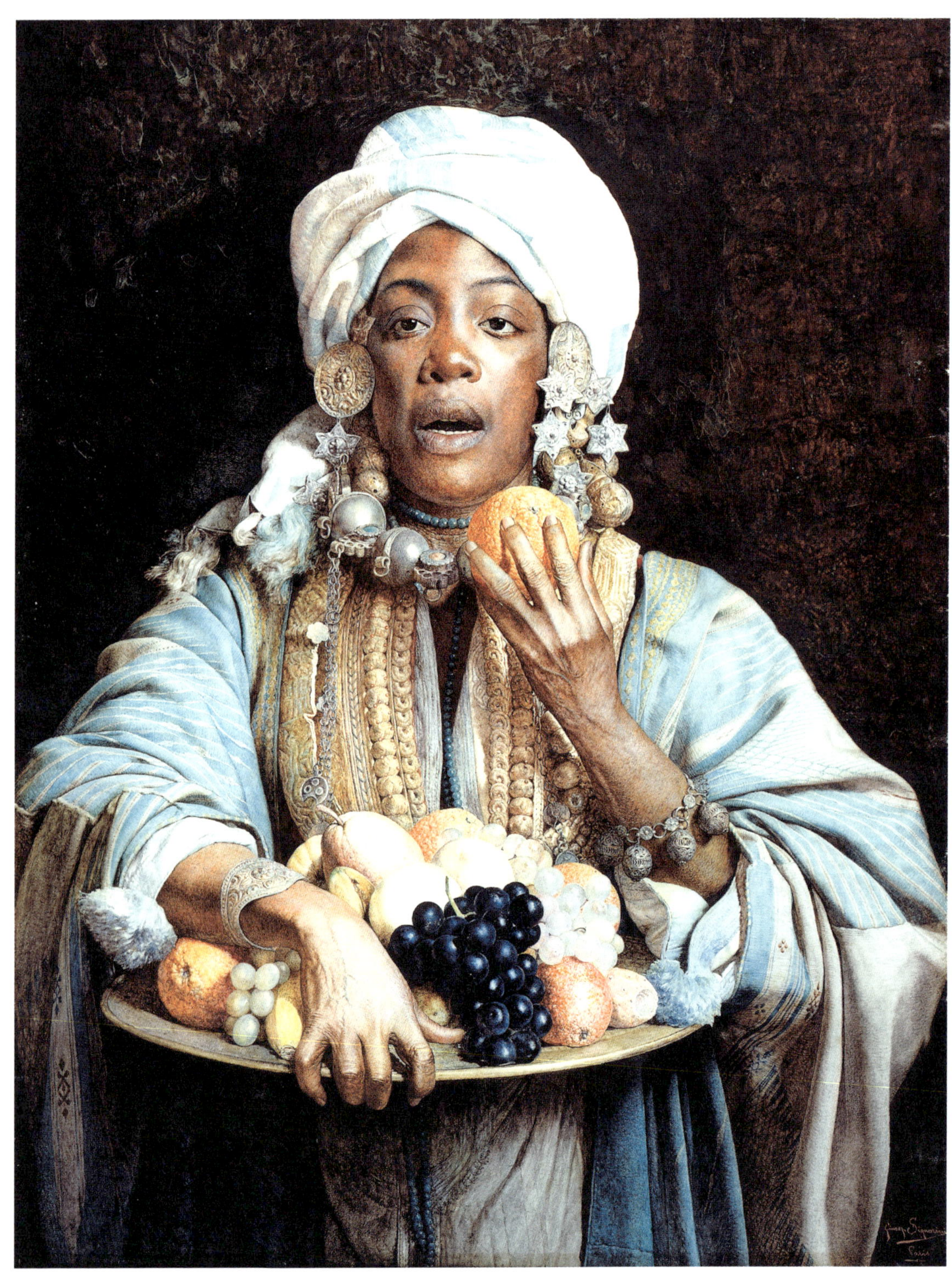

'Love is all there is. It is why you are here, to love and be loved. But first, feel what it is to love yourself. Self-love starts with being kind and treating yourself with respect. To love yourself completely; that's the hardest part. Every moment you doubt yourself is wasted, don't throw away a single second, for now, is all you have. Think upon this, look deep into your heart and start by unconditionally loving you.'

Lisa Azarmi, from *Becoming Orla-Borla* (2022)

'Violet now, in veil on veil of evening,
The hills across from Cromwell grow dreamy and far;
A wood-thrush is singing soft as a viol
In the heart of the hollow where the dark pools are;
The primrose has opened her pale yellow flowers
And heaven is lighting star after star.

Places I love come back to me like music —
Mid-ocean, midnight, the eaves buzz drowsily;
In the ship's deep churning the eerie phosphorescence
Is like the souls of people who were drowned at sea,
And I can hear a man's voice, speaking, hushed, insistent,
At midnight, in mid-ocean, hour on hour to me.'

Sara Teasdale, 'Places', from *The Collected Poems* (1937)

Hans Ole Brasen,
Sunset in a Lagoon, 1897

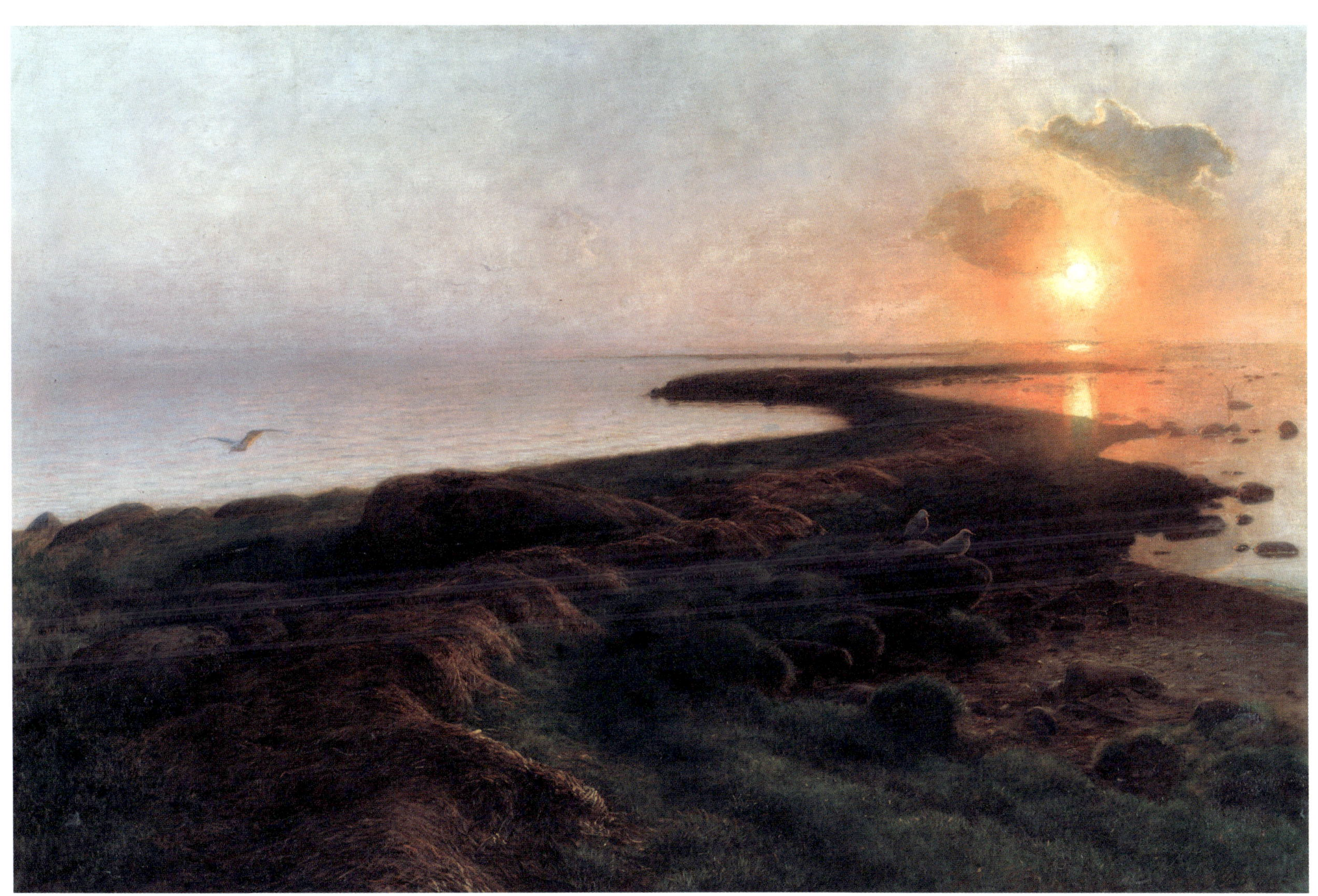

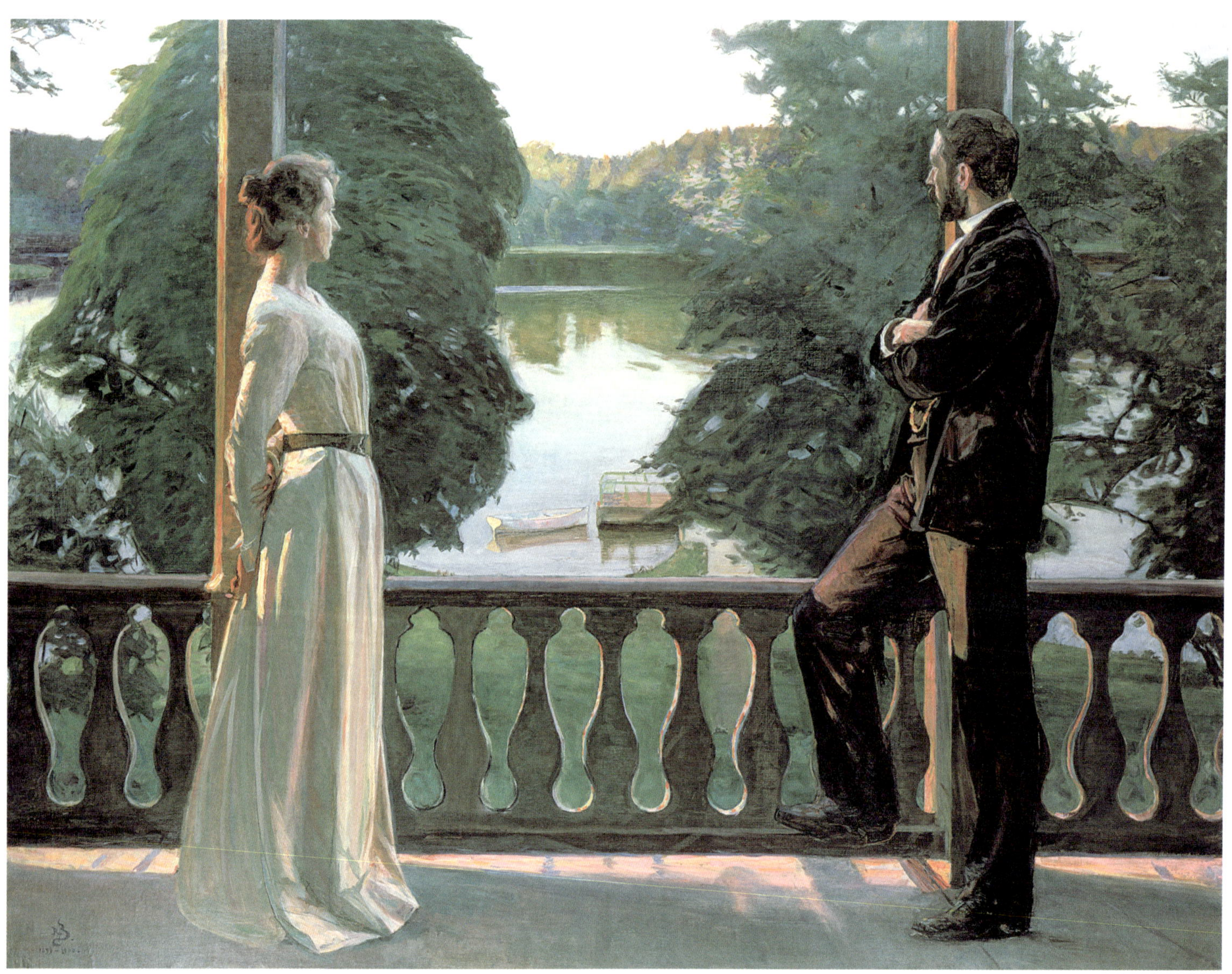

'Love one another, but make not a bond
of love:
     Let it rather be a moving sea between
the shores of your souls.
     Fill each other's cup but drink not from
one cup.
     Give one another of your bread but eat
not from the same loaf.
     Sing and dance together and be joyous,
but let each one of you be alone,
     Even as the strings of a lute are alone
though they quiver with the same music.

Give your hearts, but not into each
other's keeping.
     For only the hand of Life can contain
your hearts.
     And stand together yet not too near
together:
     For the pillars of the temple stand apart,
     And the oak tree and the cypress grow
not in each other's shadow.'

Kahlil Gibran, from *On Marriage* (1923)

Sven Richard Bergh,
Nordic Summer Evening, 1890

'We all have our time machines, don't we.
Those that take us back are memories …
And those that carry us forward, are dreams.'

Pierre-Auguste Renoir,
The Sleeper, 1880

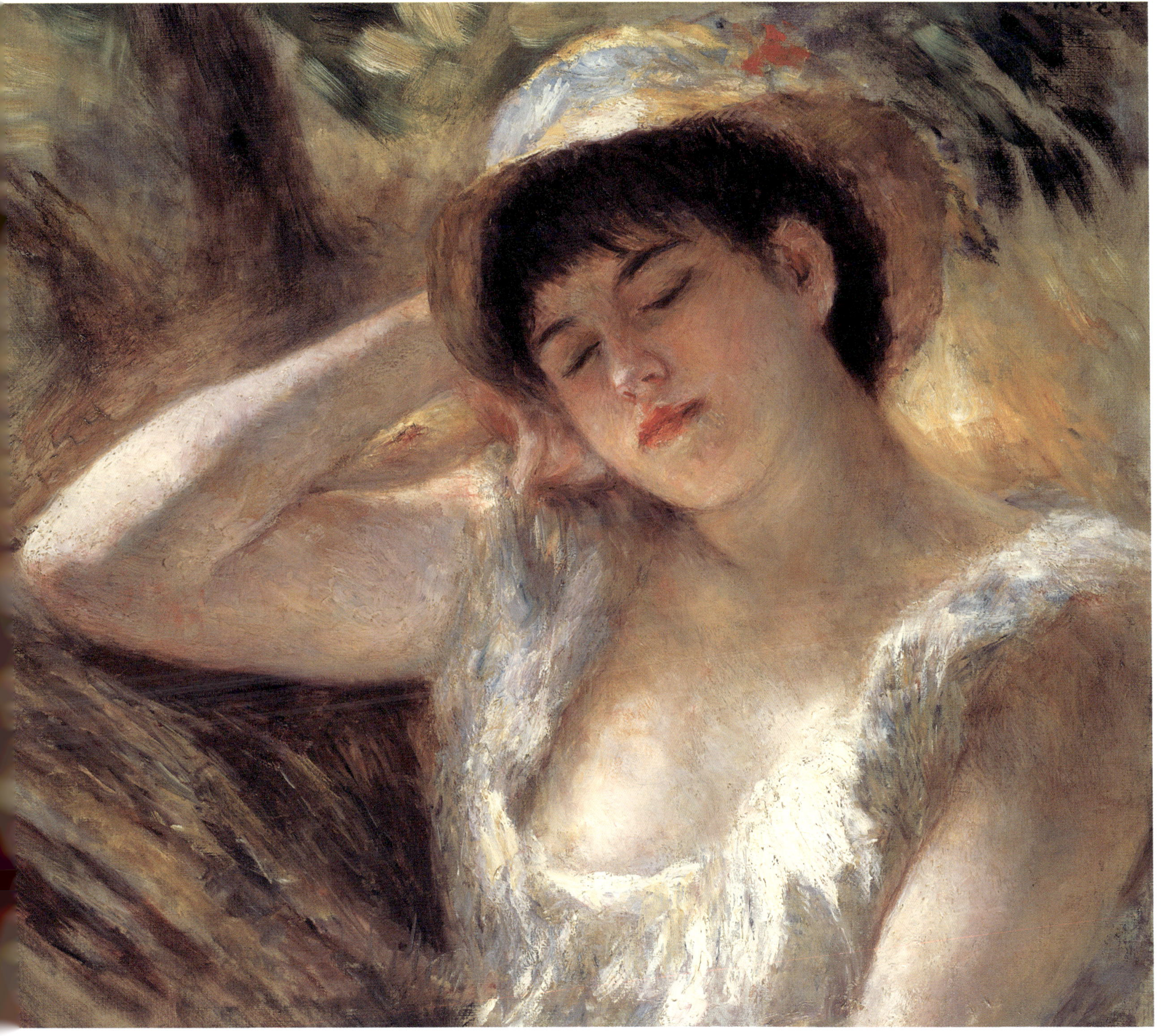

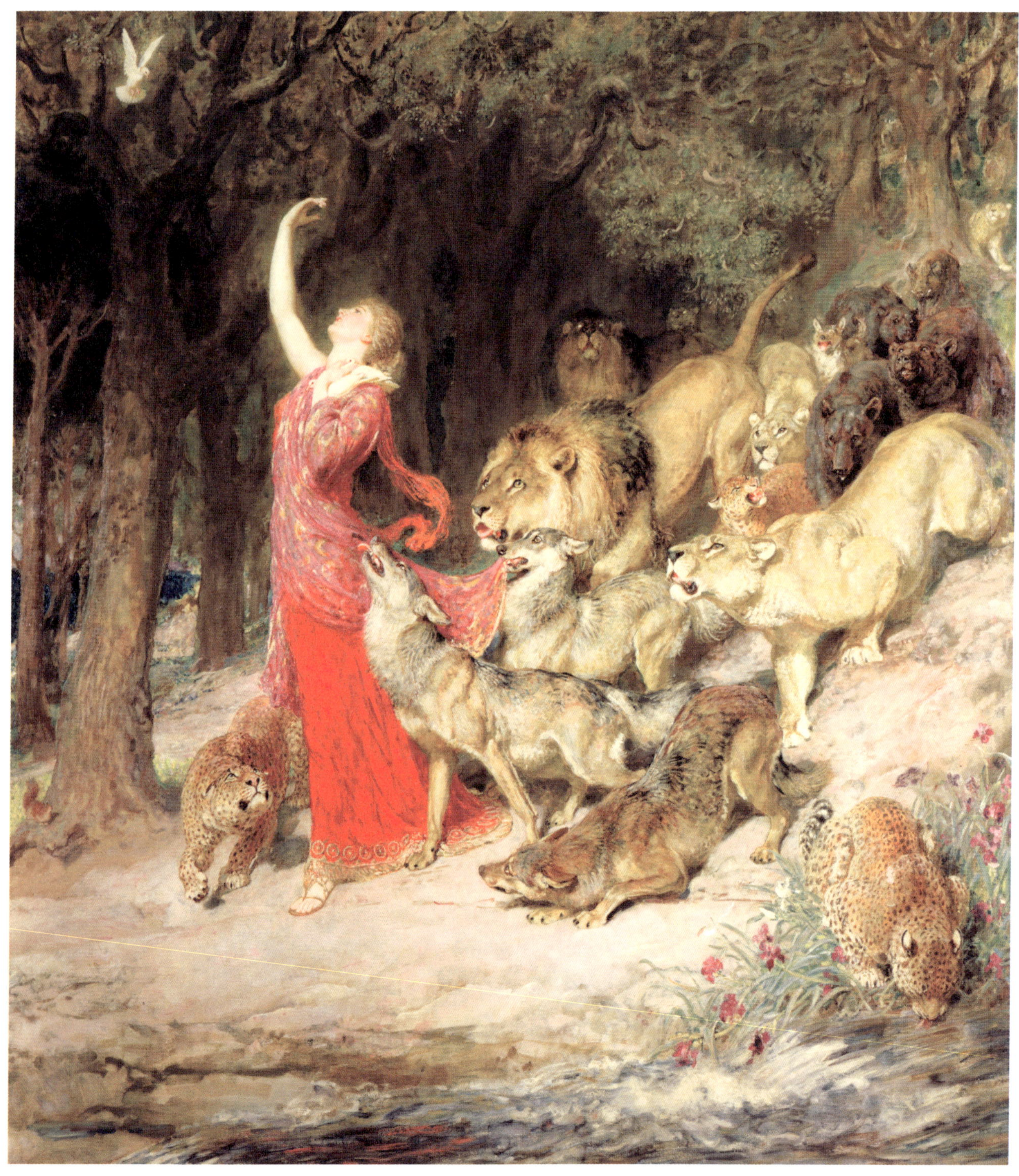

'Until one has loved an animal a part of one's soul remains unawakened.'

Briton Rivière,
Aphrodite, 1902

'Those that go searching for love only make
manifest their own lovelessness, and the
loveless never find love, only the loving find
love, and they never have to seek for it.'

D.H. Lawrence, from *Search for Love*, taken from the author's notebook
'More Pansies' (1932)

Arthur Hacker,
The Temptation of Sir Percival, 1894

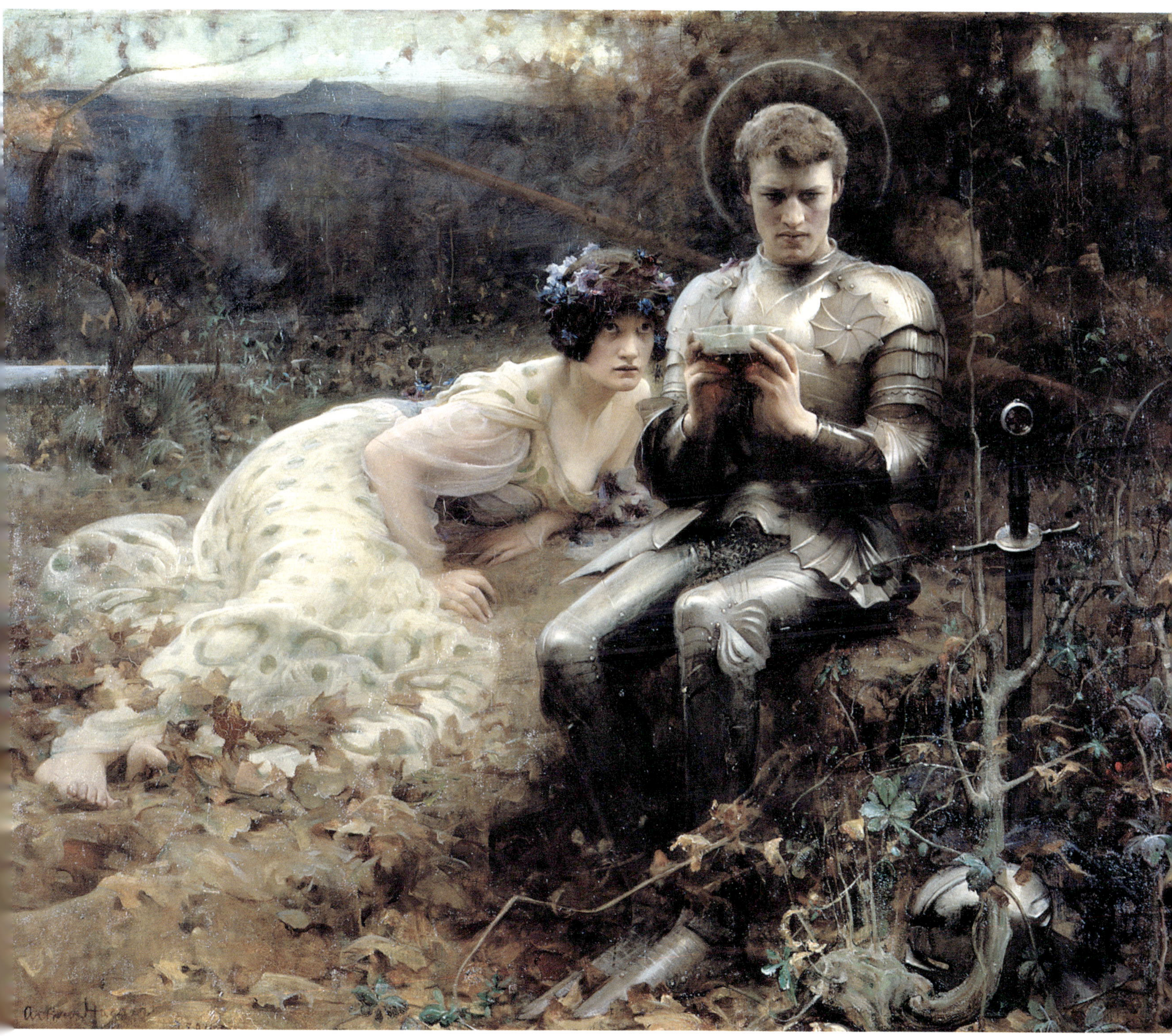

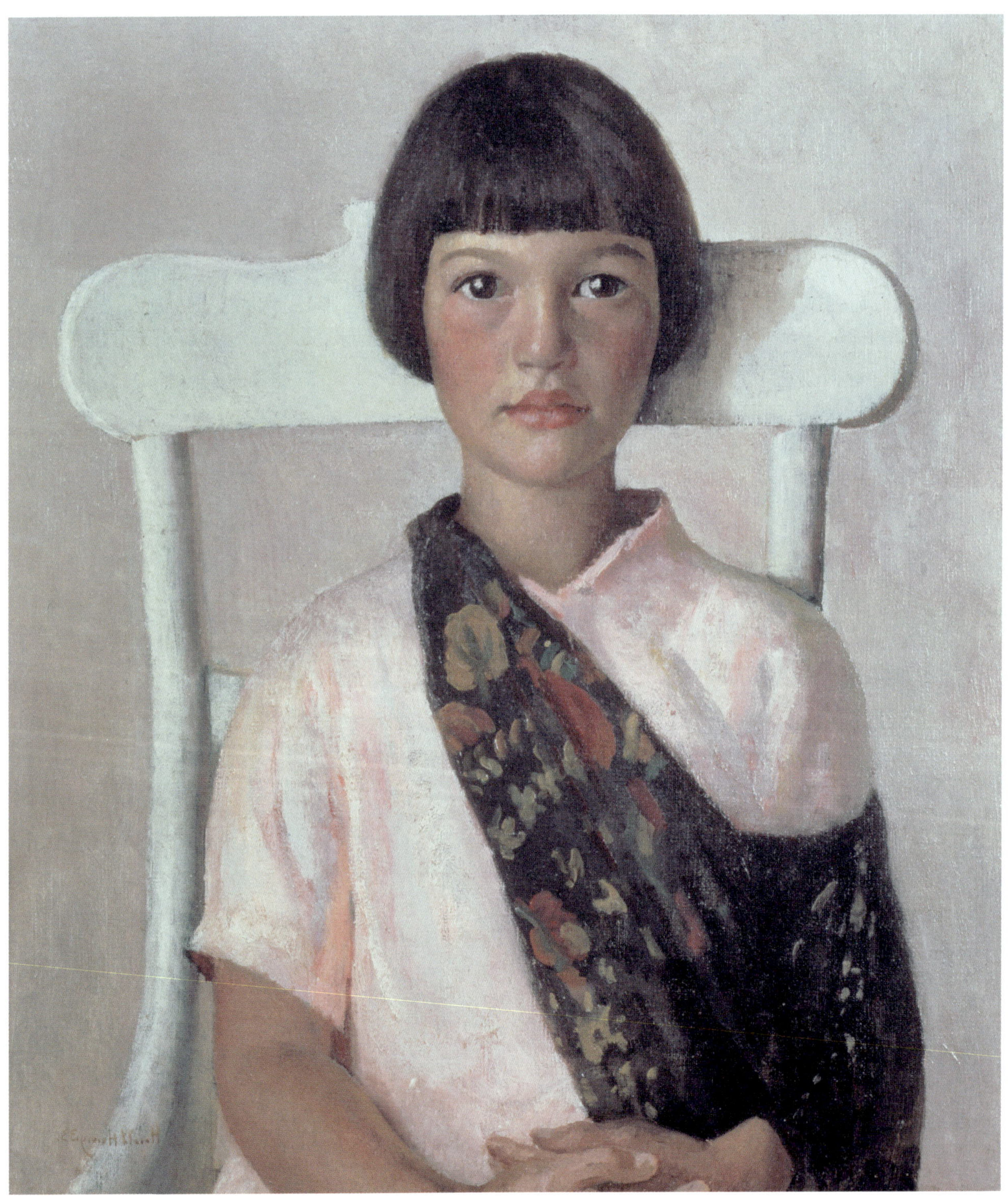

'The old woman I shall become will be
quite different from the woman I am now.
Another I is beginning.'

Harold Harvey,
Zena, 1933

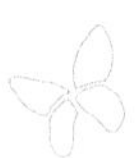

'Two roads diverged in a yellow wood,
And sorry I could not travel both
And be one traveler, long I stood
And looked down one as far as I could
To where it bent in the undergrowth;

Then took the other, as just as fair,
And having perhaps the better claim,
Because it was grassy and wanted wear;
Though as for that the passing there
Had worn them really about the same,

And both that morning equally lay
In leaves no step had trodden black.
Oh, I kept the first for another day!
Yet knowing how way leads on to way,
I doubted if I should ever come back.

I shall be telling this with a sigh
Somewhere ages and ages hence:
Two roads diverged in a wood, and I —
I took the one less traveled by,
And that has made all the difference.'

Robert Frost, *The Road Not Taken* (1915)

Paul Ranson,
Pommier aux Fruits Rouges, 1902

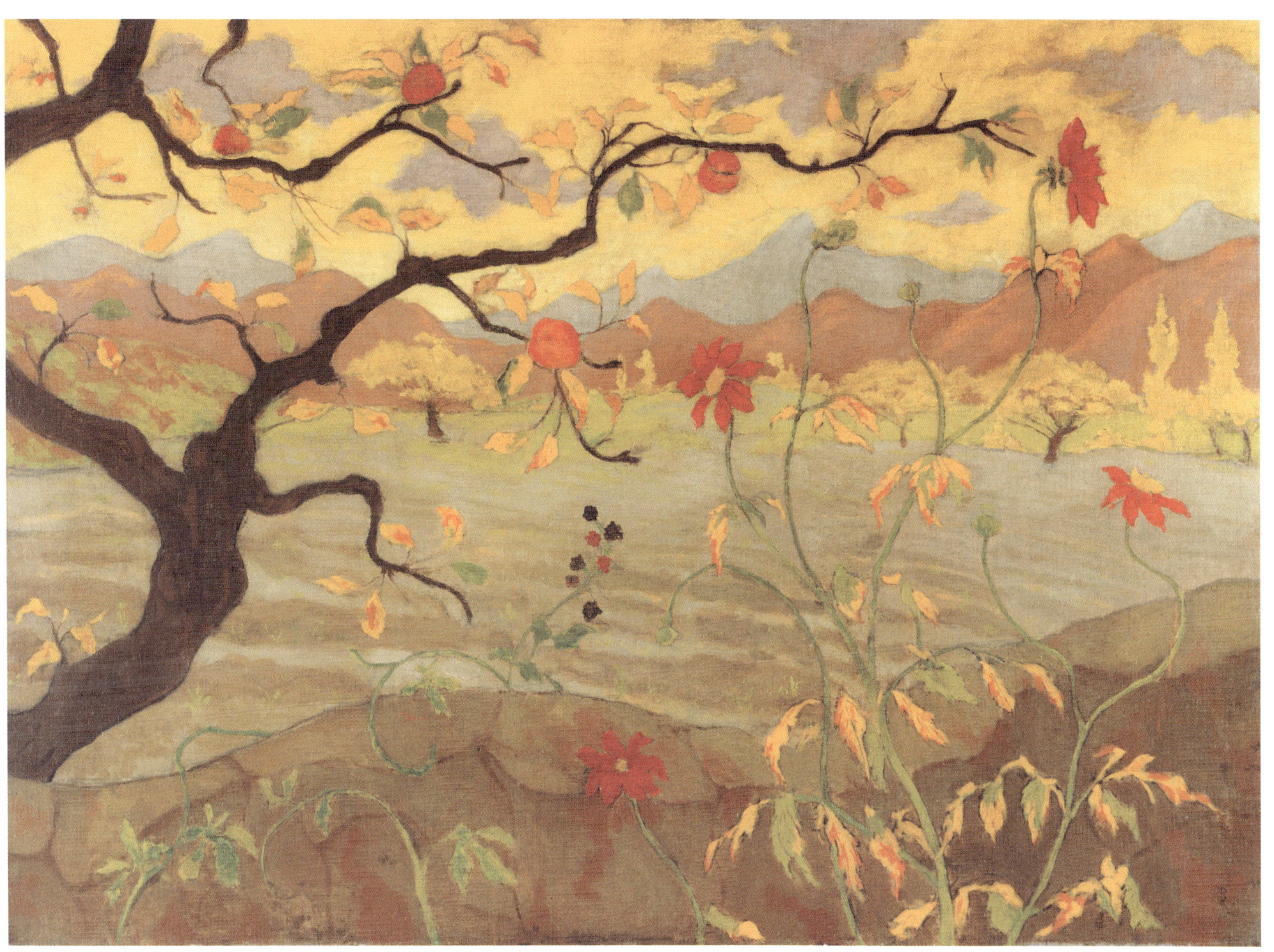

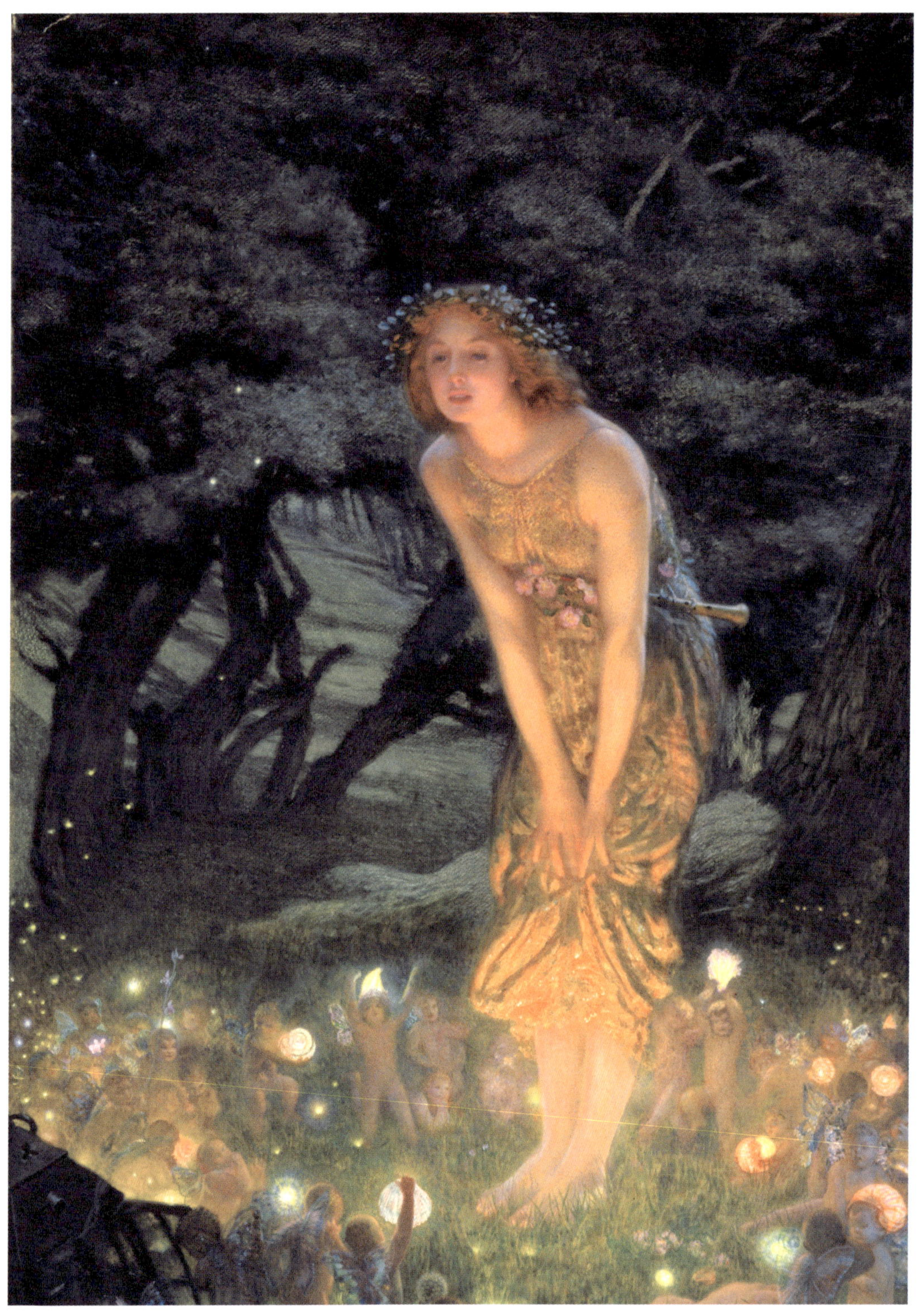

'Faeries, come take me out of this dull world,
For I would ride with you upon the wind,
Run on the top of the dishevelled tide,
And dance upon the mountains like a flame.'

William Butler Yeats, from *The Land of Heart's Desire* (1894)

Edward Robert Hughes,
Midsummer Eve, 1908

'Touch me, touch the palm of your hand to my body as I pass,
Be not afraid of my body.'

Henri Lebasque,
Nude Lying Against a Bed

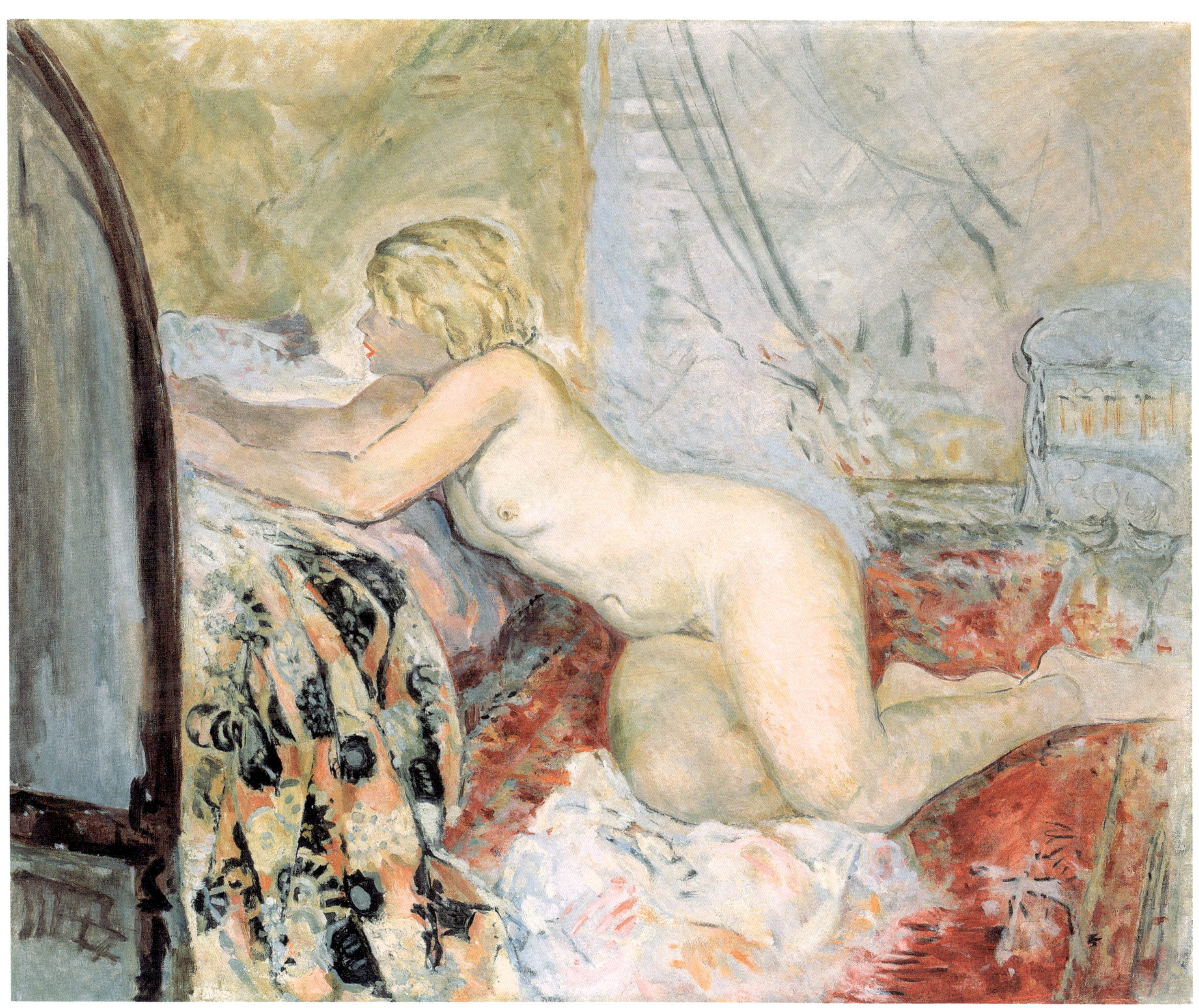

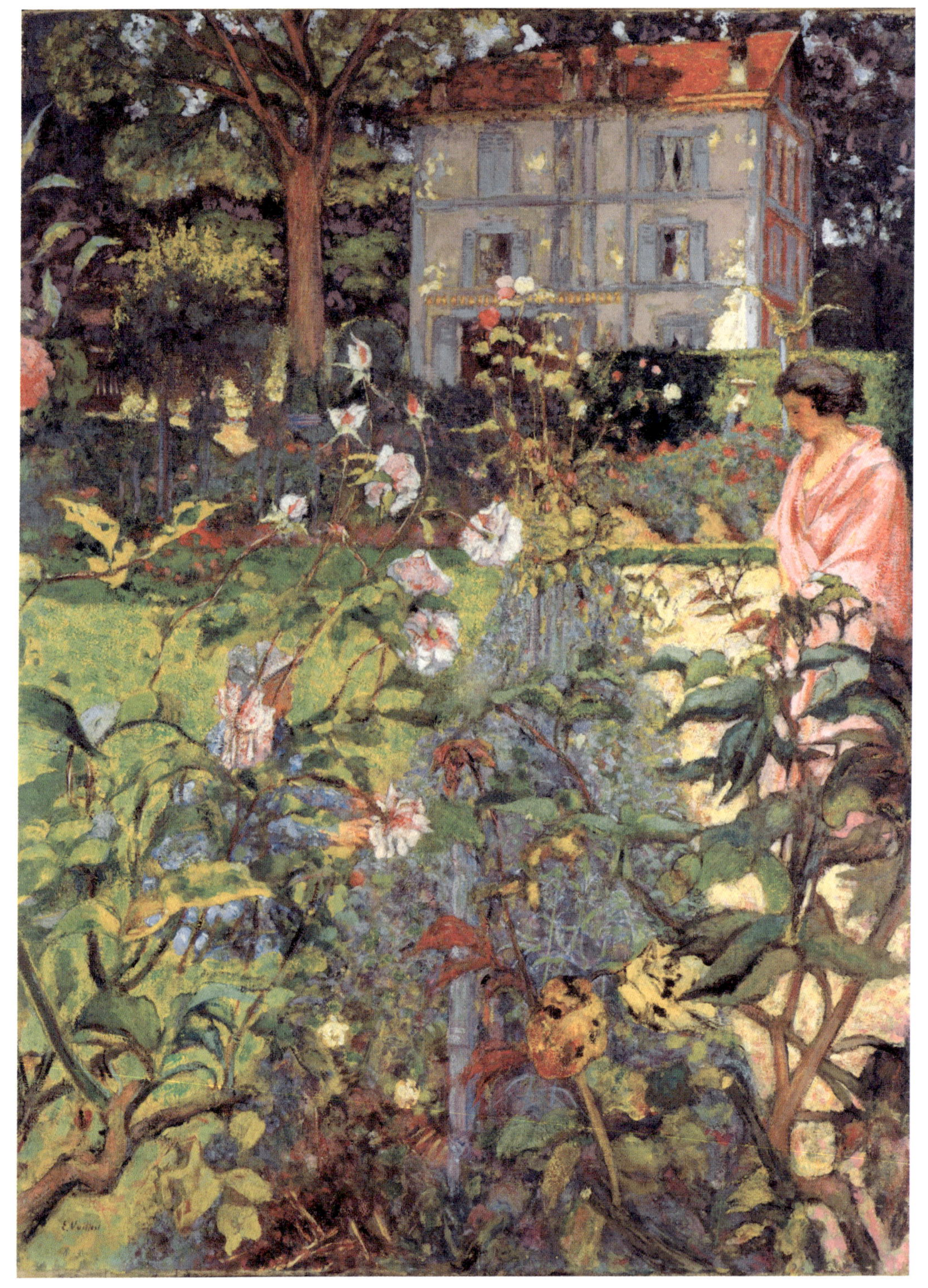

'To know someone here or there
with whom you can feel there is
understanding in spite of distances
or thoughts expressed ... That can
make life a garden.'

Édouard Vuillard,
Garden at Vaucresson, 1920

'When one door of happiness closes, another opens; but often we look so long at the closed door that we do not see the one which has been opened for us.'

Abram Efimovich Arkhipov,
Les Visiteurs (The Visitors), 1914

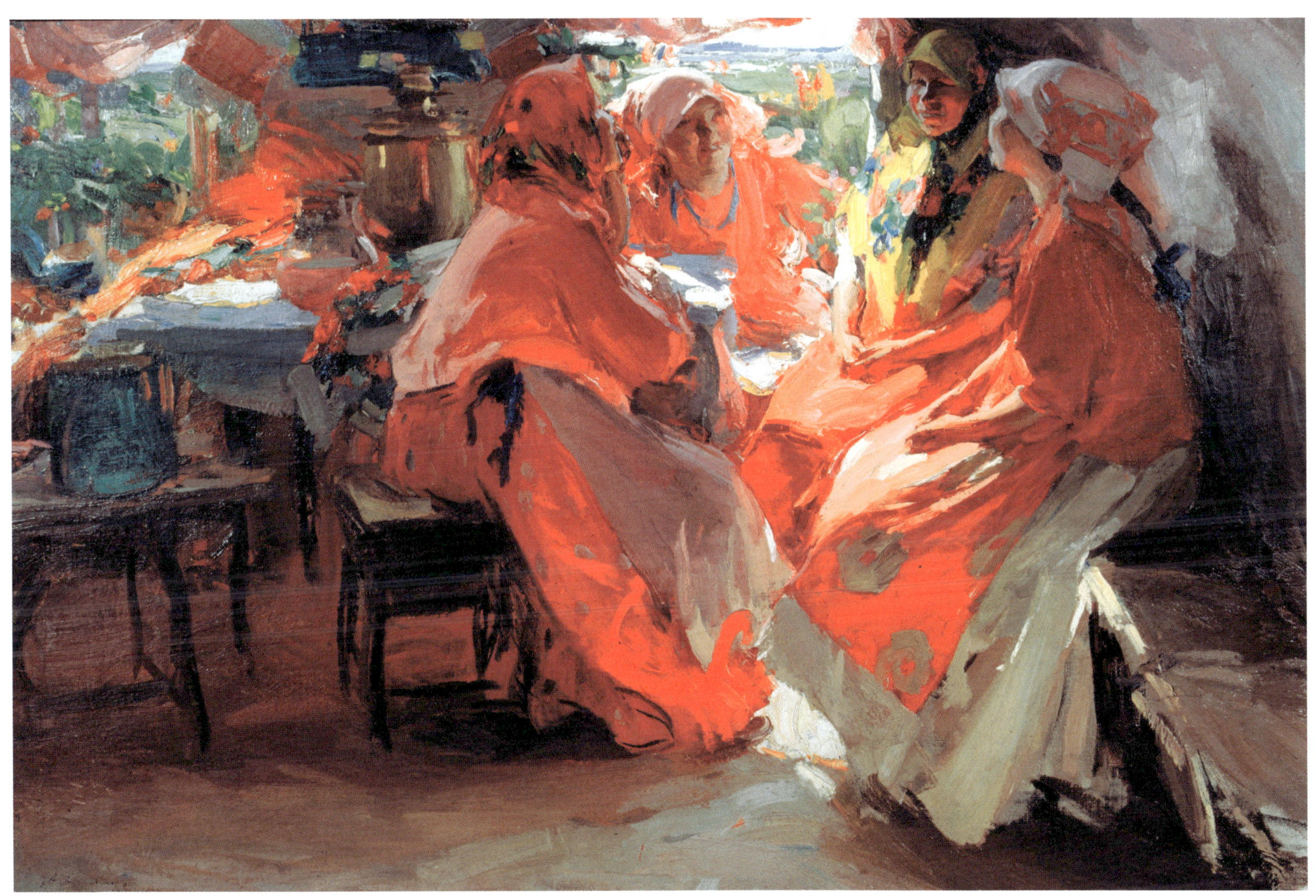

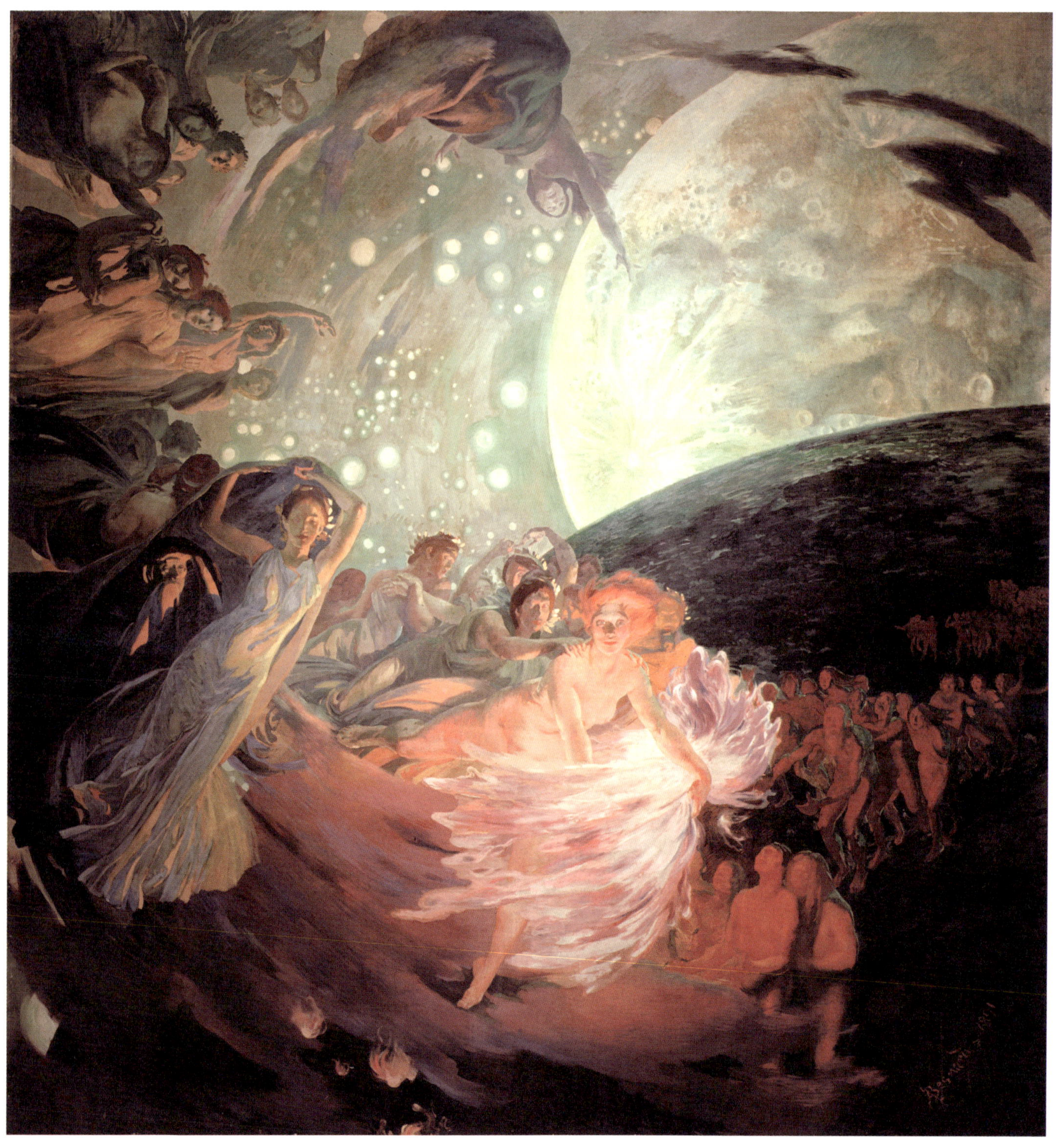

'And with dream-awakened eyes, she saw all the beauty
around her, saw the sea, felt the sun, and knew she had to
vanish for a while from the human plane and make every
sacrifice in order to create her world anew out of the depths.'

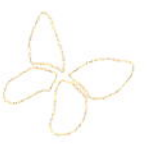

'It isn't what you have or who you are or where you are or what you are doing that makes you happy or unhappy. It is what you think about it.'

Francesc Masriera,
Moorish Girl, c.1889

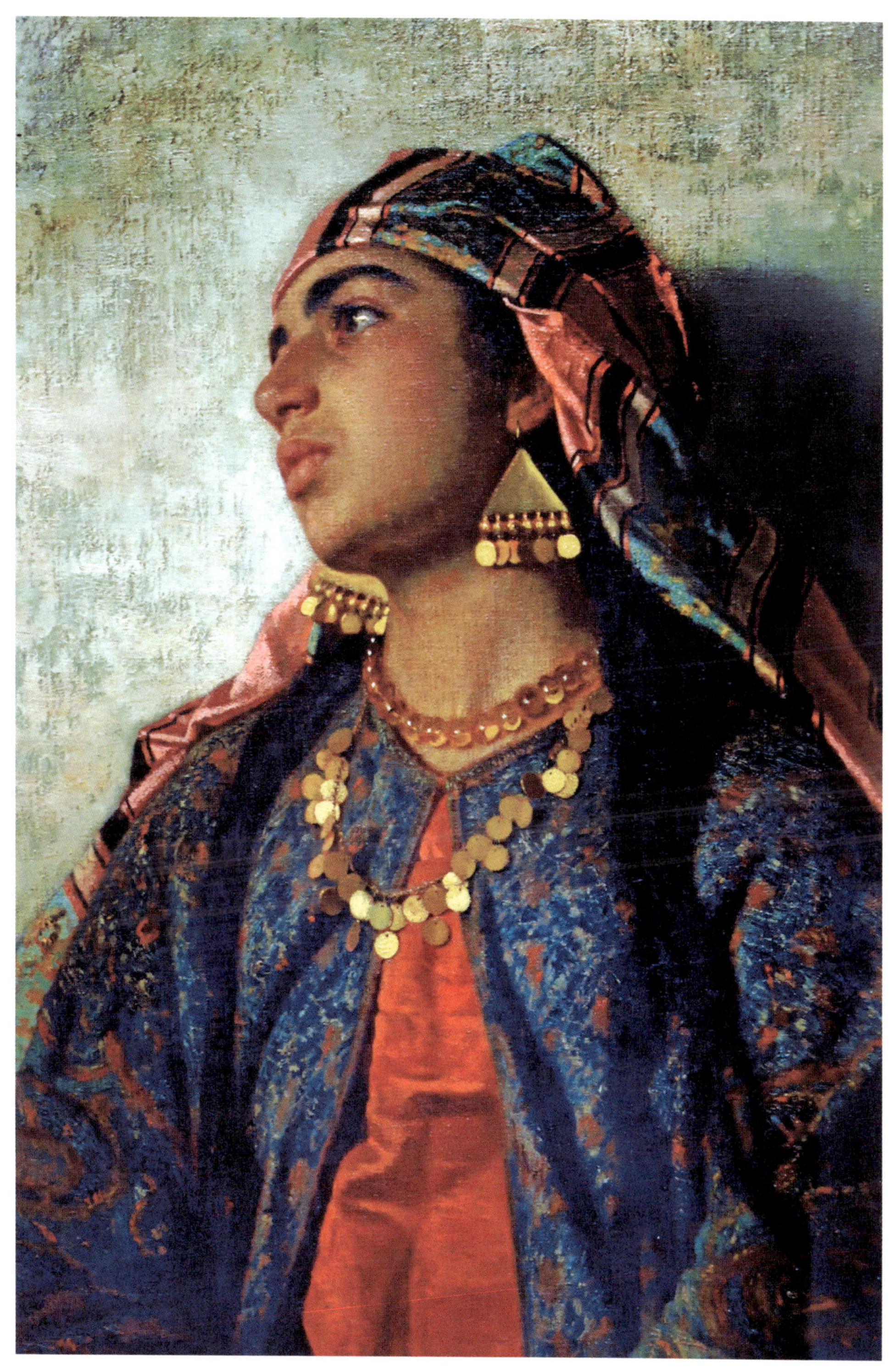

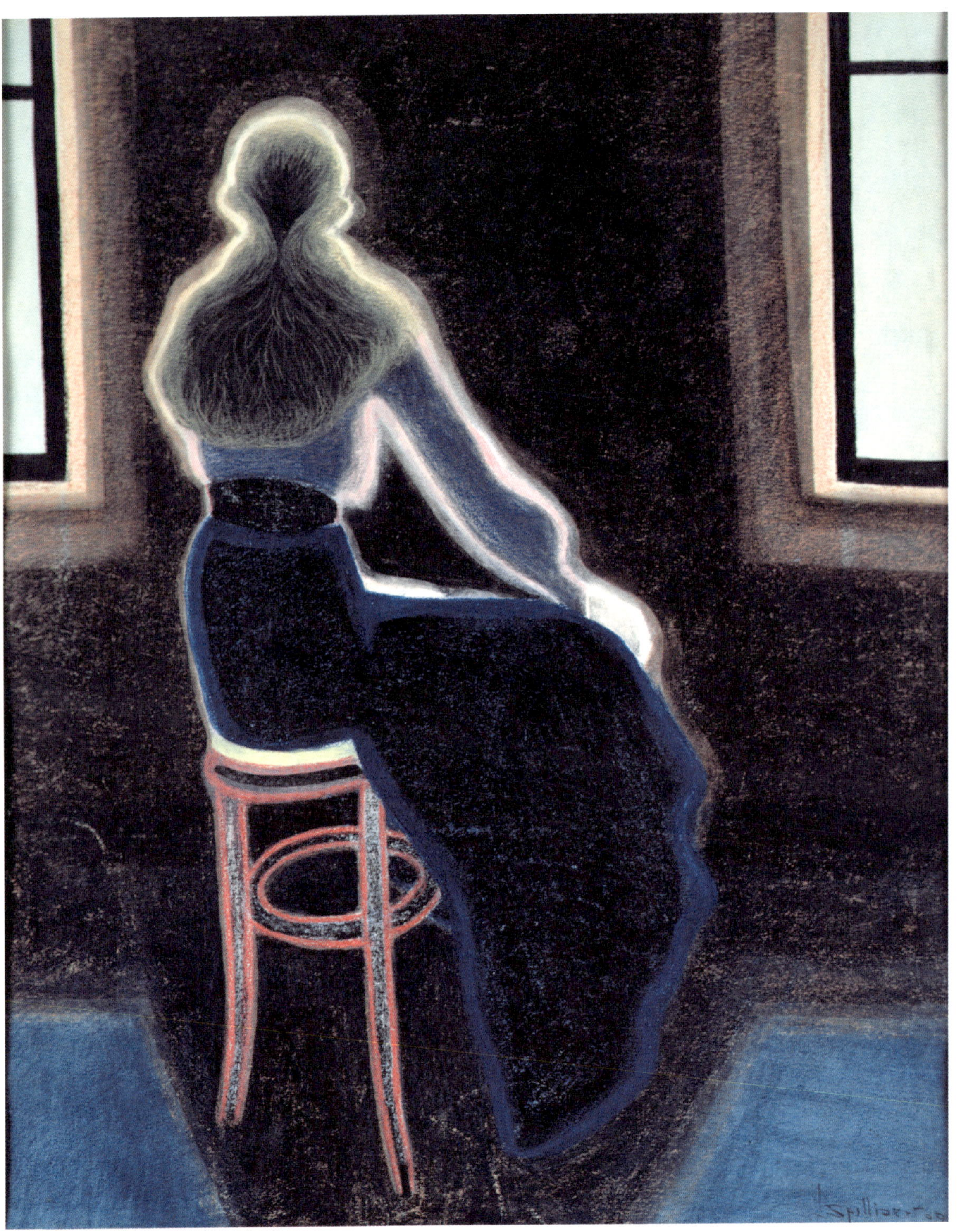

'It may be that you are not yourself luminous, but that you are a conductor of light.
Some people without possessing genius have a remarkable power of stimulating it.'

Arthur Conan Doyle, from *The Hound of the Baskervilles* (1902)

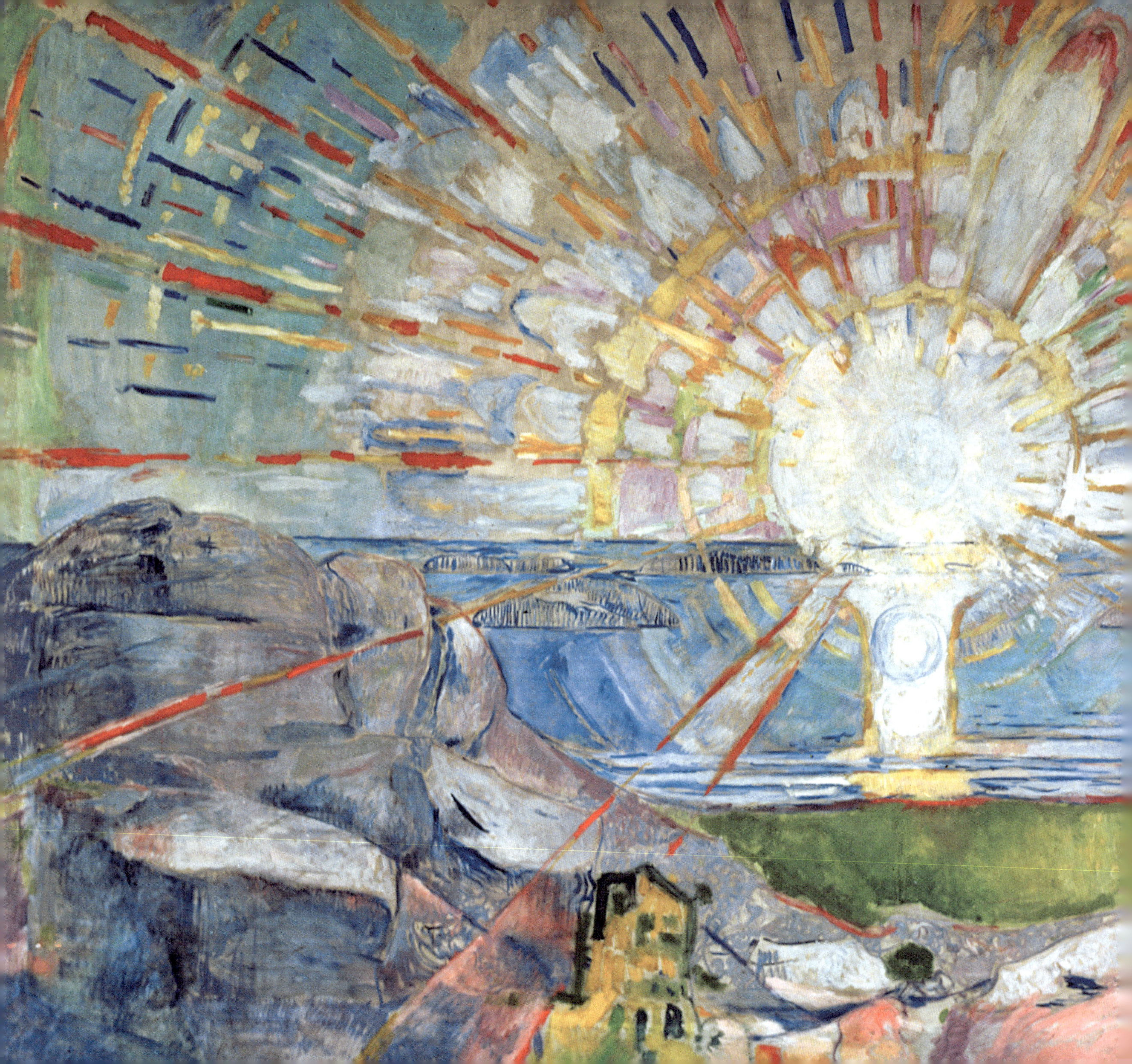

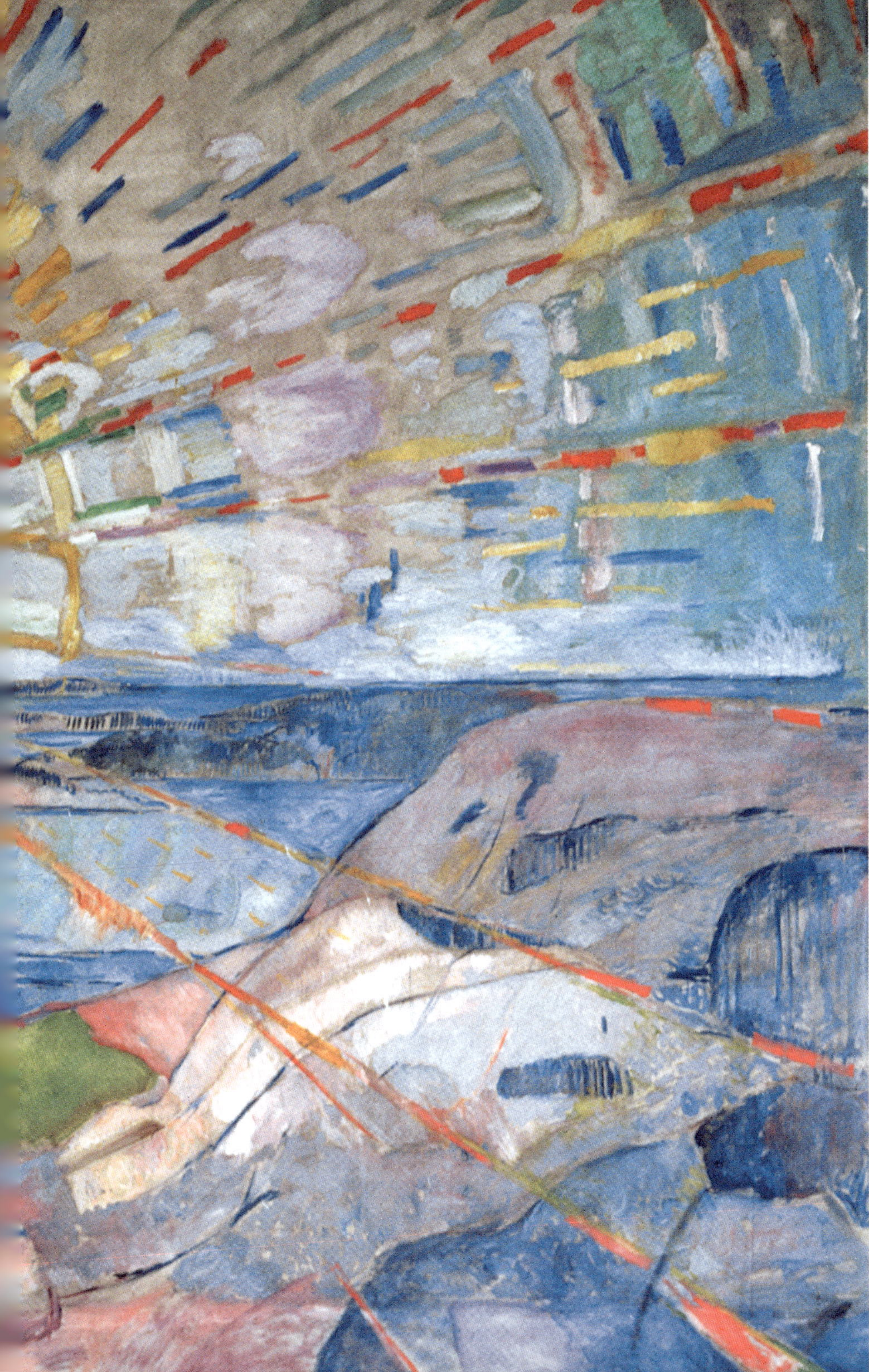

'Laughter is a sunbeam
of the soul.'

Thomas Mann, from *The Magic Mountain* (1924)

Edvard Munch,
The Sun, 1911–1916

'Every heart sings a song,
incomplete, until another heart
whispers back. Those who wish to
sing always find a song. At the touch
of a lover, everyone becomes a poet.'

Plato (c.428–c.348BCE)

Elisabeth Jerichau-Baumann,
An Egyptian Pot Seller at Gizeh, 1876–1878

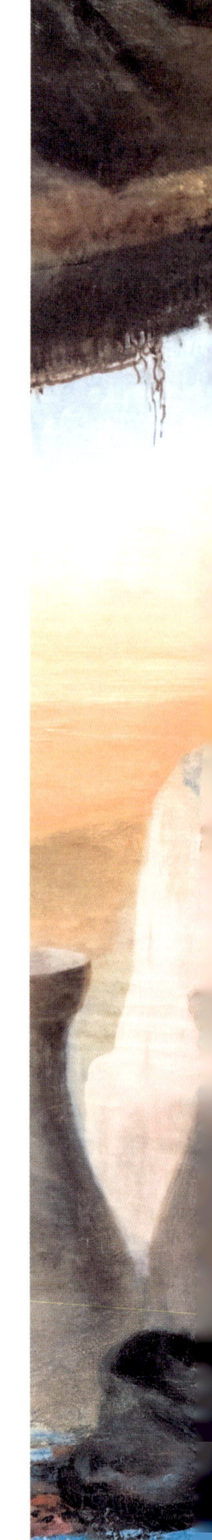

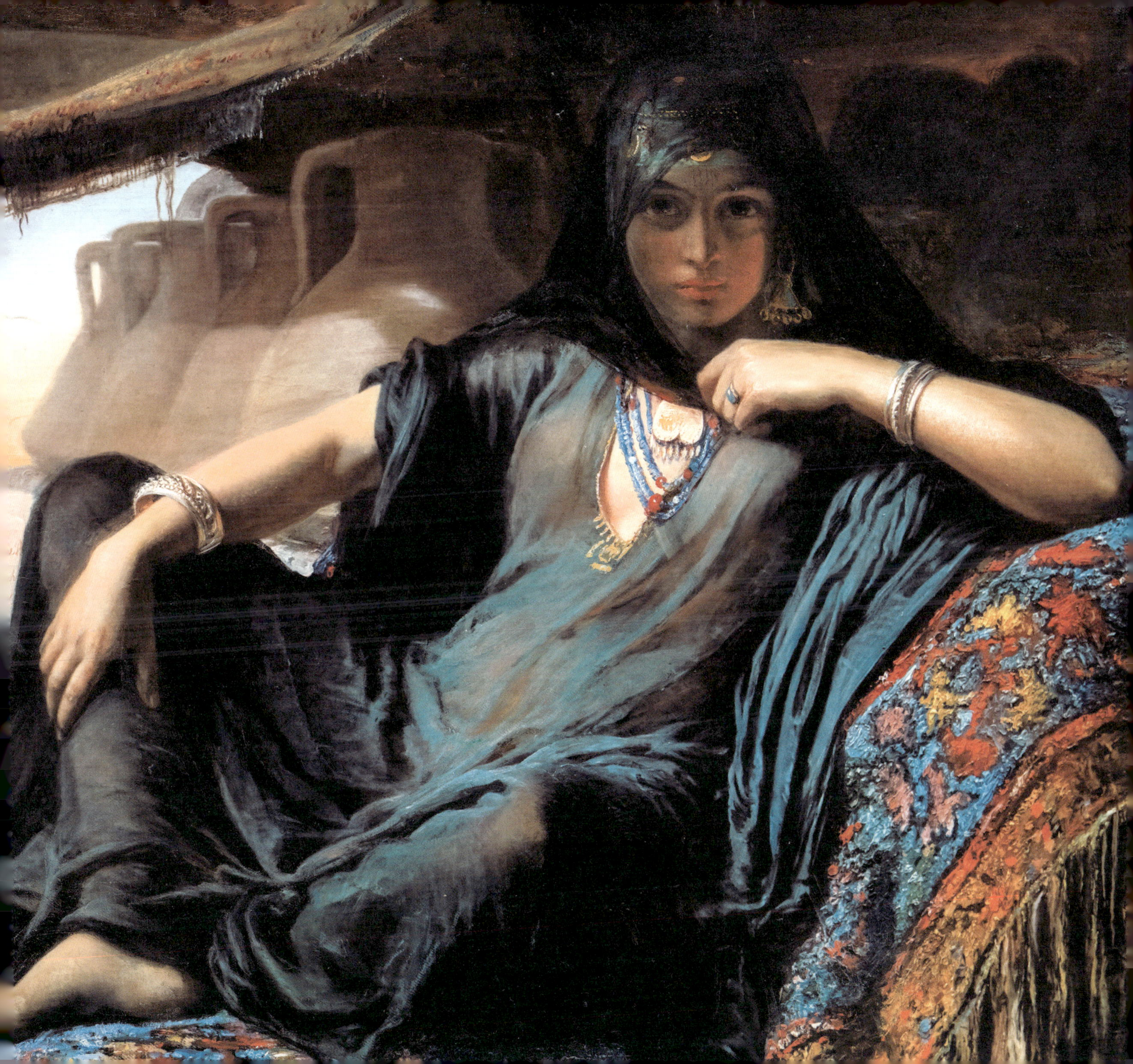

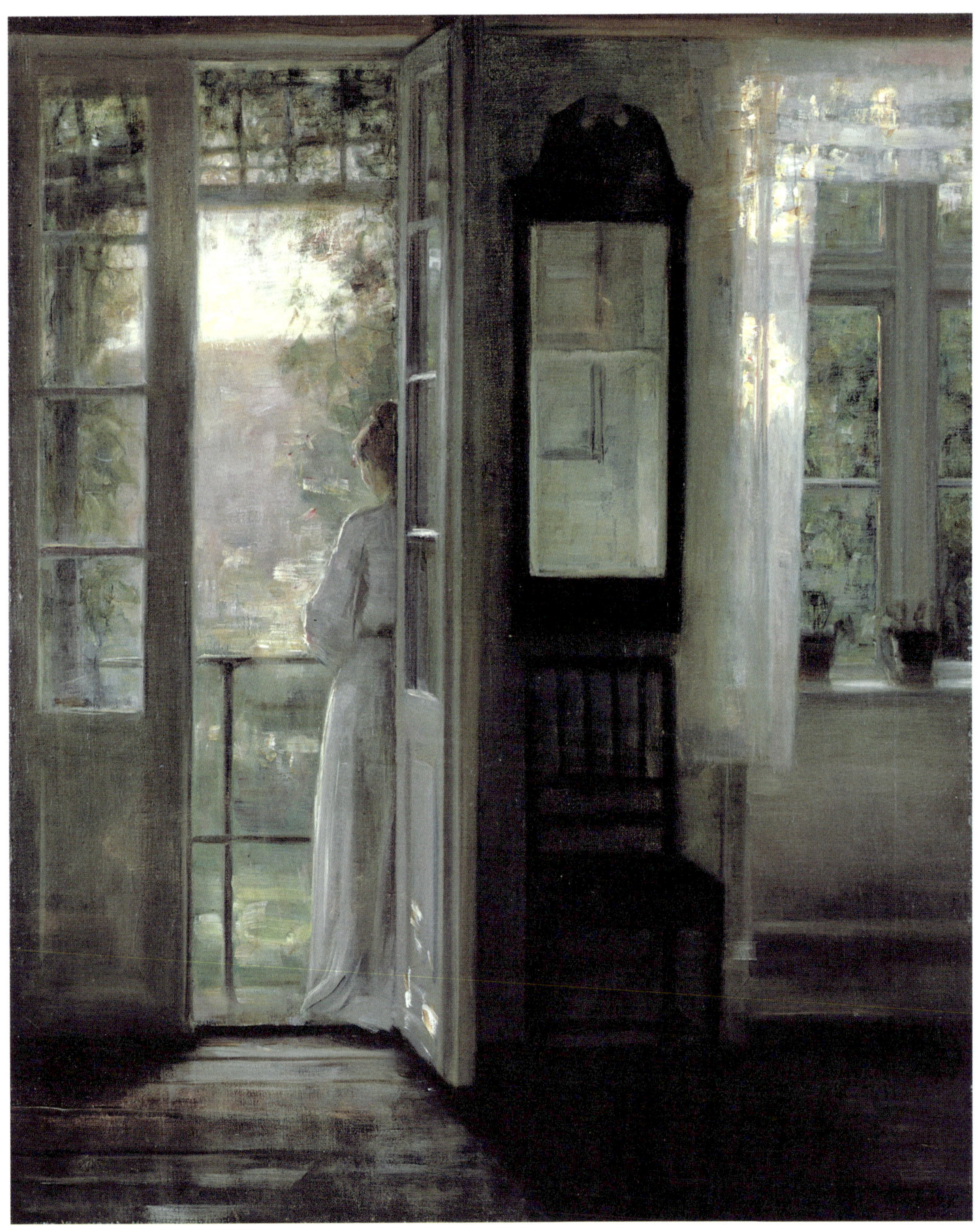

'The most beautiful people we have known are those who have known defeat, known suffering, known struggle, known loss, and have found their way out of the depths. These persons have an appreciation, a sensitivity, and an understanding of life that fills them with compassion, gentleness, and a deep loving concern. Beautiful people do not just happen.'

Dr Elisabeth Kübler-Ross, from *Death: The Final Stage of Growth* (1974)

Carl Vilhelm Holsøe,
Girl Standing on a Balcony

'I wondered whether music might not be the
unique example of what might have been — if
the invention of language, the formation of
words, the analysis of ideas had not intervened
— the means of communication between souls.'

Marcel Proust, from *The Captive* / *The Fugitive* (1923 / 1925)

Frank Xavier Leyendecker,
The Flapper, 1922

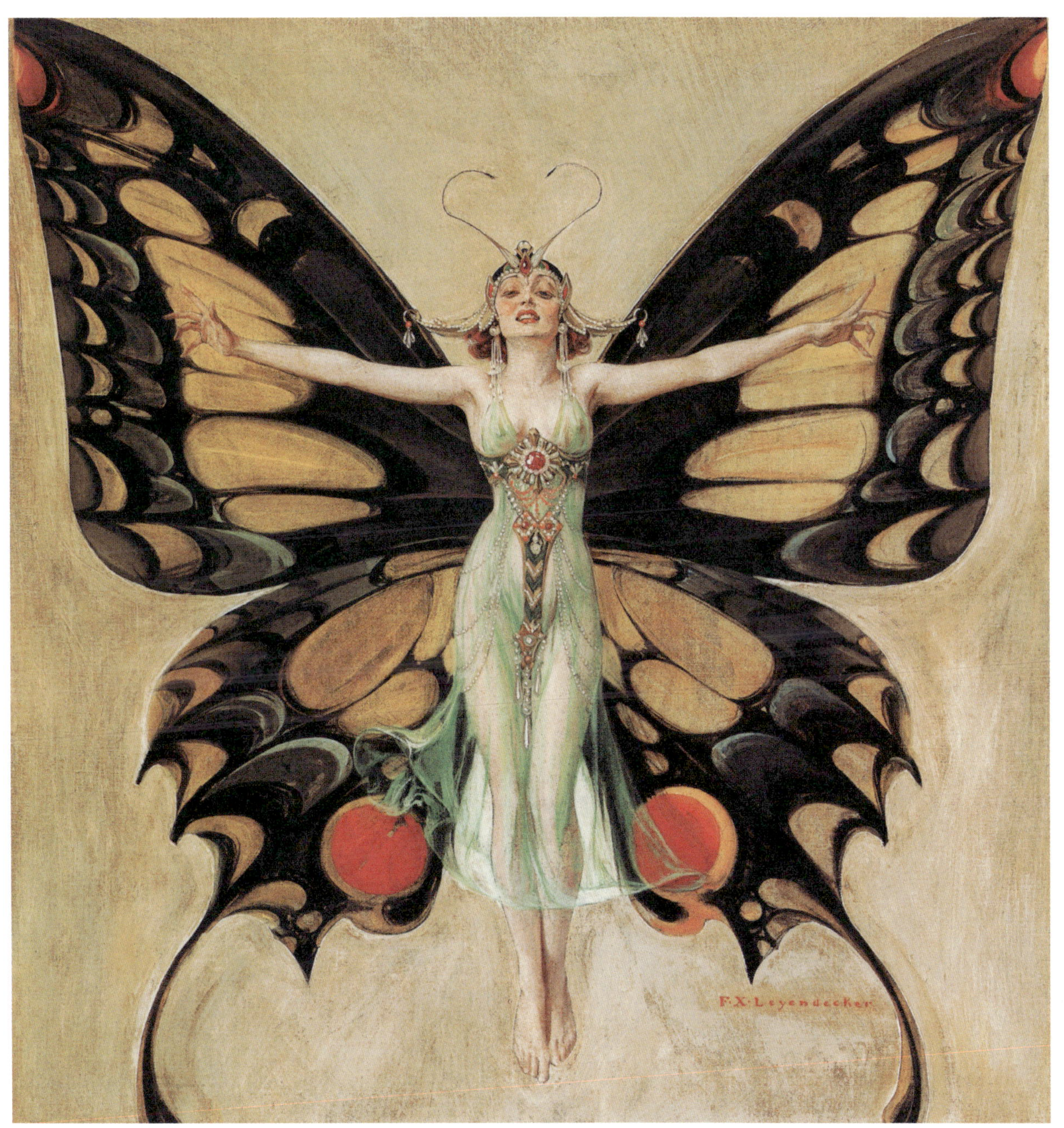
F.X.Leyendecker

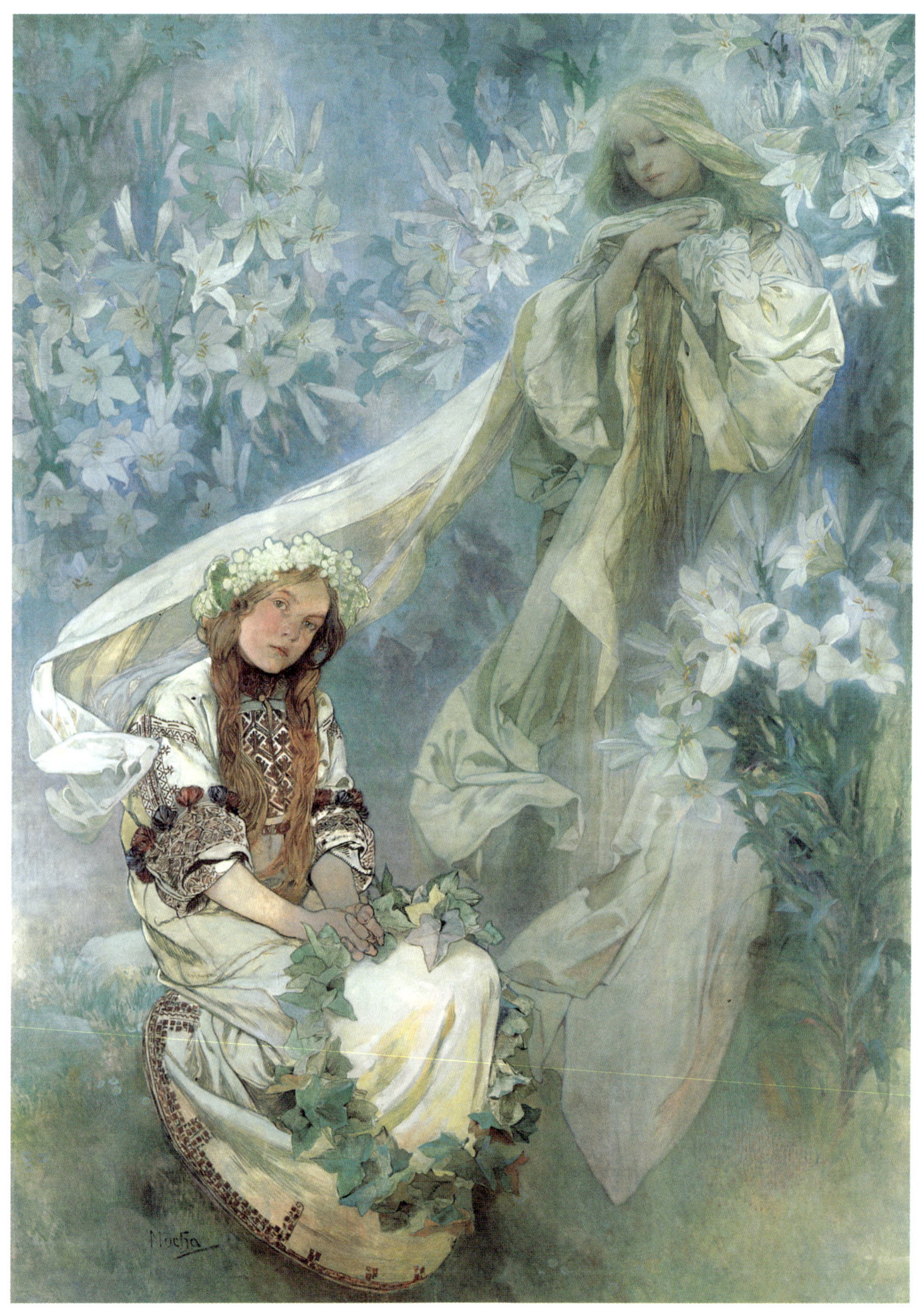

'If you look the right way, you can see that the whole world is a garden.'

Frances Hodgson Burnett, from *The Secret Garden* (1911)

Alphonse Mucha,
Madonna of the Lilies, 1905

'The minute I heard my first love story, I
started looking for you, not knowing how
blind that was. Lovers don't finally meet
somewhere. They're in each other all along.'

Rumi (1207–1273)

Henry Scott Tuke,
The Promise, 1888

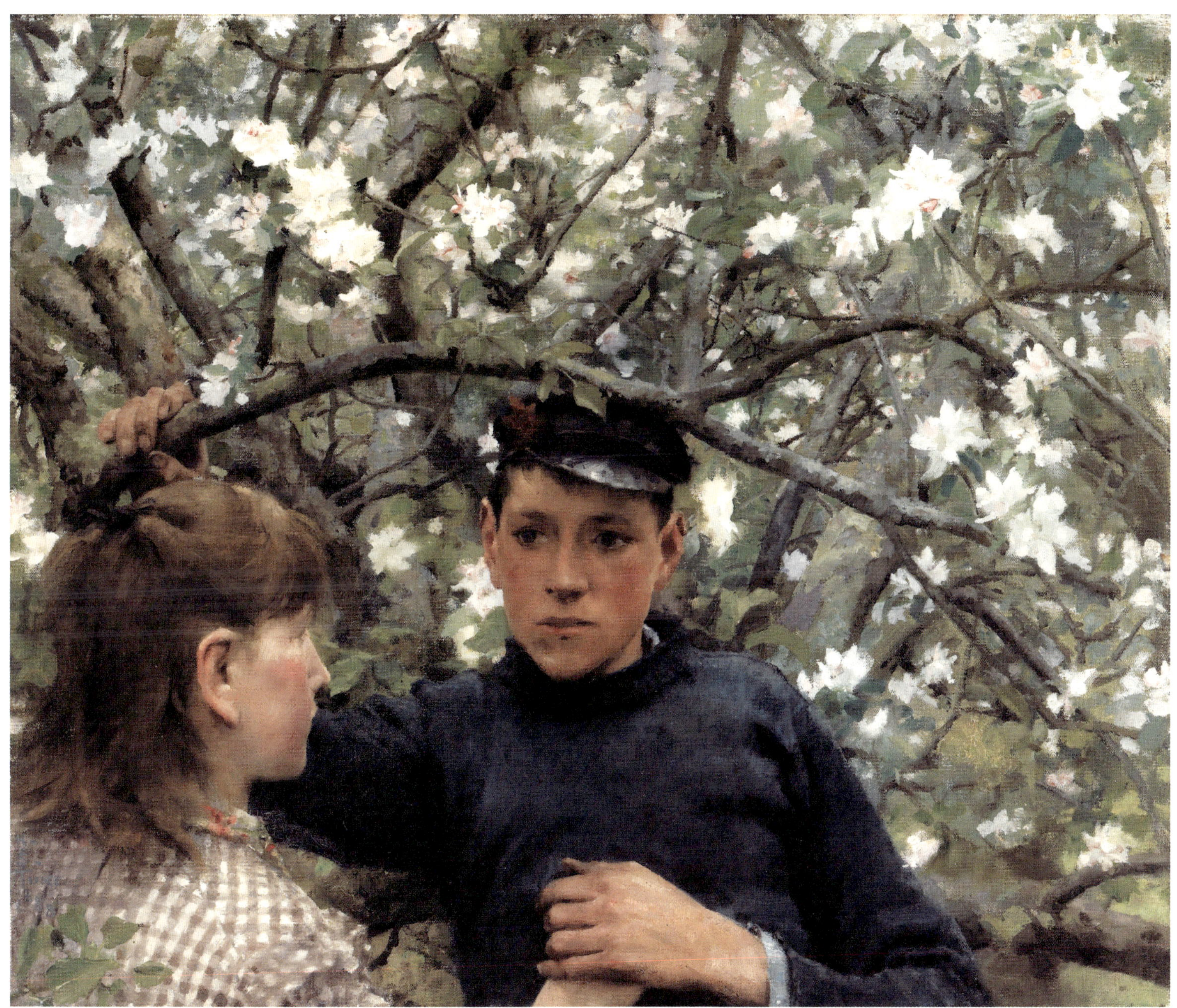

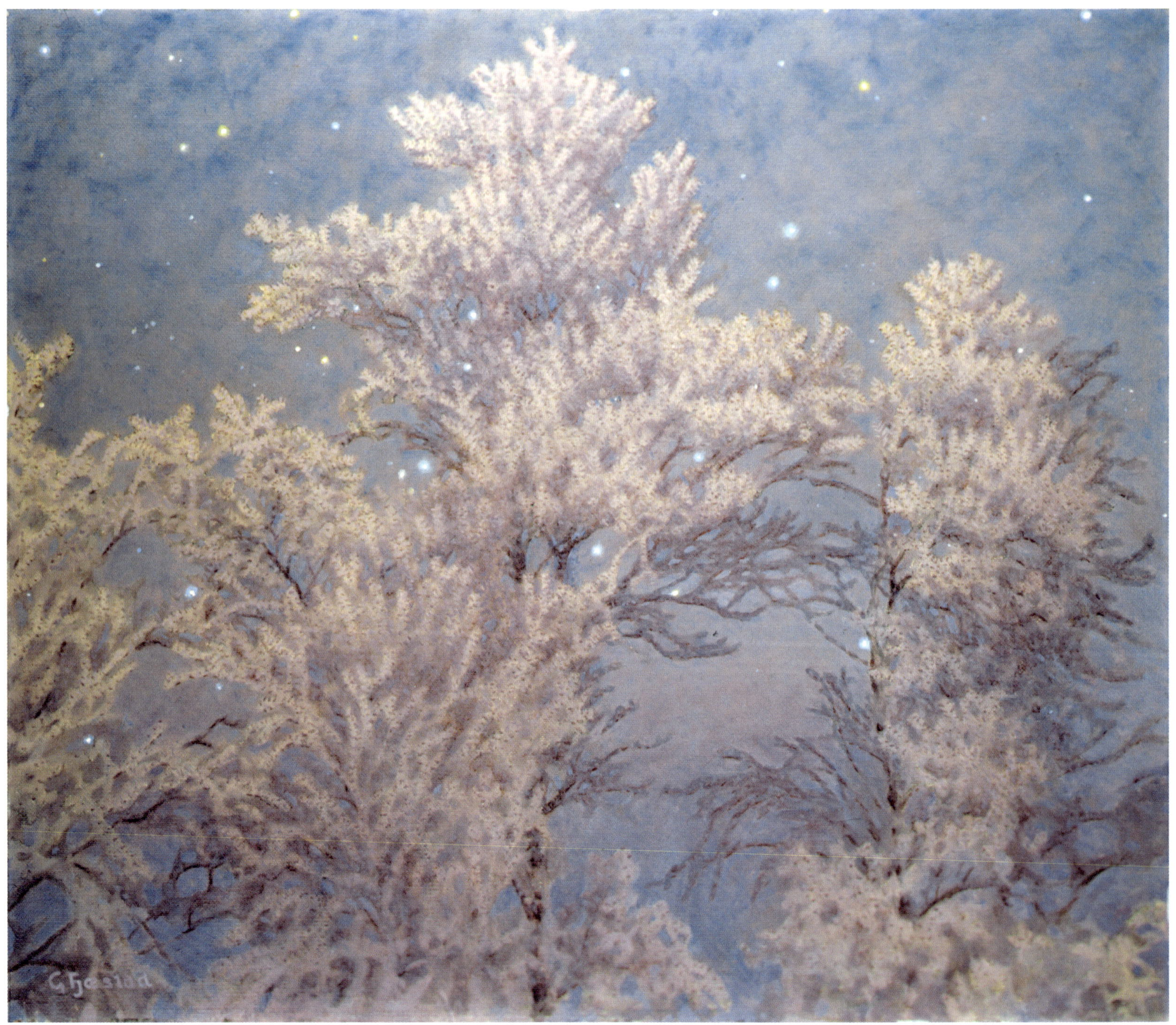
G Hessing

'Tonight I can write the saddest lines.
To think that I do not have her. To feel that I have lost her.
To hear the immense night, still more immense without her,
And the verse falls to the snow like dew to the pasture.'

Pablo Neruda, from *Tonight I Can Write* (1924)

Gustaf Fjaestad,
Hoar Frost and Stars

'When despair for the world grows in me
and I wake in the night at the least sound
in fear of what my life and my children's lives may be,
I go and lie down where the wood drake
rests in his beauty on the water, and the great heron feeds.
I come into the peace of wild things
who do not tax their lives with forethought
of grief. I come into the presence of still water.
And I feel above me the day-blind stars
waiting with their light. For a time
I rest in the grace of the world, and am free.'

Wendell Berry, *The Peace of Wild Things* (2018)

Henri Lebasque,
Hammock, 1923

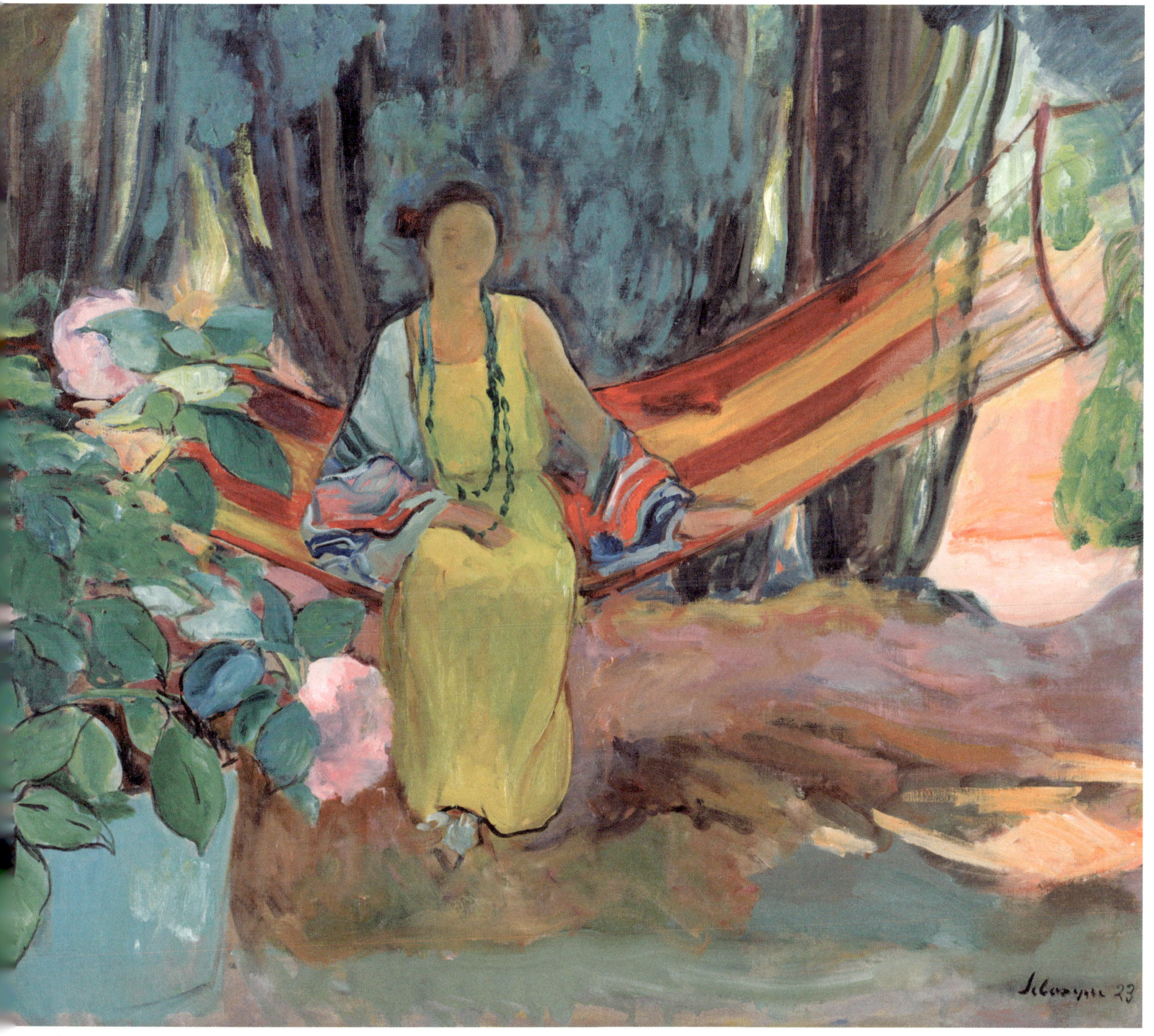

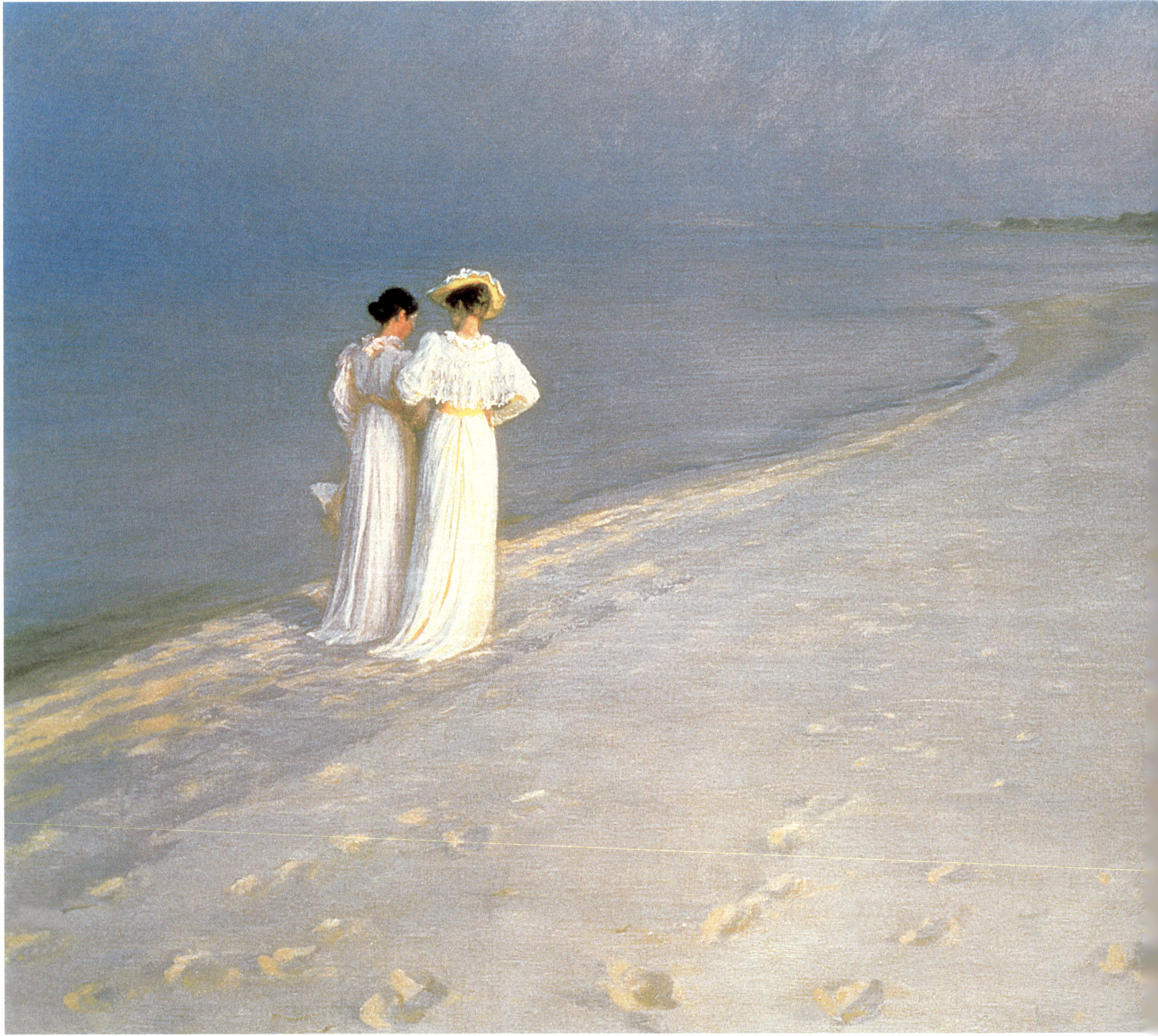

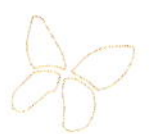

'What greater thing is there for two human souls, than to feel that they are joined for life — to strengthen each other in all labour, to rest on each other in all sorrow, to minister to each other in all pain, to be one with each other in silent unspeakable memories at the moment of the last parting?'

George Eliot, from *Adam Bede* (1859)

Peder Severin Krøyer,
Summer Evening on Skagen's Southern Beach, 1893

'Don't be afraid. There are exquisite things in store for you.
This is merely the beginning.'

Oscar Wilde, from *The Picture of Dorian Gray* (1890)

Simon Maris,
Isabella, 1906

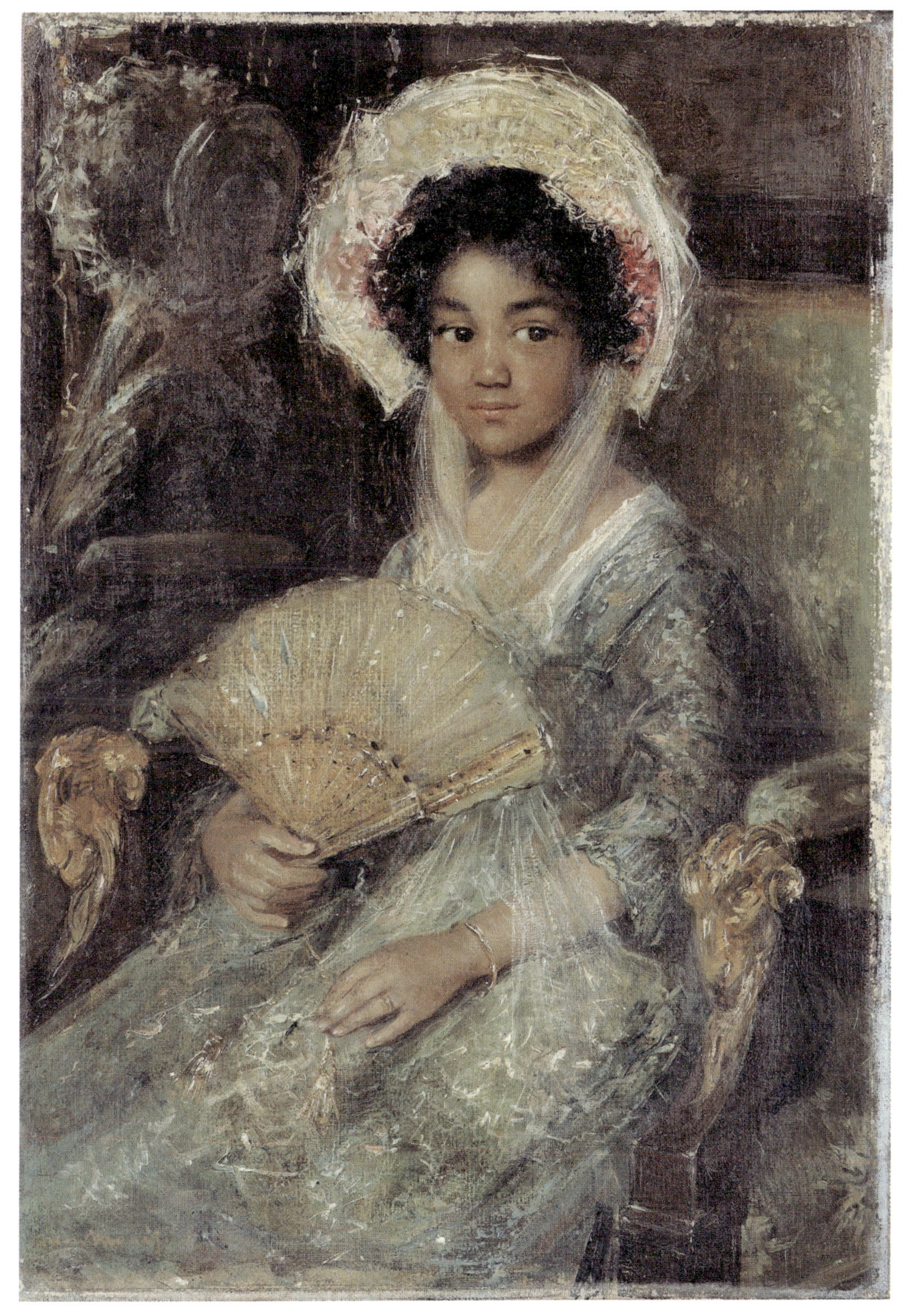

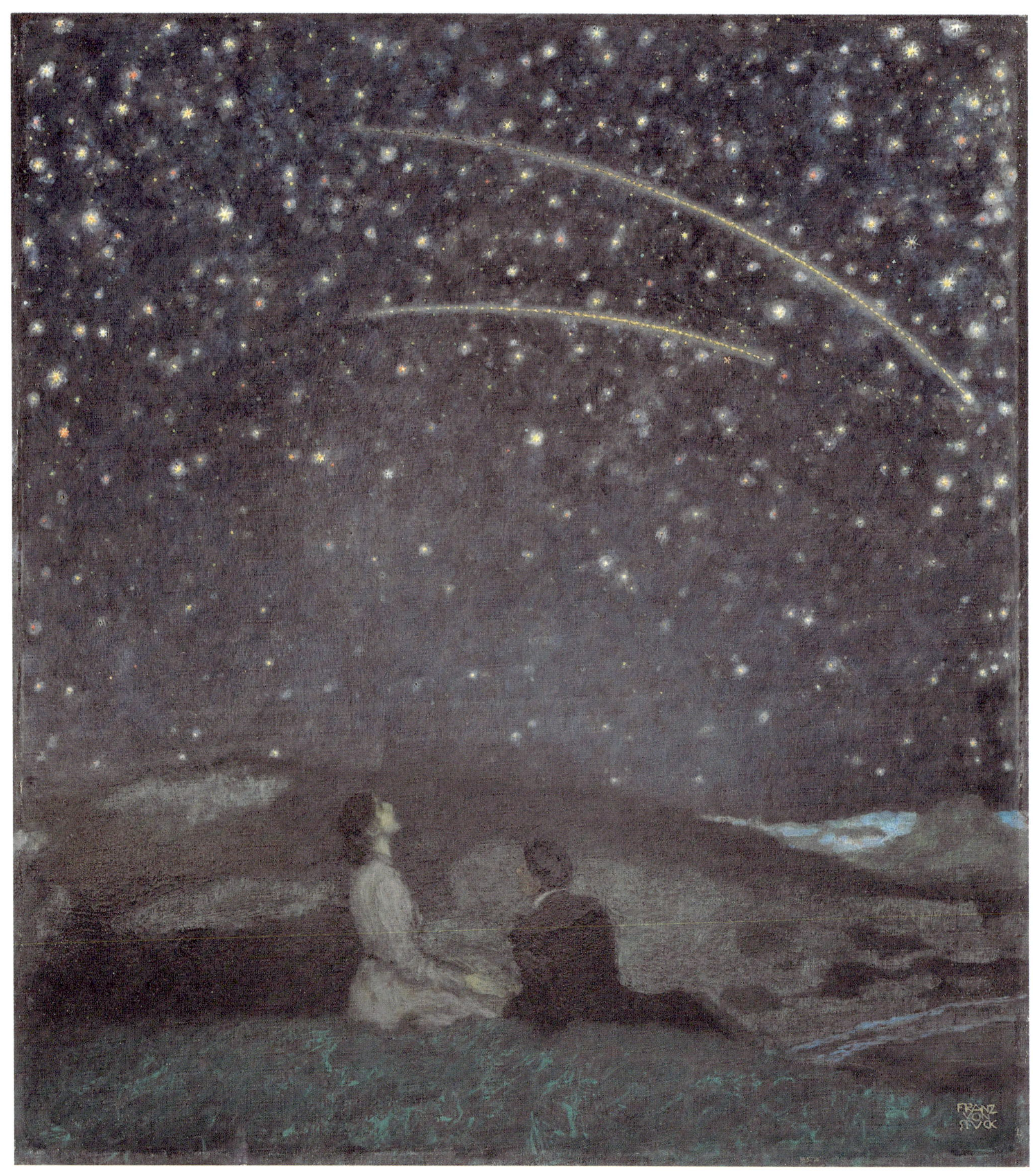

FRANZ
VON
STVCK

'Every great dream begins with a dreamer. Always remember, you have within you the strength, the patience, and the passion to reach for the stars to change the world.'

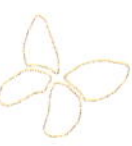

Franz von Stuck,
Falling Stars, 1912

'I do know that for the sympathy of one living being, I would make peace with all. I have love in me the likes of which you can scarcely imagine and rage the likes of which you would not believe. If I cannot satisfy the one, I will indulge the other.'

Thomas Cooper Gotch,
The Exile, 1930

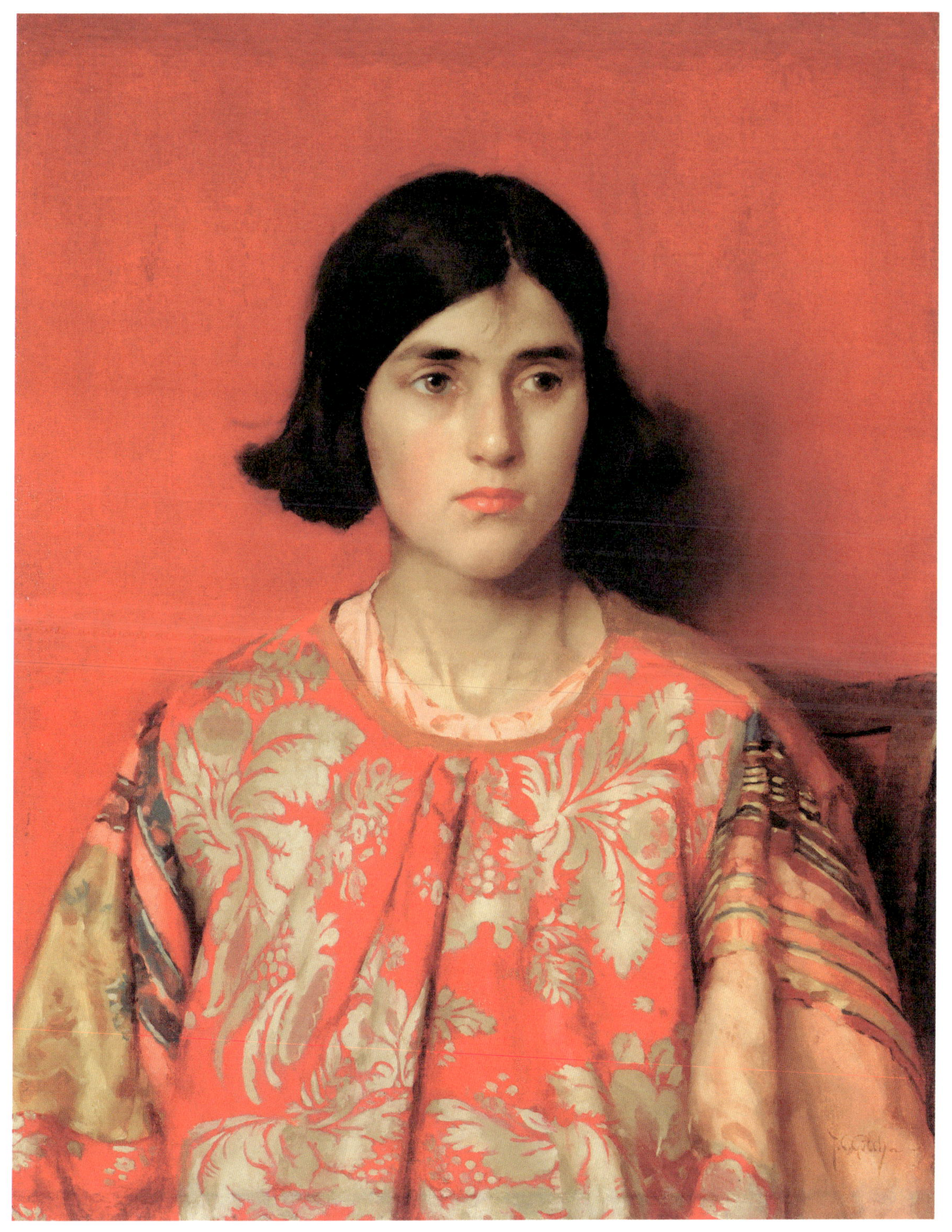

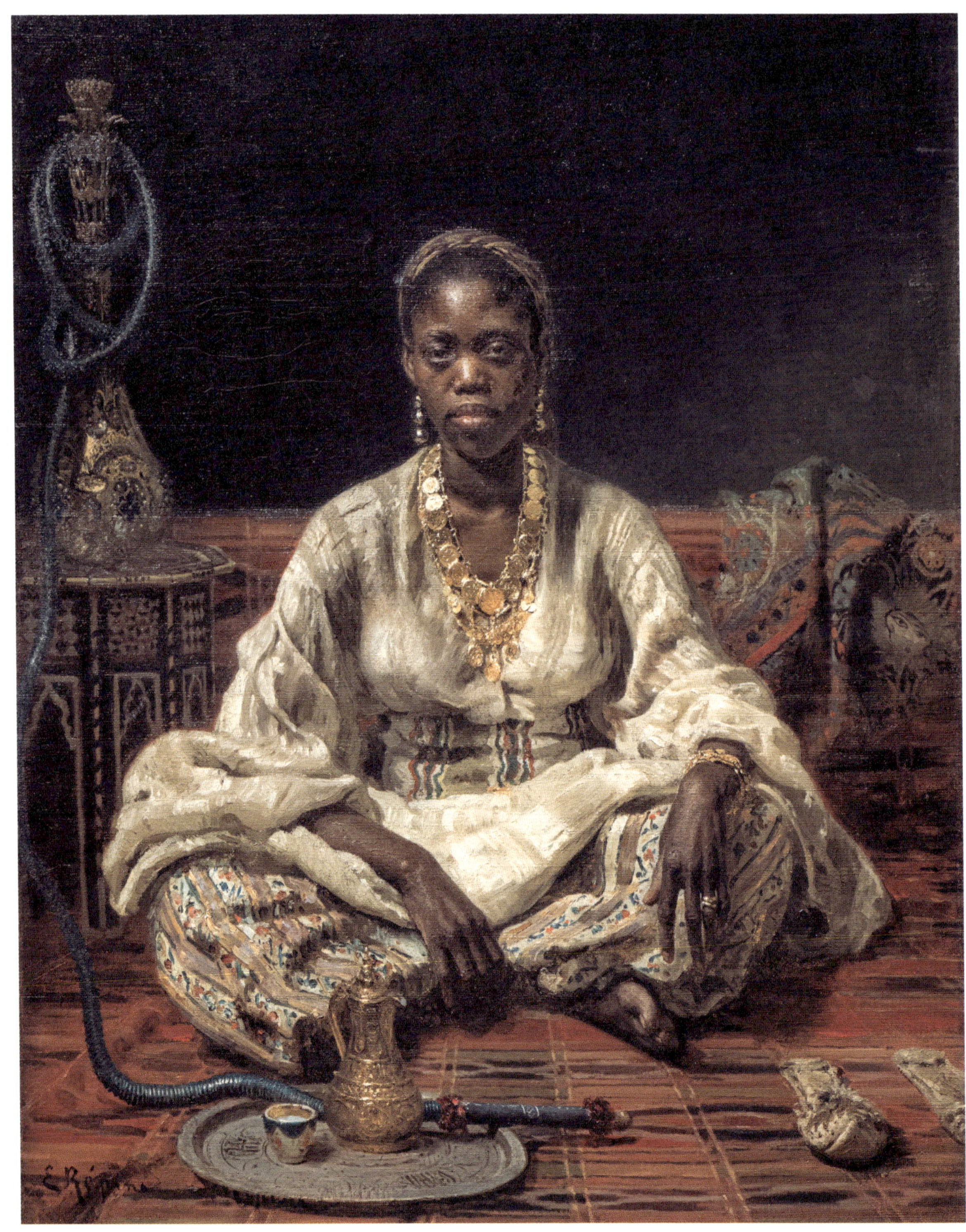

'I love to be alone. I never found the companion that was so companionable as solitude.'

Henry David Thoreau, from *Walden* (1854)

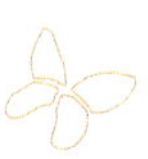

Ilya Yefimovich Repin,
Black Woman (1876)

'Your children are not your children. They are sons and daughters of Life's longing for itself. They come through you but not from you. And though they are with you yet they belong not to you. You may give them your love but not your thoughts, For they have their own thoughts. You may house their bodies but not their souls, For their souls dwell in the house of tomorrow, which you cannot visit, not even in your dreams. You may strive to be like them, but seek not to make them like you. For life goes not backward nor tarries with yesterday.'

Kahlil Gibran, from *The Prophet* (1923)

Virginie Demont-Breton,
Into the water, 1898

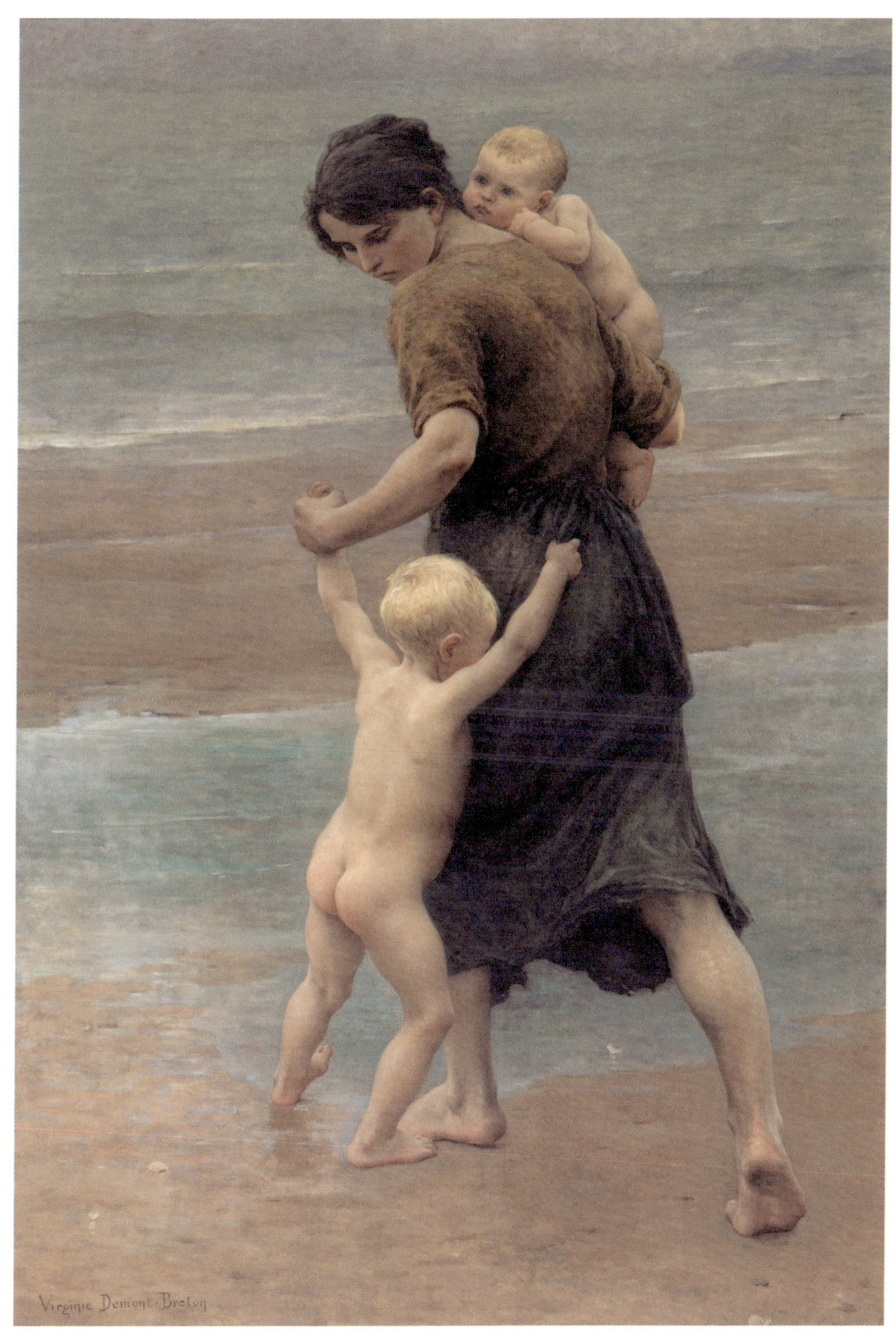

Virginie Demont-Breton

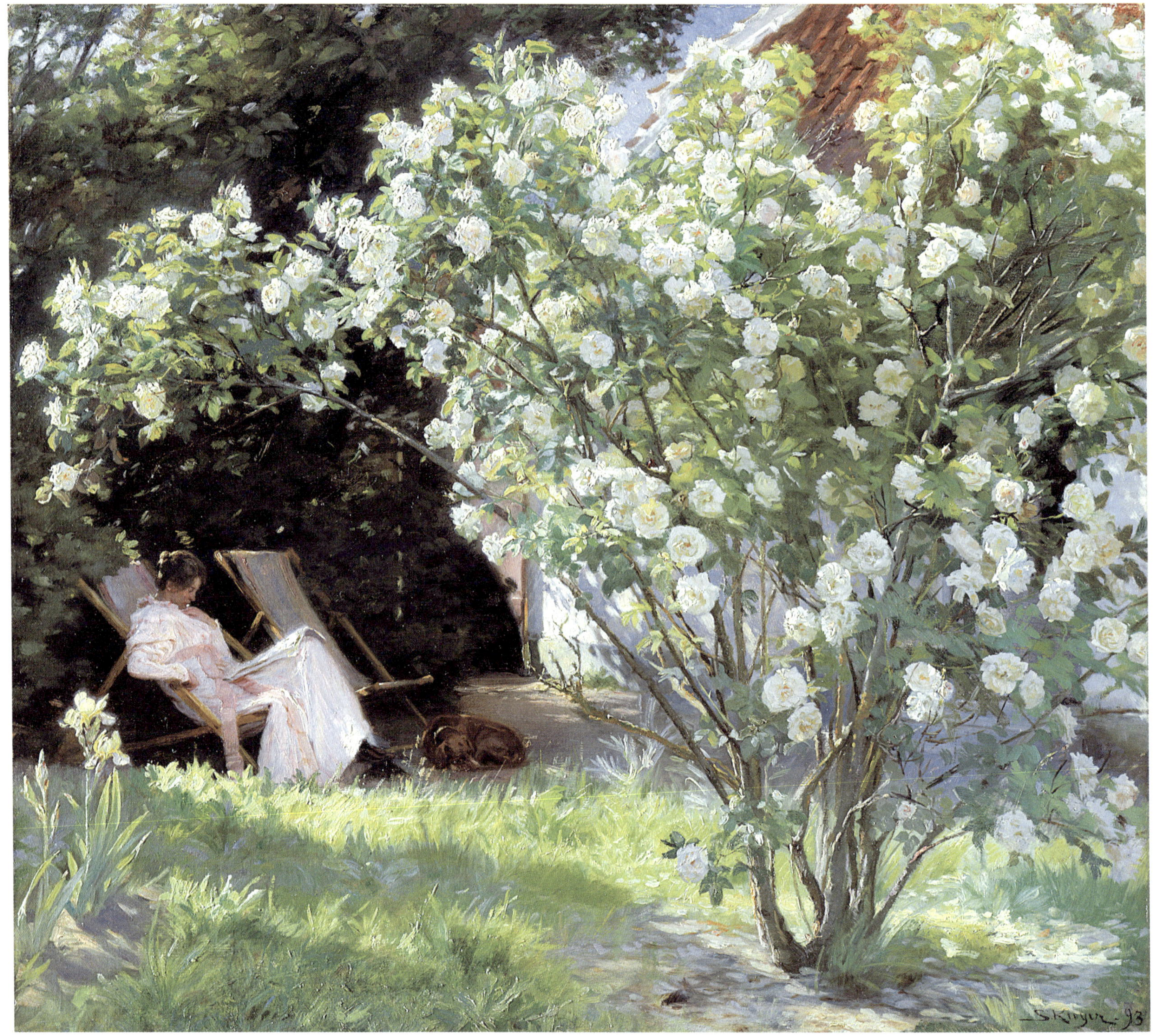

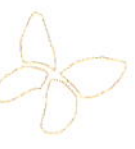

‘The greatest thing in the world is to
know how to belong to oneself.’

Michel de Montaigne, *The Complete Essays* (1572–1592)

Peder Severin Krøyer,
Roses, or The Artist's Wife in the Garden at Skagen, 1883

'Have you also learned that secret from the
river; that there is no such thing as time? That
the river is everywhere at the same time, at the
source and at the mouth, at the waterfall, at
the ferry, at the current, in the ocean and in the
mountains, everywhere and that the present
only exists for it, not the shadow of the past
nor the shadow of the future.'

Hermann Hesse, from *Siddhartha* (1922)

Frits Thaulow,
A Stream in Spring, 1901

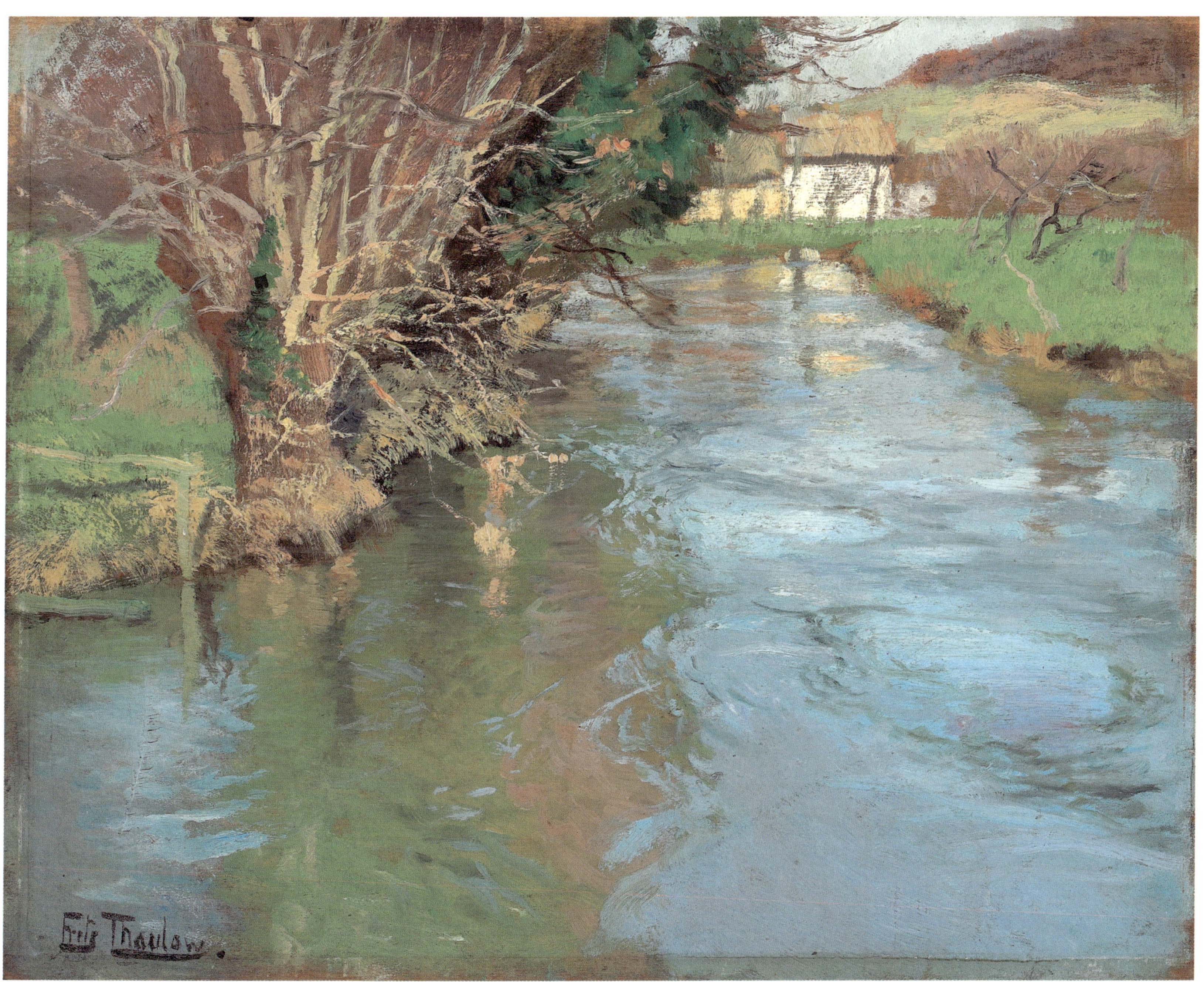
Frits Thaulow

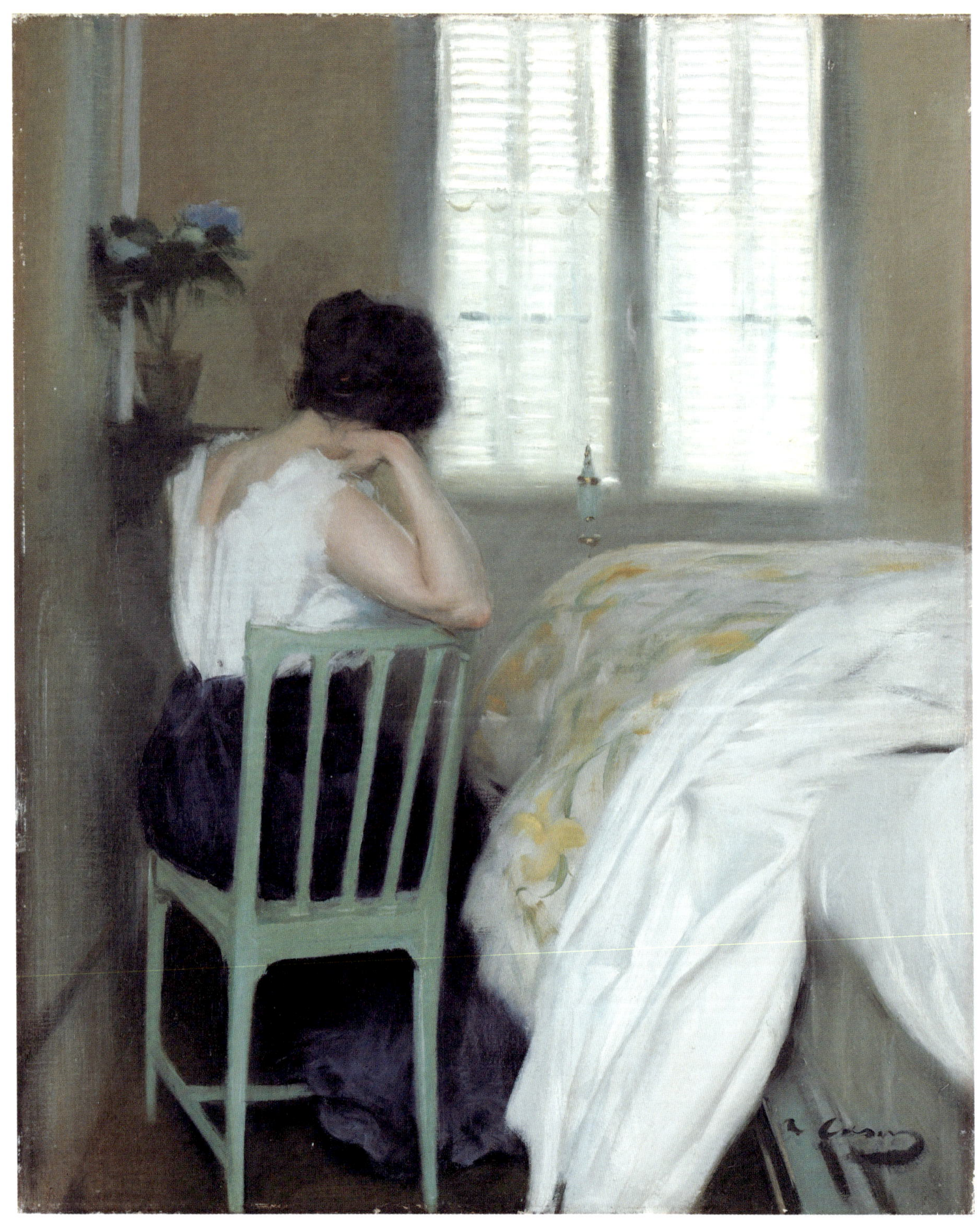

'I would like to beg you, dear Sir, as well as I can, to have patience with everything unresolved in your heart and to try to love the questions themselves as if they were locked rooms or books written in a very foreign language. Don't search for the answers, which could not be given to you now, because you would not be able to live them. And the point is, to live everything. Live the questions now. Perhaps then, someday far in the future, you will gradually, without even noticing it, live your way into the answer.'

Ramon Casas i Carbó,
Las Horas Tristes, c.1900

'She never failed to affect me profoundly.
Her art, although brilliant, had a quality
pale and luminous, as delicate as a white
rose-petal. As she danced every move was
the centre of gravity. The moment she
made her entrance, no matter how gay or
winsome she was, I wanted to weep … It was
a tragedy that the speed of the old cinema
failed to capture the lyricism of her dancing,
and because of that her great art has been
lost to the world.'

Charlie Chaplin, from *My Autobiography* (1964)

Evelyn De Morgan,
Night and Sleep, 1878

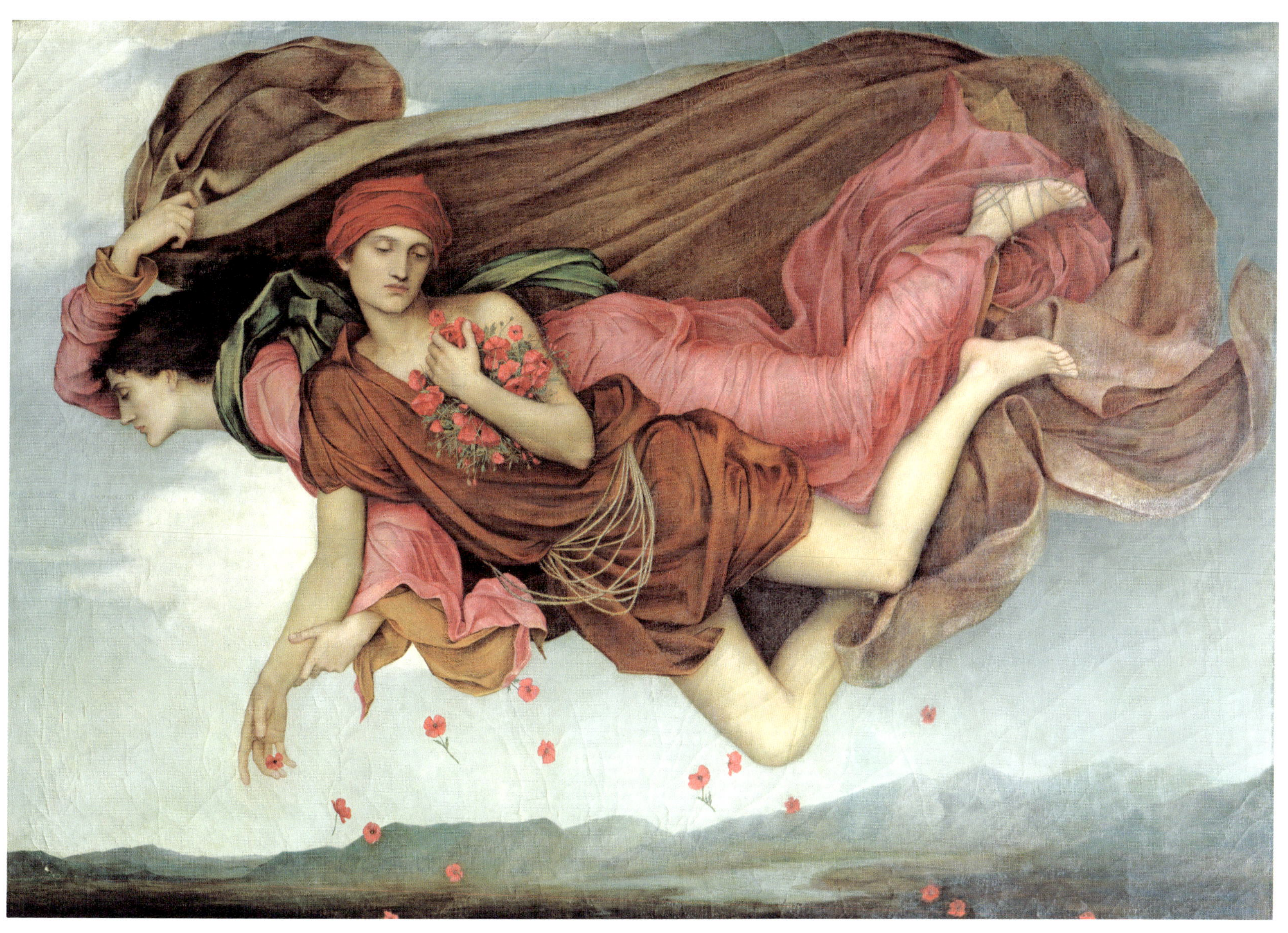

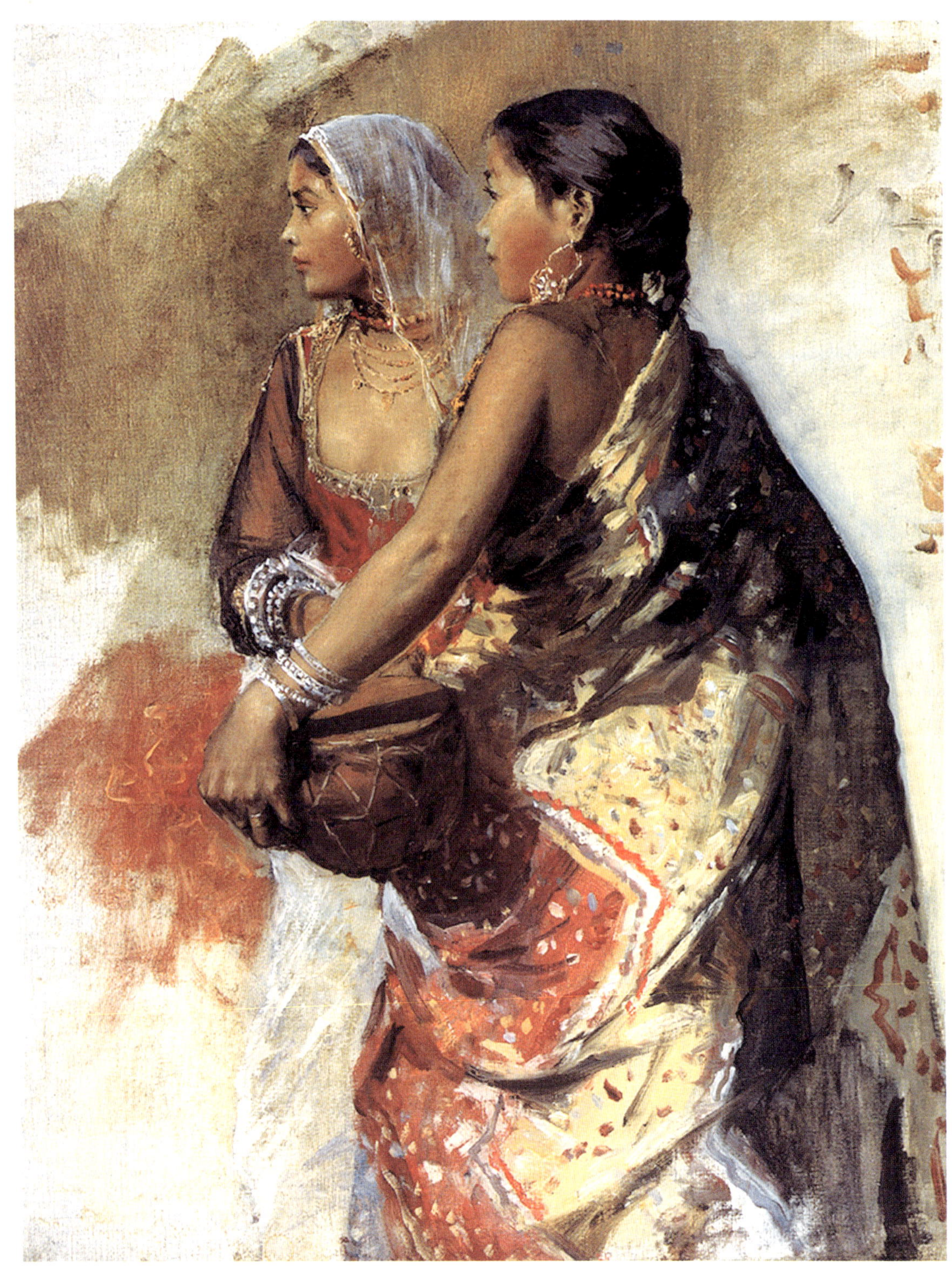

'To love. To be loved. To never forget your own insignificance. To never get used to the unspeakable violence and the vulgar disparity of life around you. To seek joy in the saddest places. To pursue beauty to its lair. To never simplify what is complicated or complicate what is simple. To respect strength, never power. Above all, to watch. To try and understand. To never look away. And never, never to forget.'

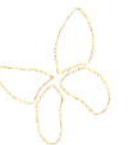

Edwin Lord Weeks,
Two Nautch Girls, c.1880

'Are my stories true, you ask? No, they are imaginary tales ... But real life is only one kind of life ... there is also the life of the imagination.'

Dame Laura Knight,
Summertime Cornwall

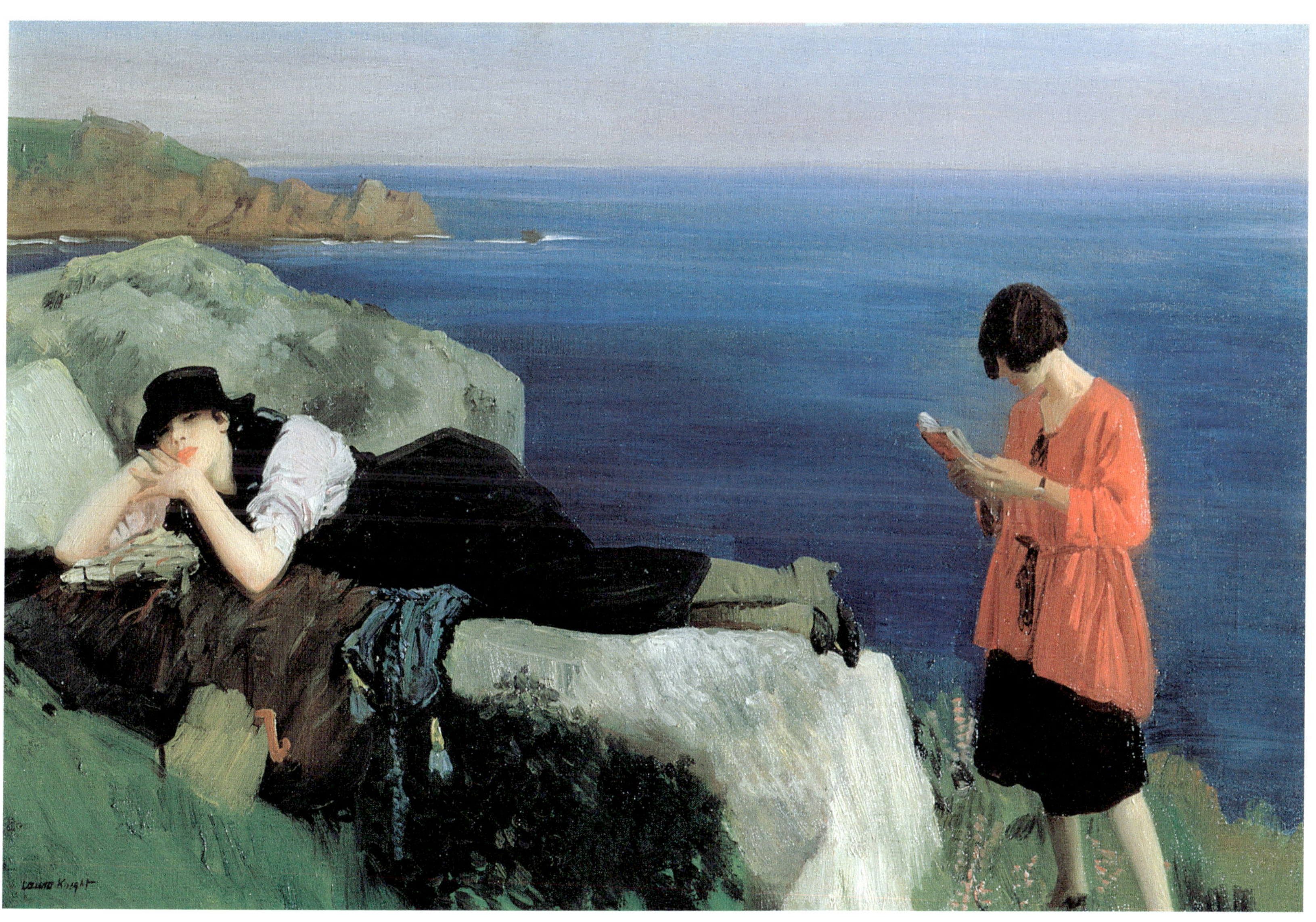

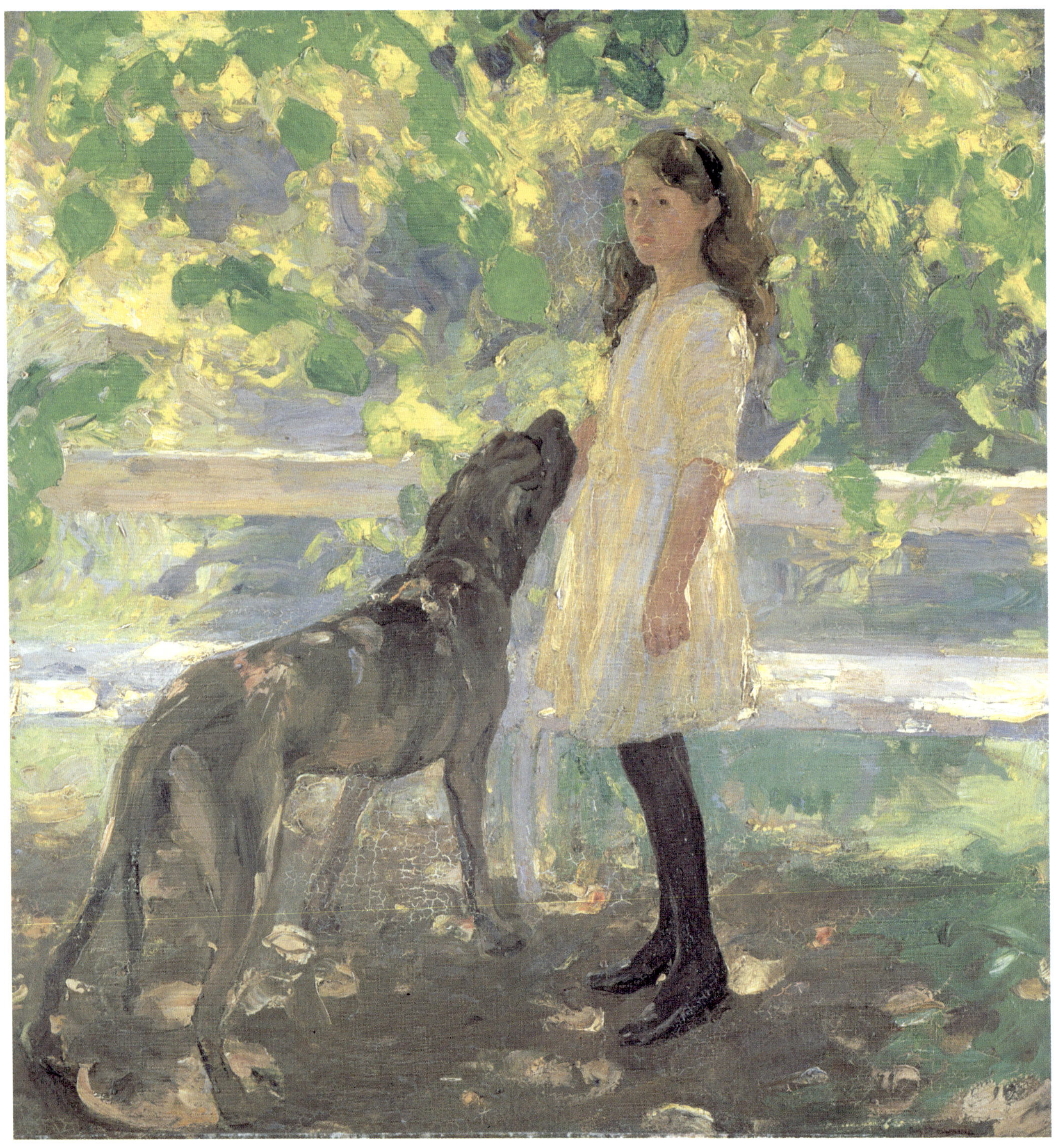

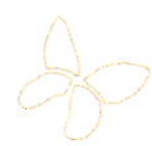

'A dog will teach you more about yourself than you ever knew possible. Through their boundless enthusiasm, tail wagging and play, you'll learn the language of "canine". Canine is very simple; it is the language of love.'

Lisa Azarmi, from *Thoughts on a Dog* (2022)

Amy Katherine Browning,
Lime Tree Shade, 1913

'You were once wild here.
Don't let them tame you.'

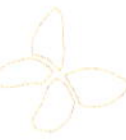

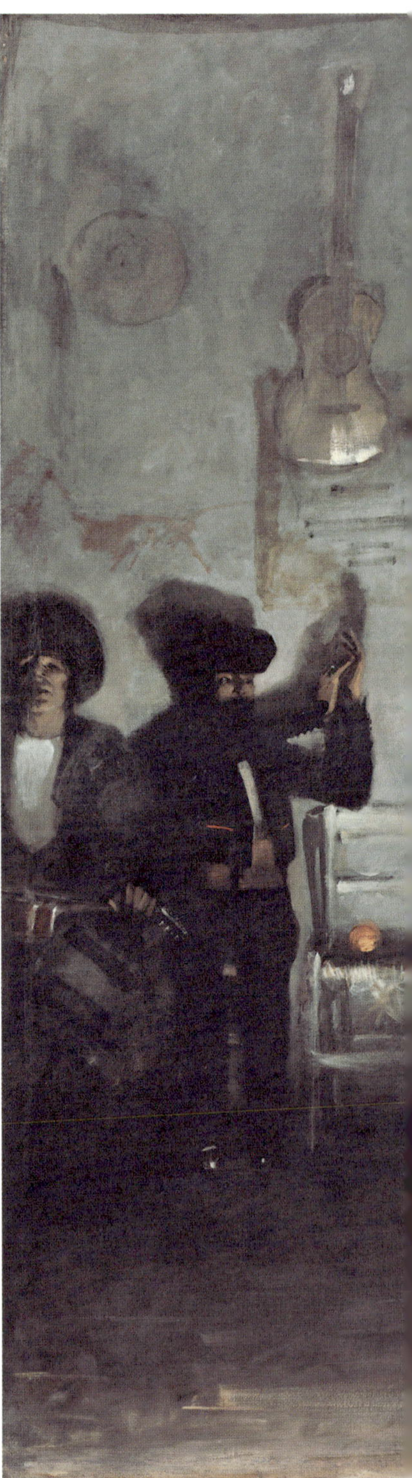

John Singer Sargent,
El Jaleo, 1882

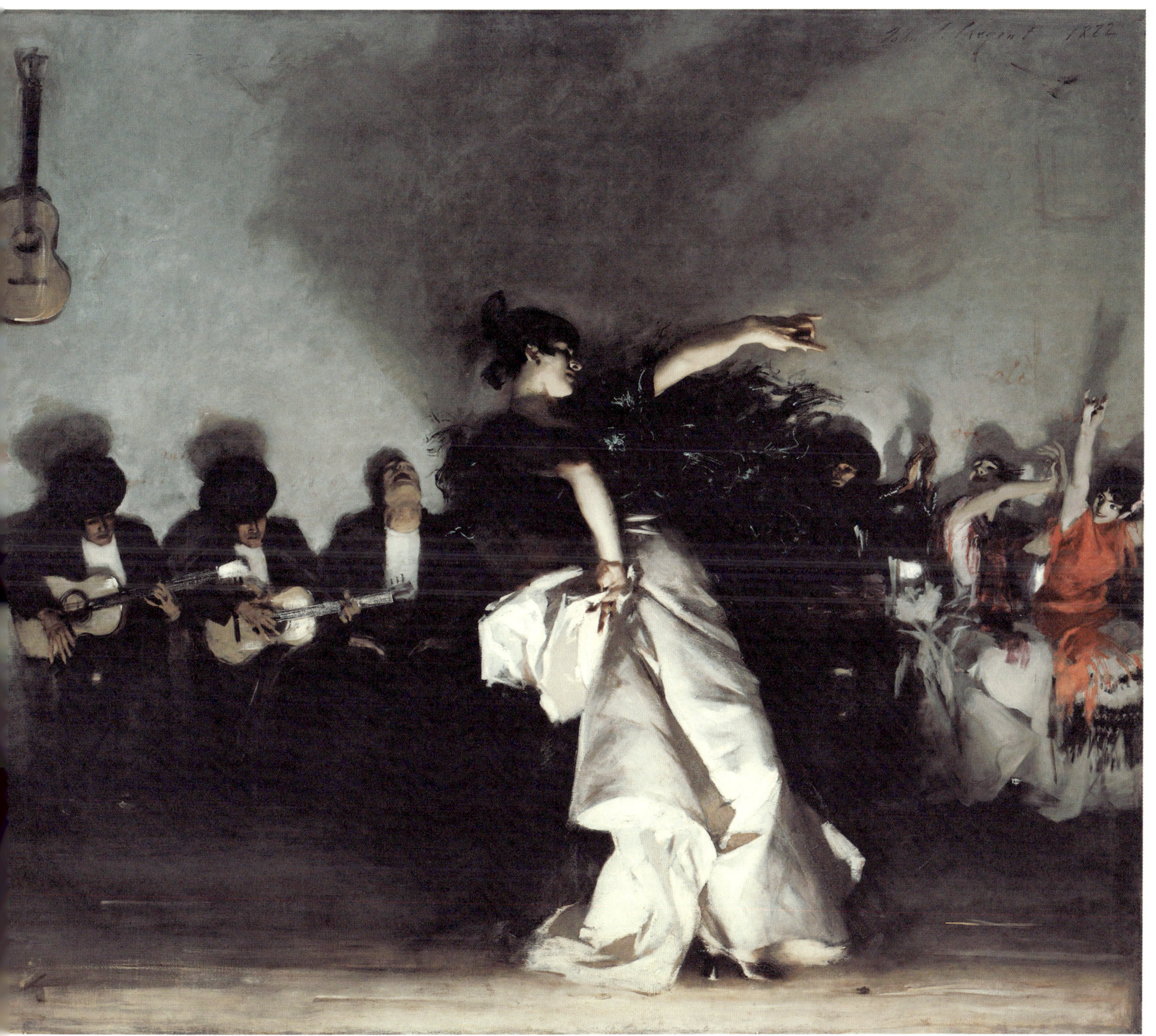

John S. Sargent 1882

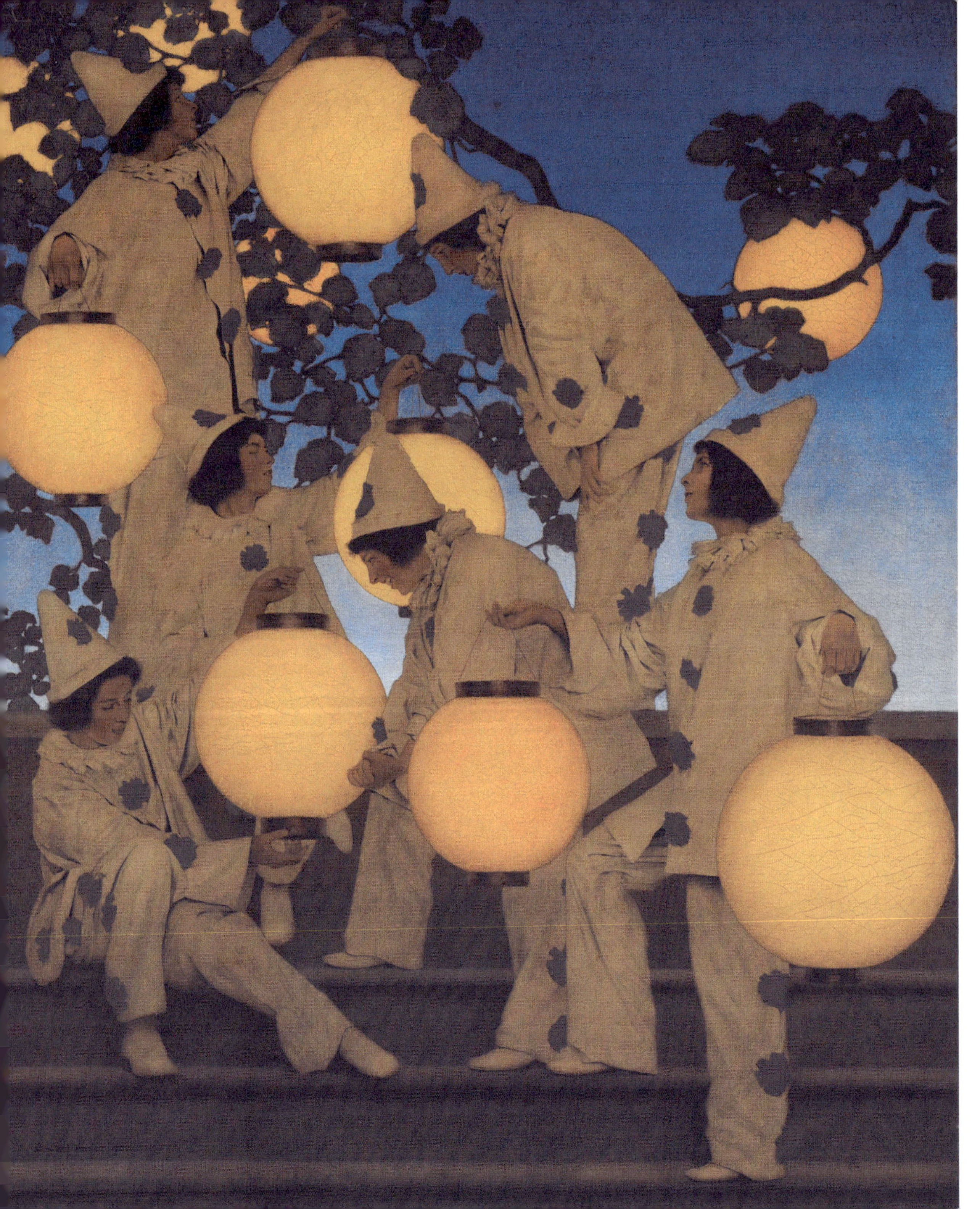

'Imagination is the beginning of creation.
You imagine what you desire, you will
what you imagine and at last you create
what you will.'

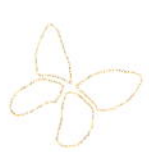

Maxfield Parrish,
The Lantern Bearers, 1908

'The clearest way into the Universe is through a forest wilderness.'

John Muir, from *John of the Mountains: The Unpublished Journals of John Muir* (1938)

James Thomas Watts,
Russet and Gray: A Welsh Beechwood, 1905

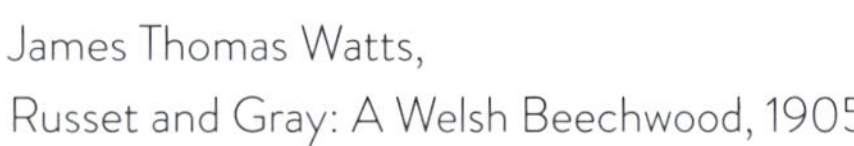

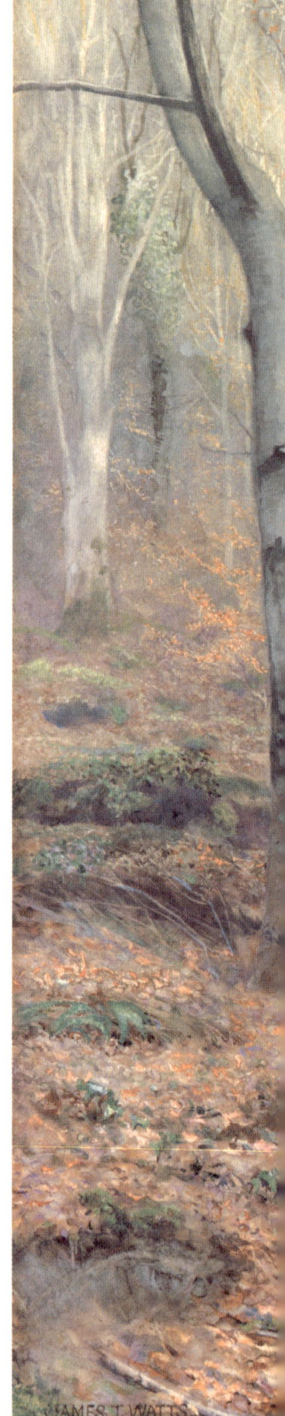

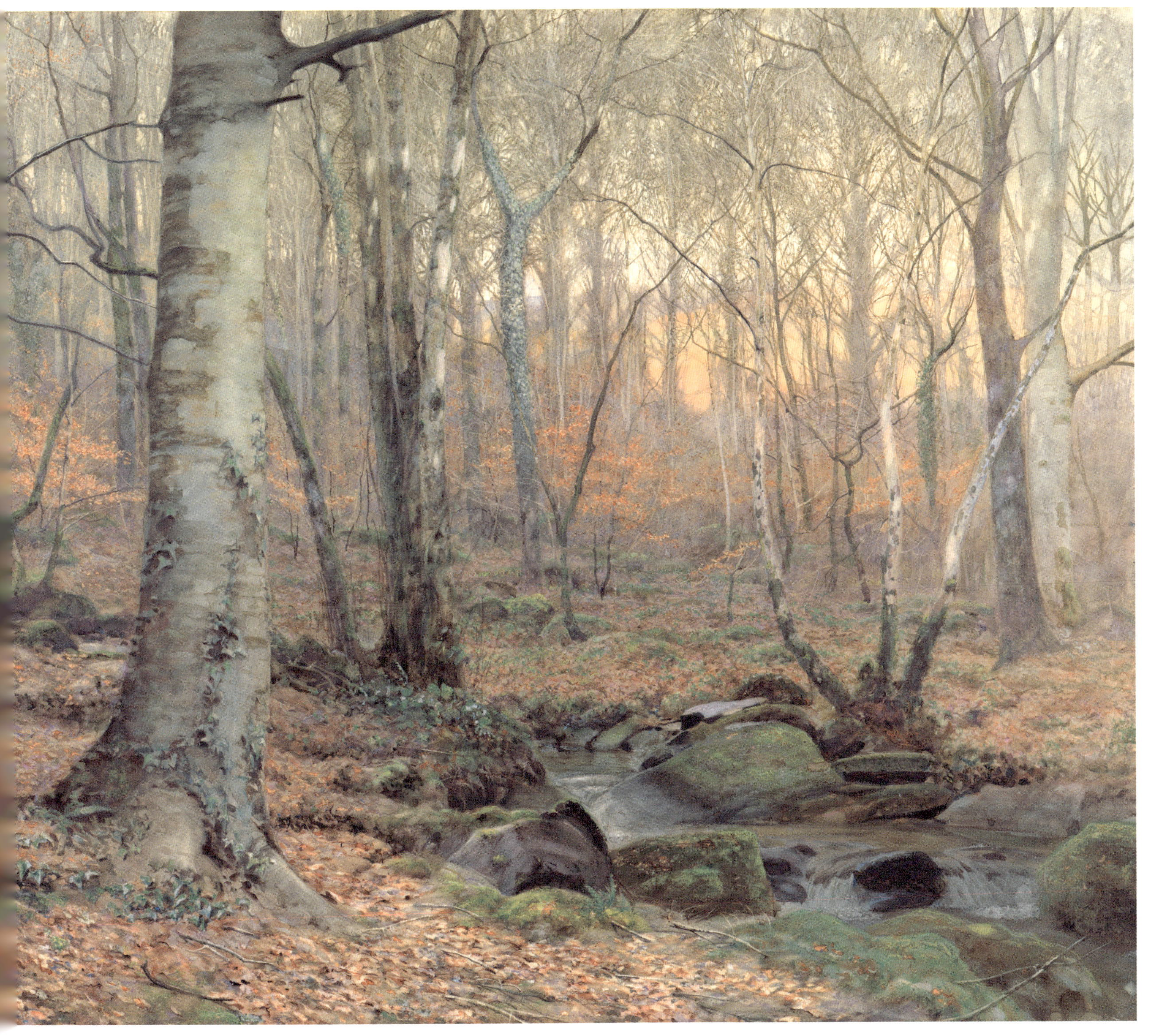

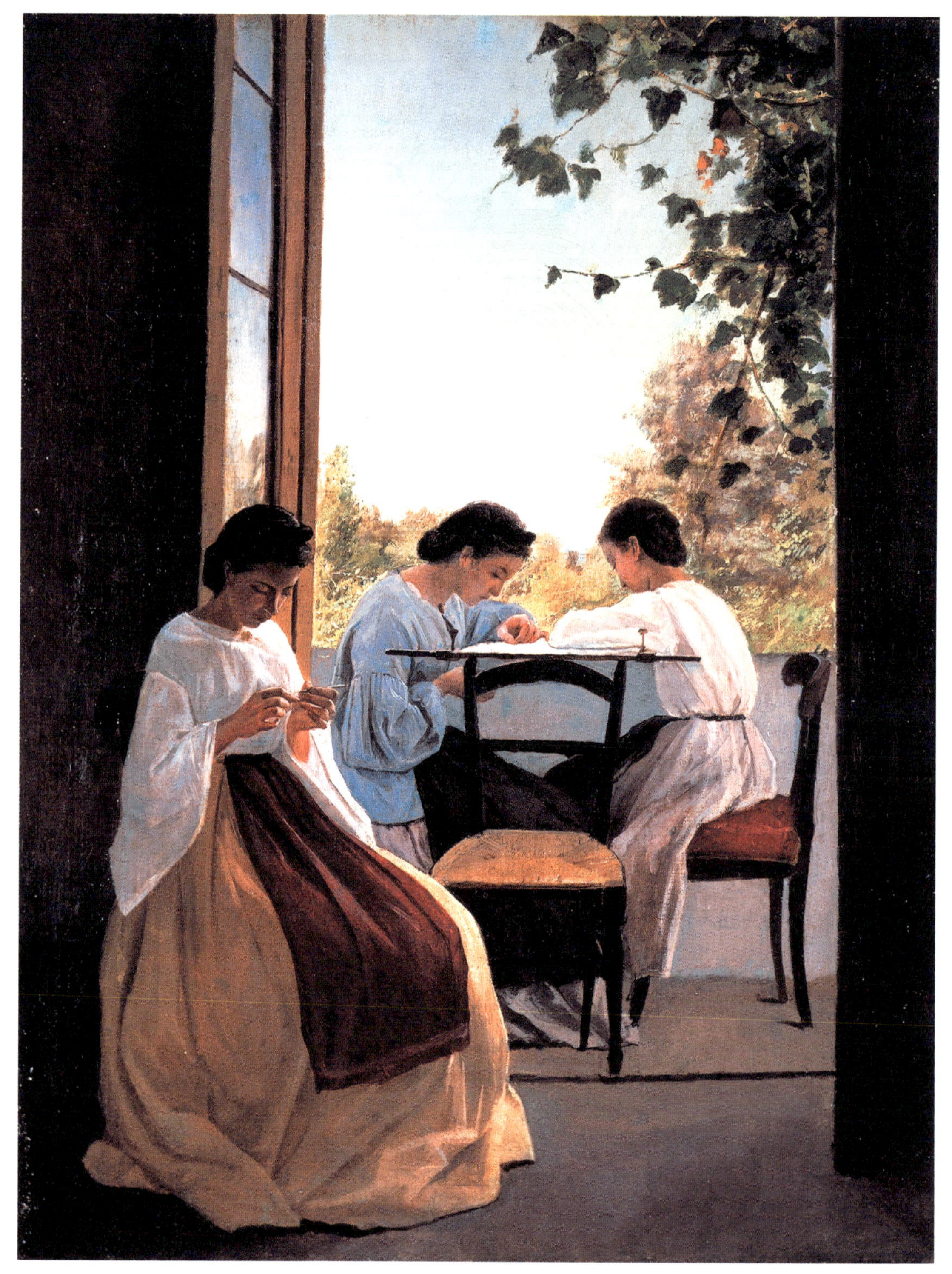

'Friendship improves
happiness and abates misery,
by the doubling of our joy and
the dividing of our grief.'

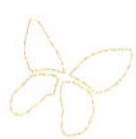

Adriano Cecioni,
The Embroiderers, 1866

'Far away there in the sunshine are
my highest aspirations. I may not
reach them, but I can look up and
see their beauty, believe in them, and
try to follow where they lead.'

Louisa May Alcott (1832–1888)

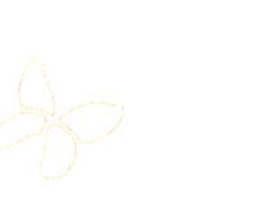

Berthe Morisot,
Shepherdess Resting, 1891

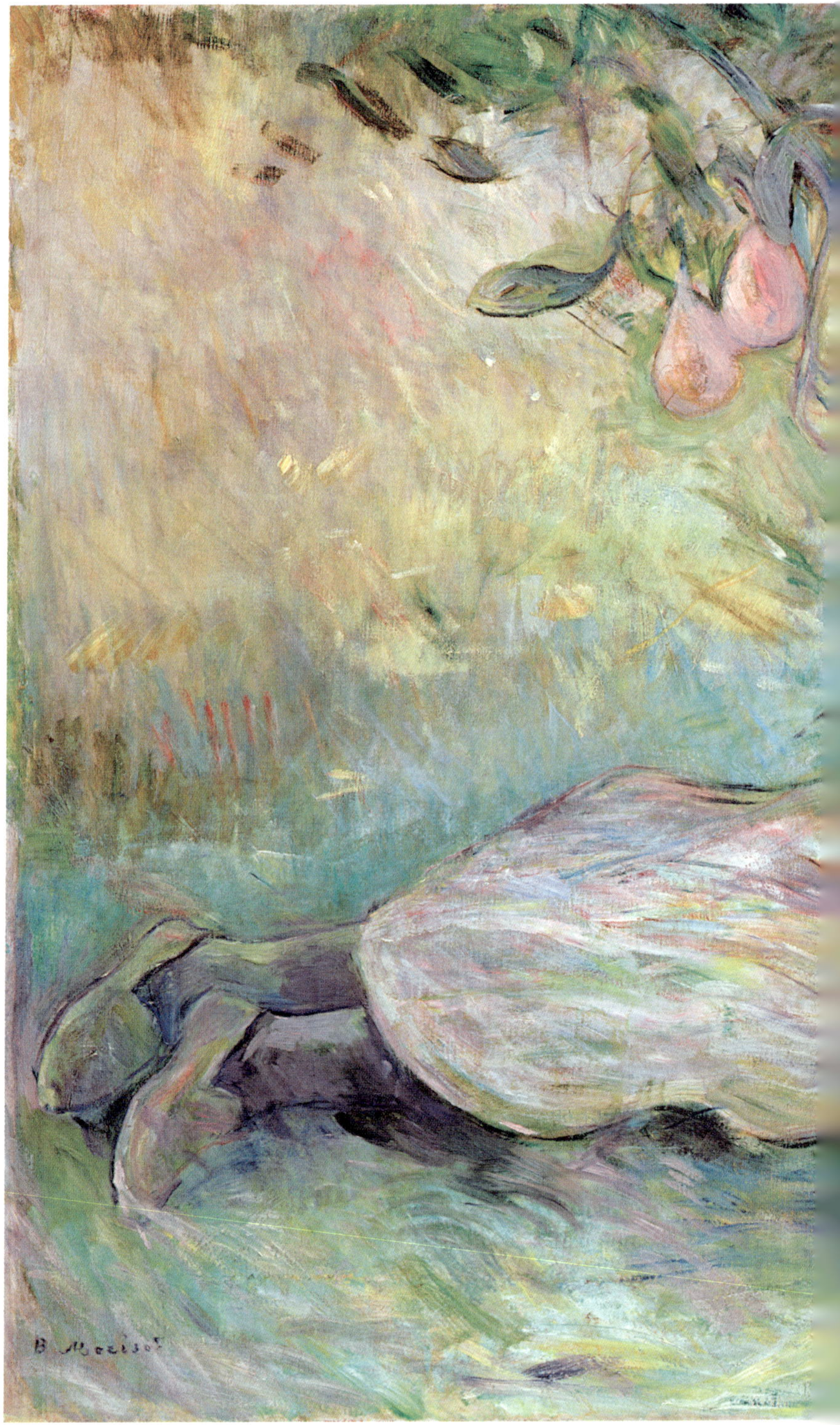

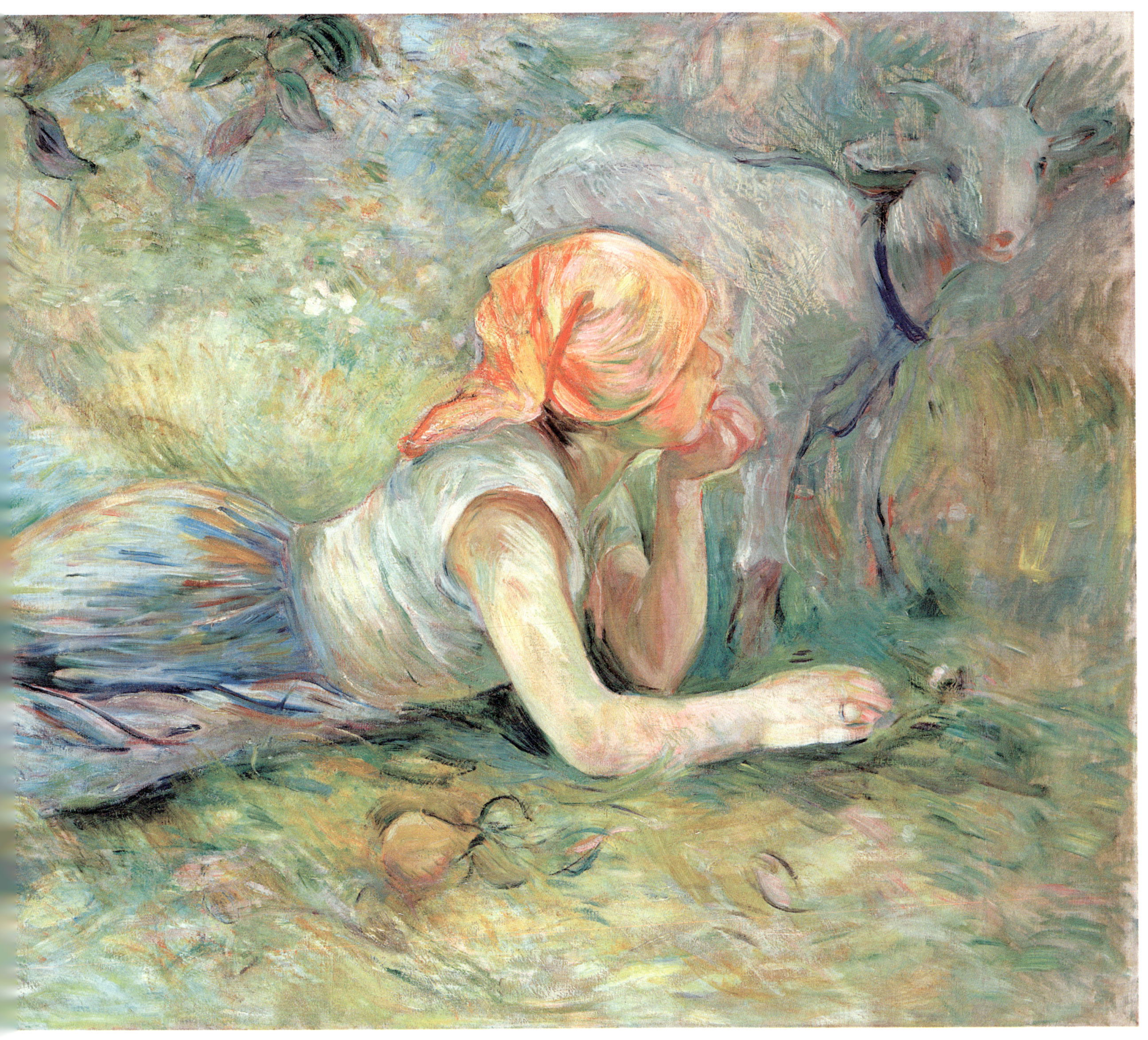

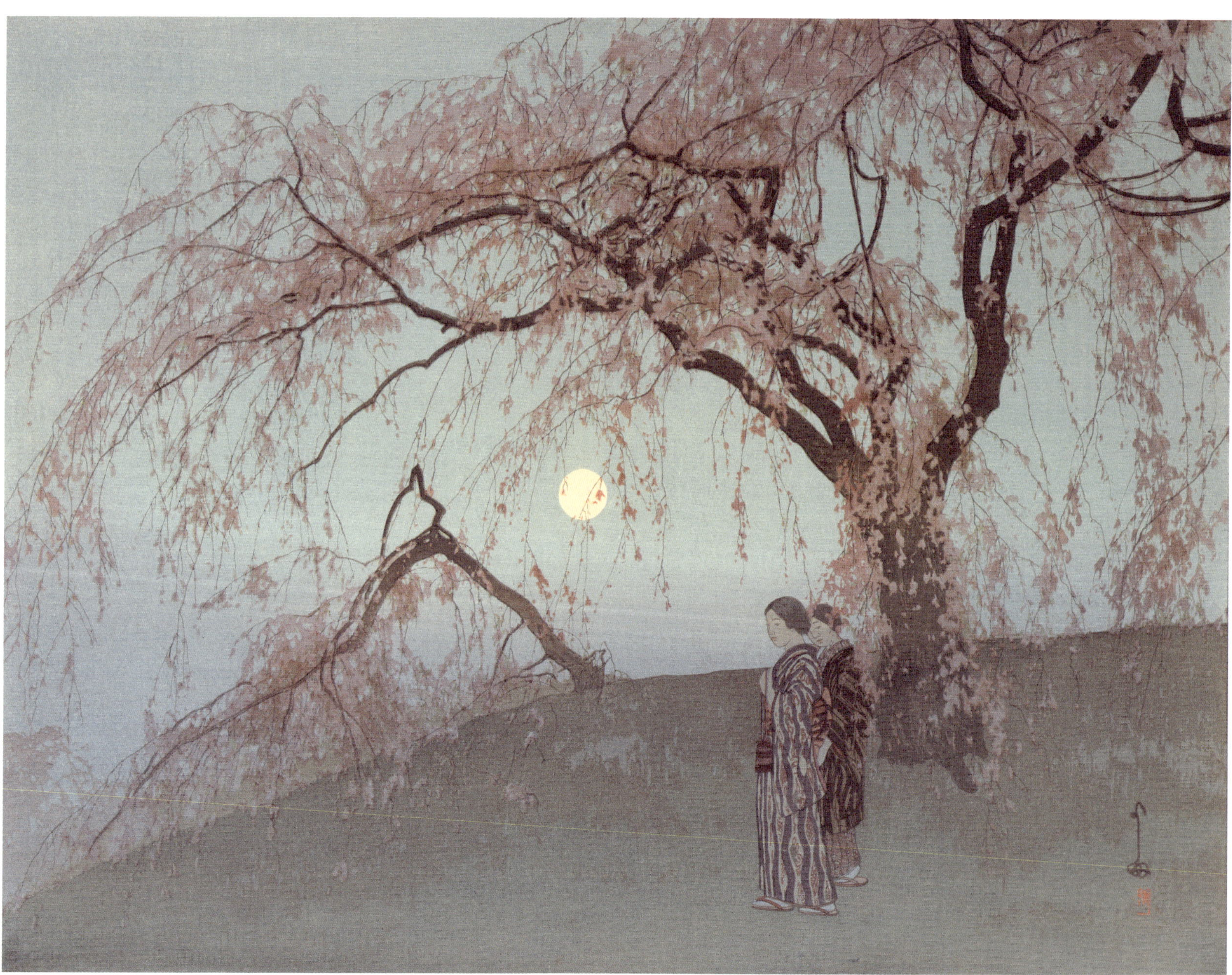

'One is not born, but rather becomes, a woman.'

Simone de Beauvoir, from *The Second Sex* (1949)

Hiroshi Yoshida,
Kumoi Cherry Trees (1920)

'I wonder if the snow loves the trees and fields, that it kisses them so gently?
And then it covers them up snug, you know, with a white quilt; and perhaps
it says, "Go to sleep, darlings, till the summer comes again."'

Lewis Carroll, from *Alice's Adventures in Wonderland & Through the Looking-Glass* (1871)

Akseli Valdemar Gallen-Kallela,
A Winter Landscape, 1917

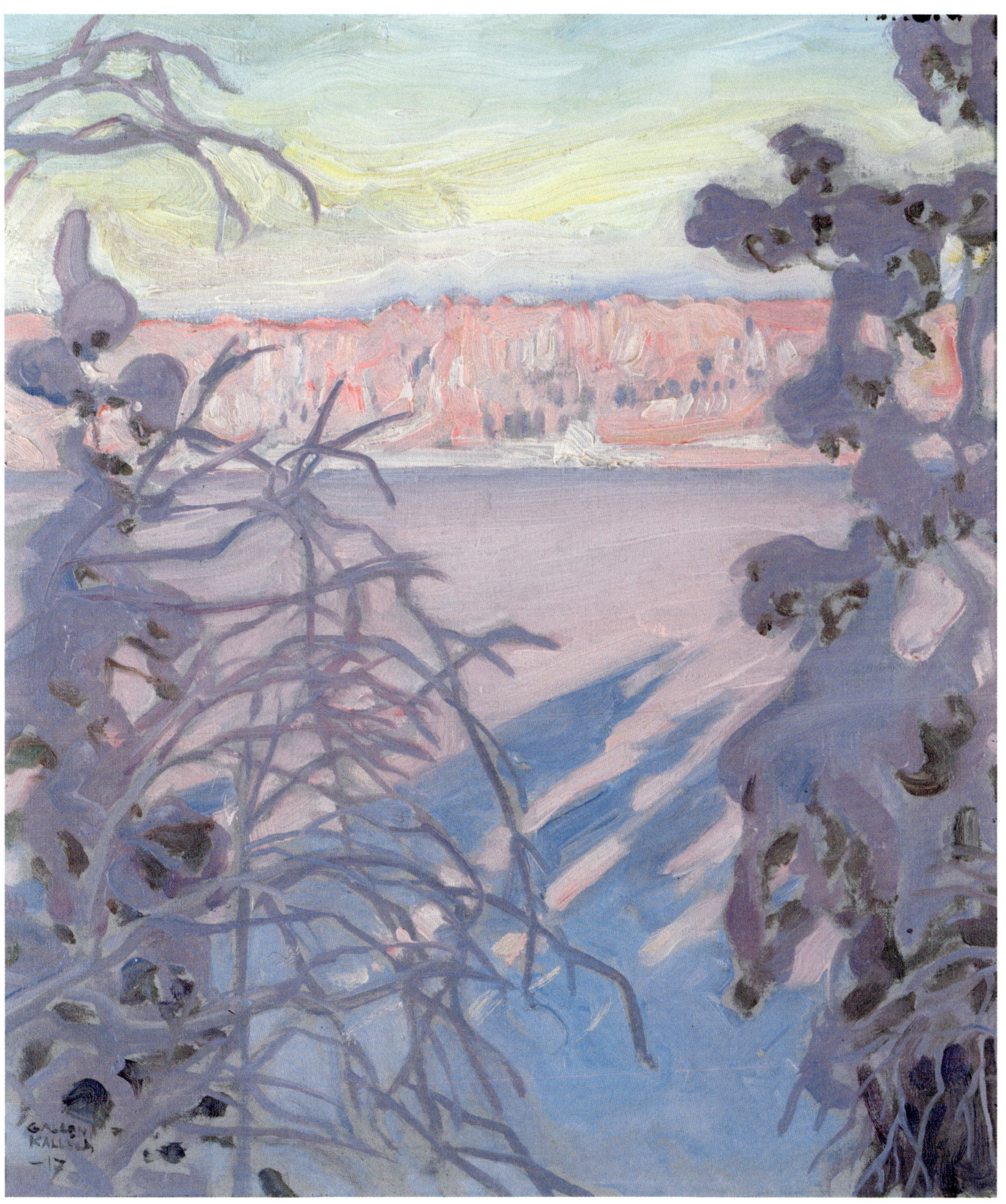

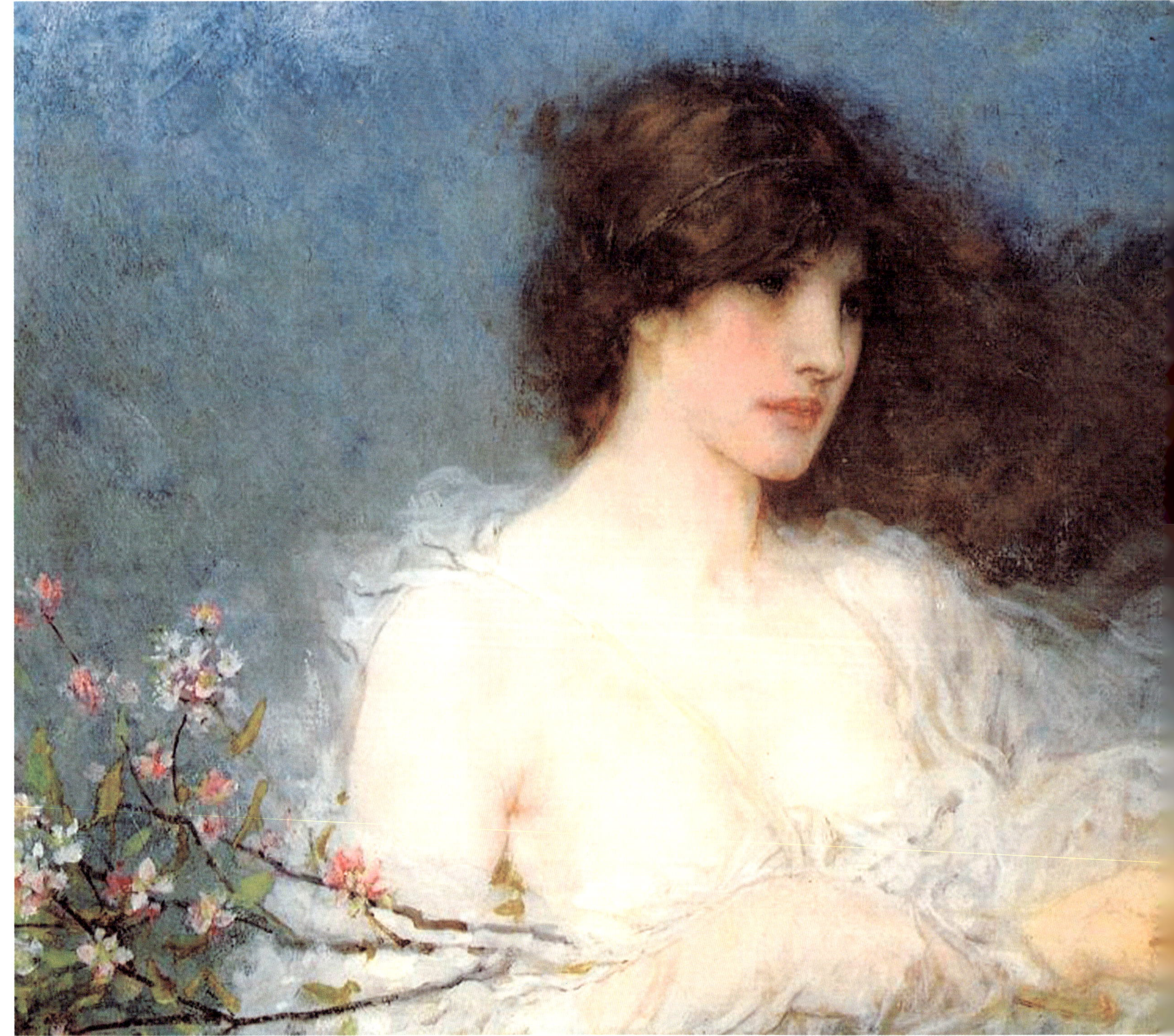

'The longer I live the more beautiful life
becomes. If you foolishly ignore beauty,
you will soon find yourself without it.
Your life will be impoverished. But if
you invest in beauty, it will remain with
you all the days of your life.'

Frank Lloyd Wright (1867–1959)

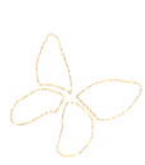

George Henry Boughton,
A Spring Idyll, 1901

'In the sweetness of friendship let there be laughter, and sharing of pleasures. For in the dew of little things the heart finds its morning and is refreshed.'

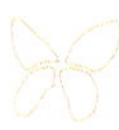

John Lavery,
Sutton Courtenay, 1917

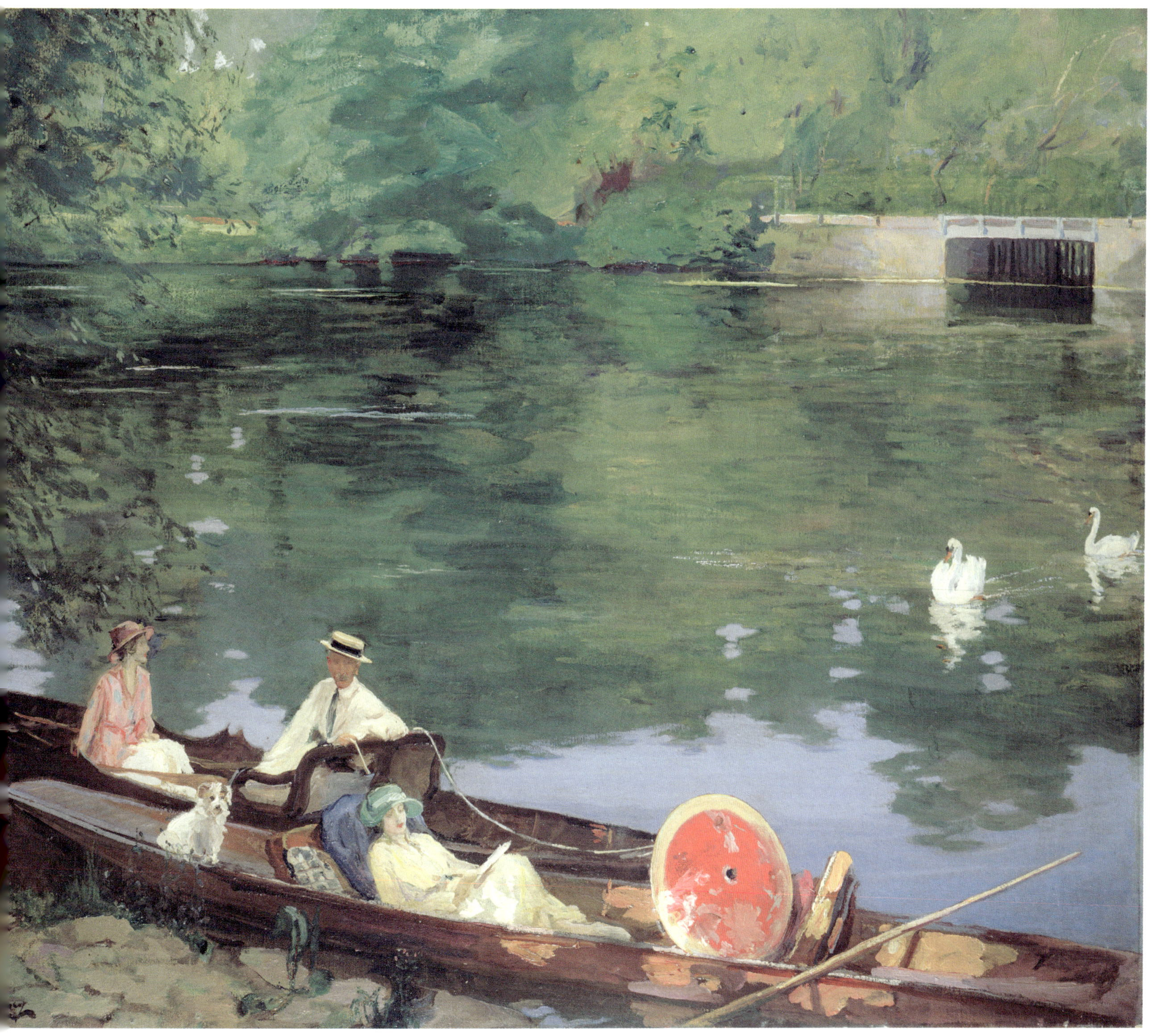

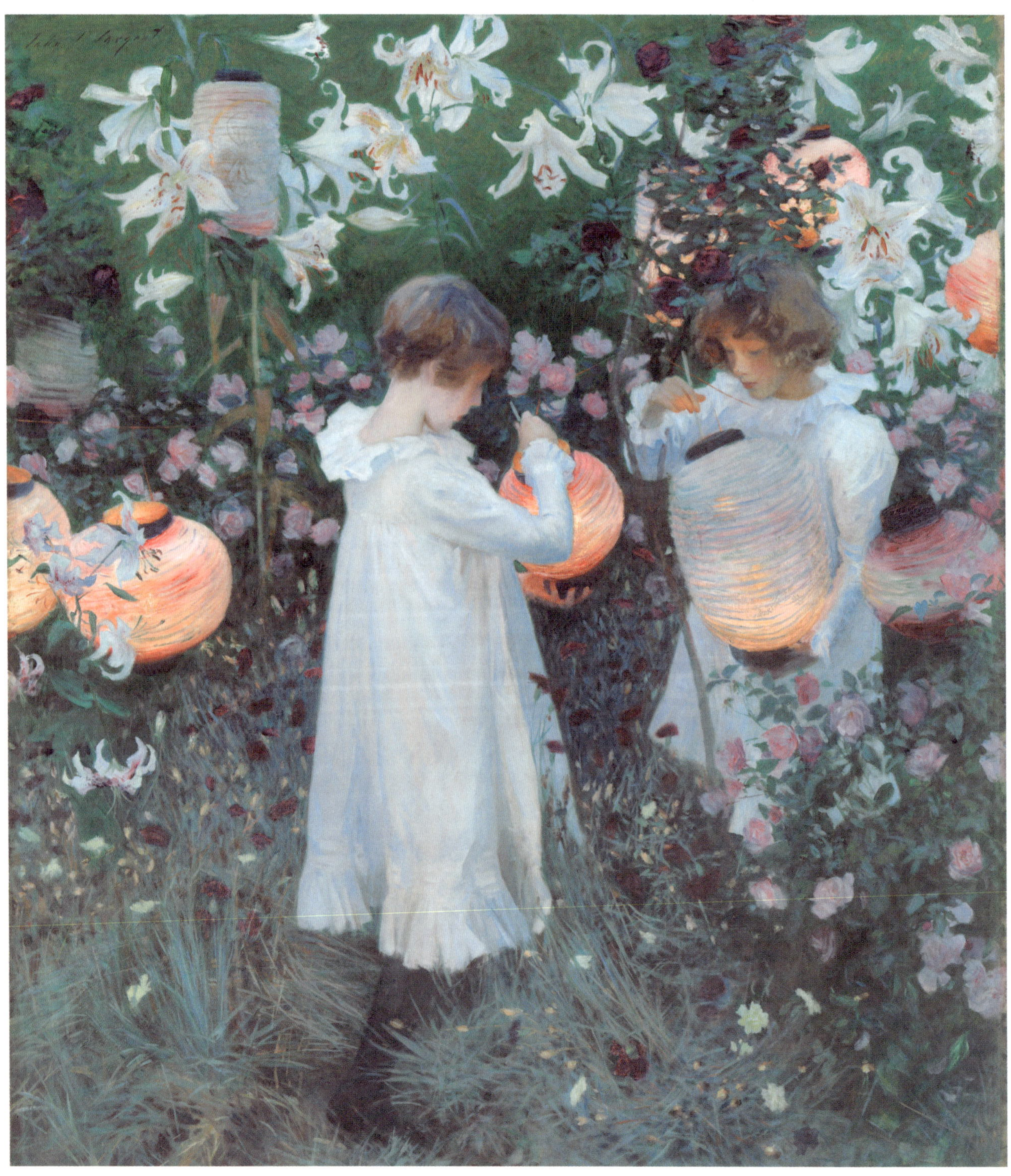

'Let us be grateful to the people who make us happy; they are the charming gardeners who make our souls blossom.'

Marcel Proust (1871–1922)

John Singer Sargent,
Carnation, Lily, Lily, Rose, 1885–1886

'One word frees us of all the weight
and pain of life: That word is love.'

Elin Danielson-Gambogi,
To Bed, 1897

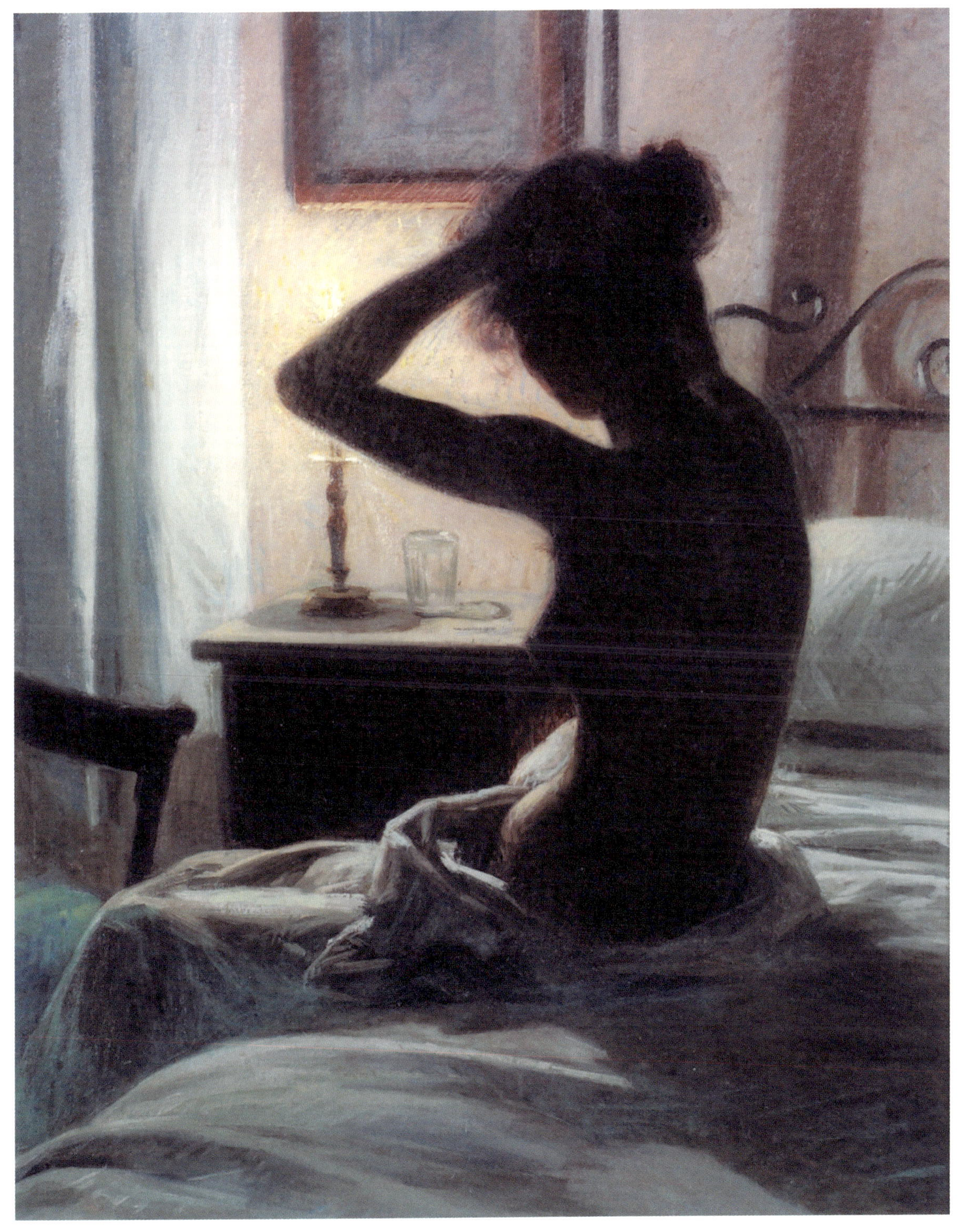

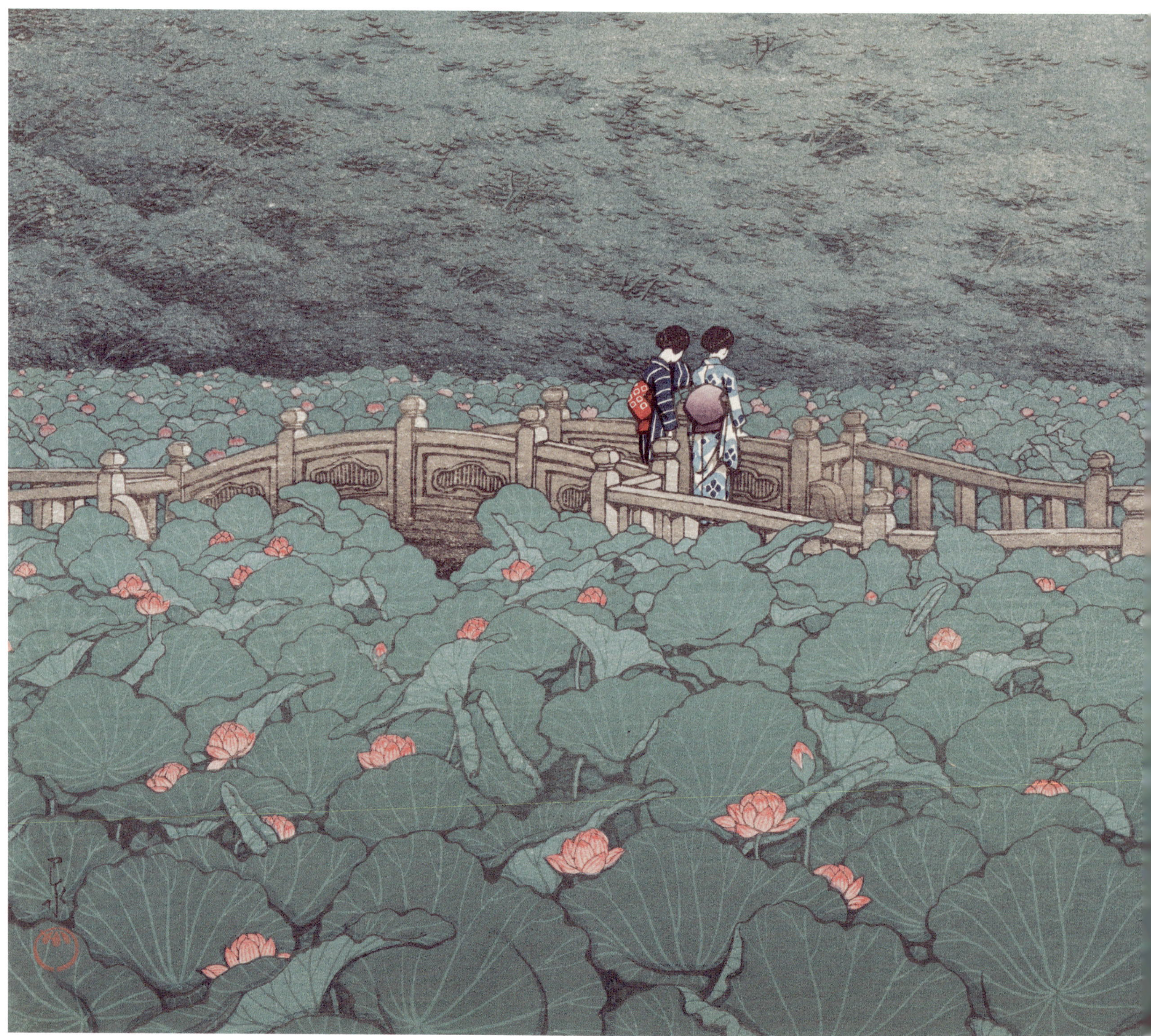

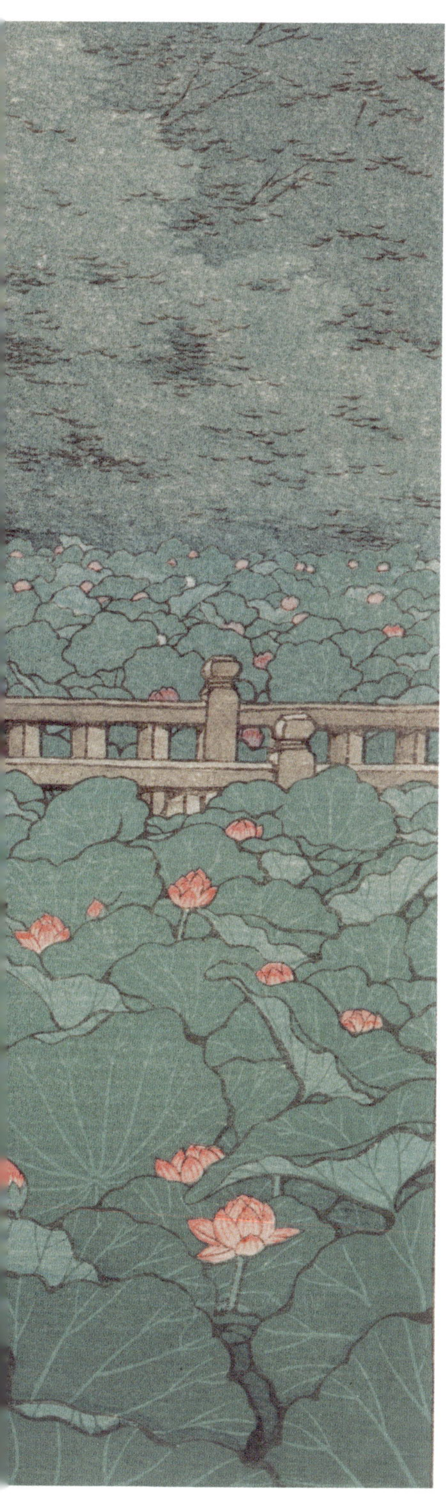

'If you feel lost, disappointed, hesitant, or weak, return to yourself, to who you are, here and now and when you get there, you will discover yourself, like a lotus flower in full bloom, even in a muddy pond, beautiful and strong.'

Masaru Emoto, from *The Secret Life of Water* (2003)

Hasui Kawase,
The Pond at Benten Shrine in Shiba, 1929

'A quiet secluded life in the country, with the
possibility of being useful to people to whom it
is easy to do good, and who are not accustomed
to have it done to them; then work which one
hopes may be of some use; then rest, nature,
books, music, love for one's neighbour — such is
my idea of happiness.'

Leo Tolstoy, from *Family Happiness* (1859)

Charles Sillem Lidderdale,
The Fern Gatherer, 1877

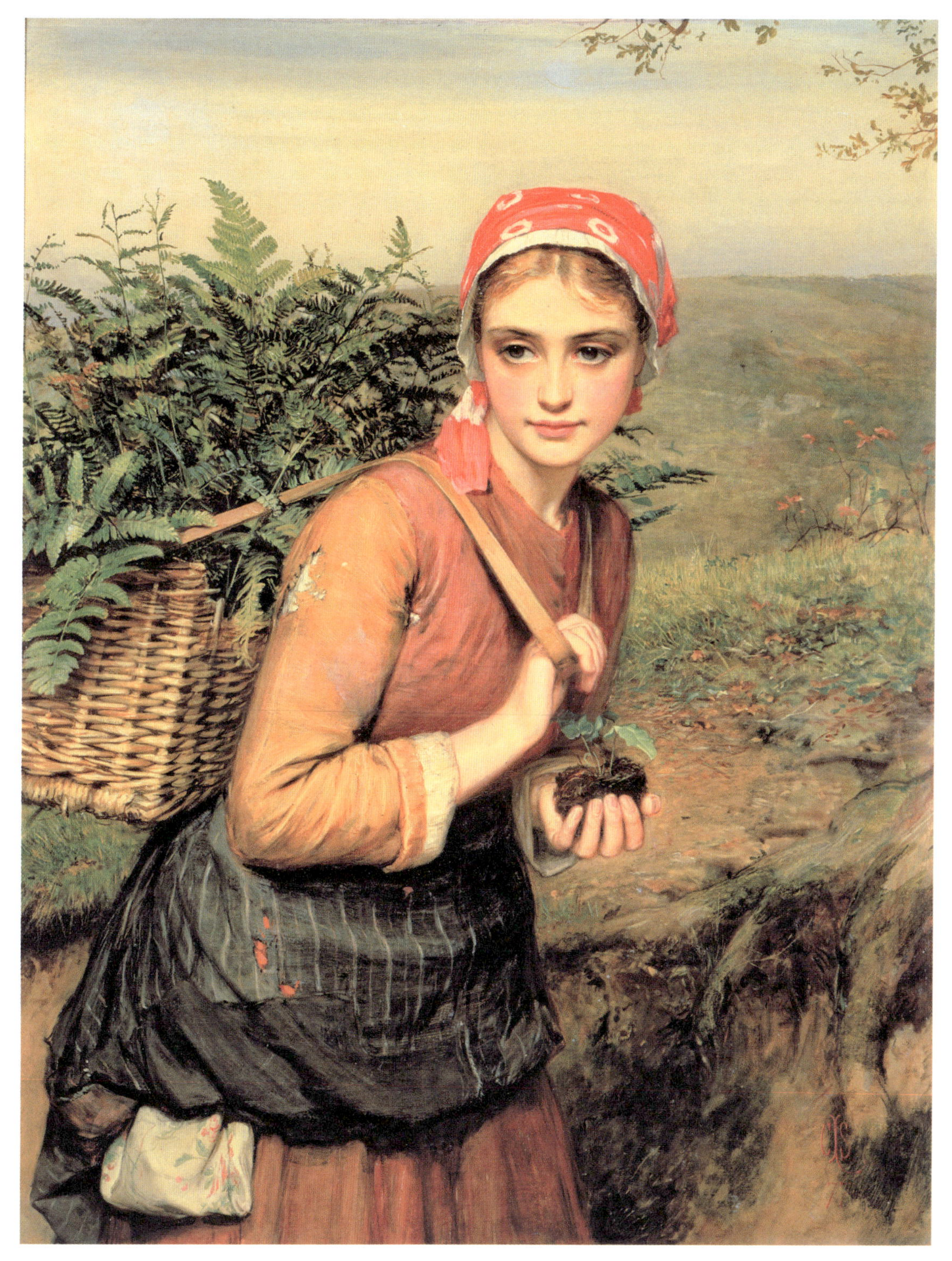

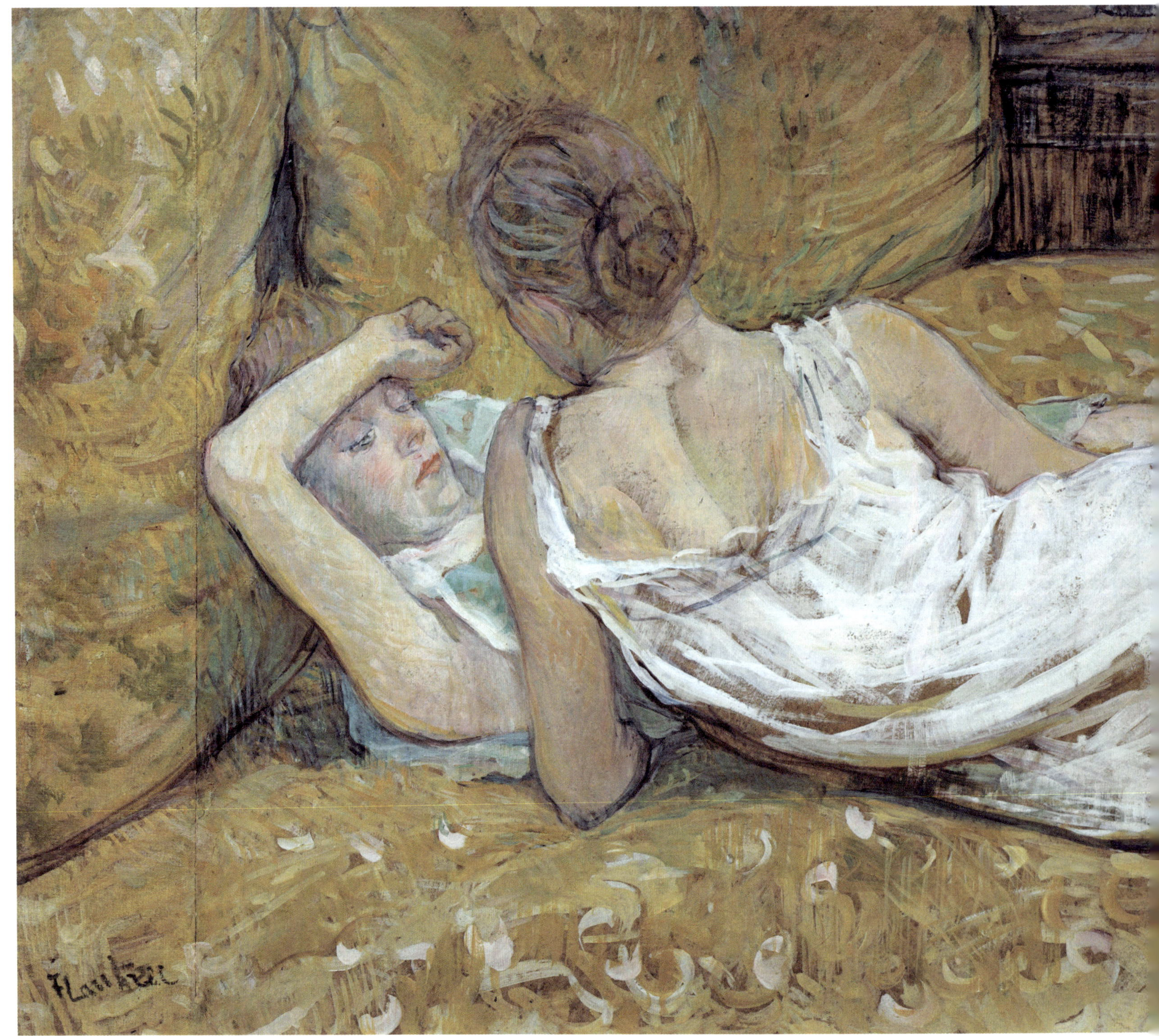

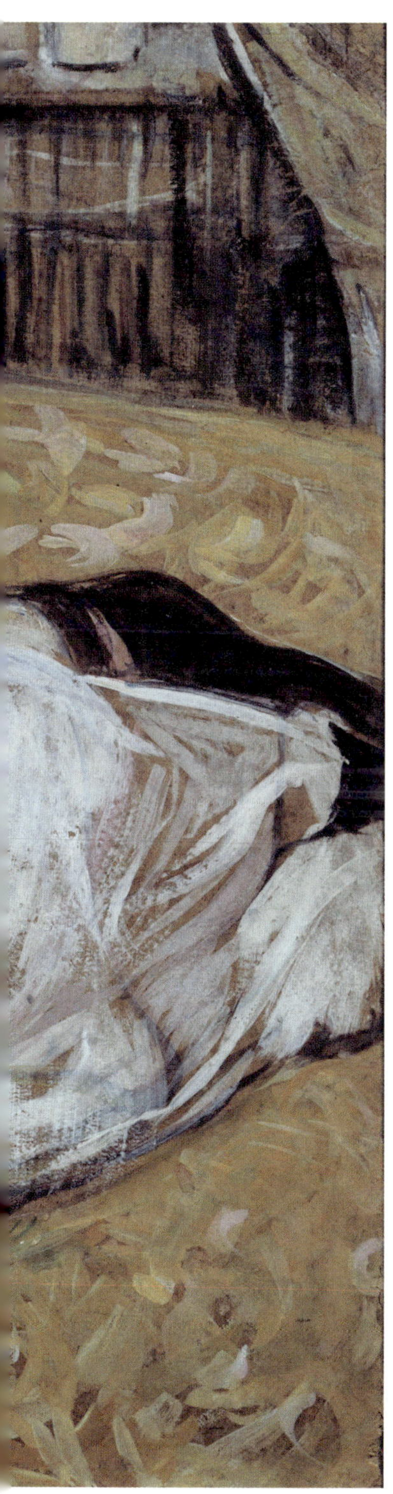

'The meeting of two personalities is like the contact of two chemical substances: if there is any reaction, both are transformed.'

Carl Jung, from *Modern Man in Search of a Soul* (1933)

Henri de Toulouse-Lautrec,
Abandonment (The Two Friends), 1895

'The human heart has hidden treasures, In secret kept, in silence sealed; The thoughts, the hopes, the dreams, the pleasures, Whose charms were broken if revealed.'

Frederic Leighton,
Flaming June, 1895

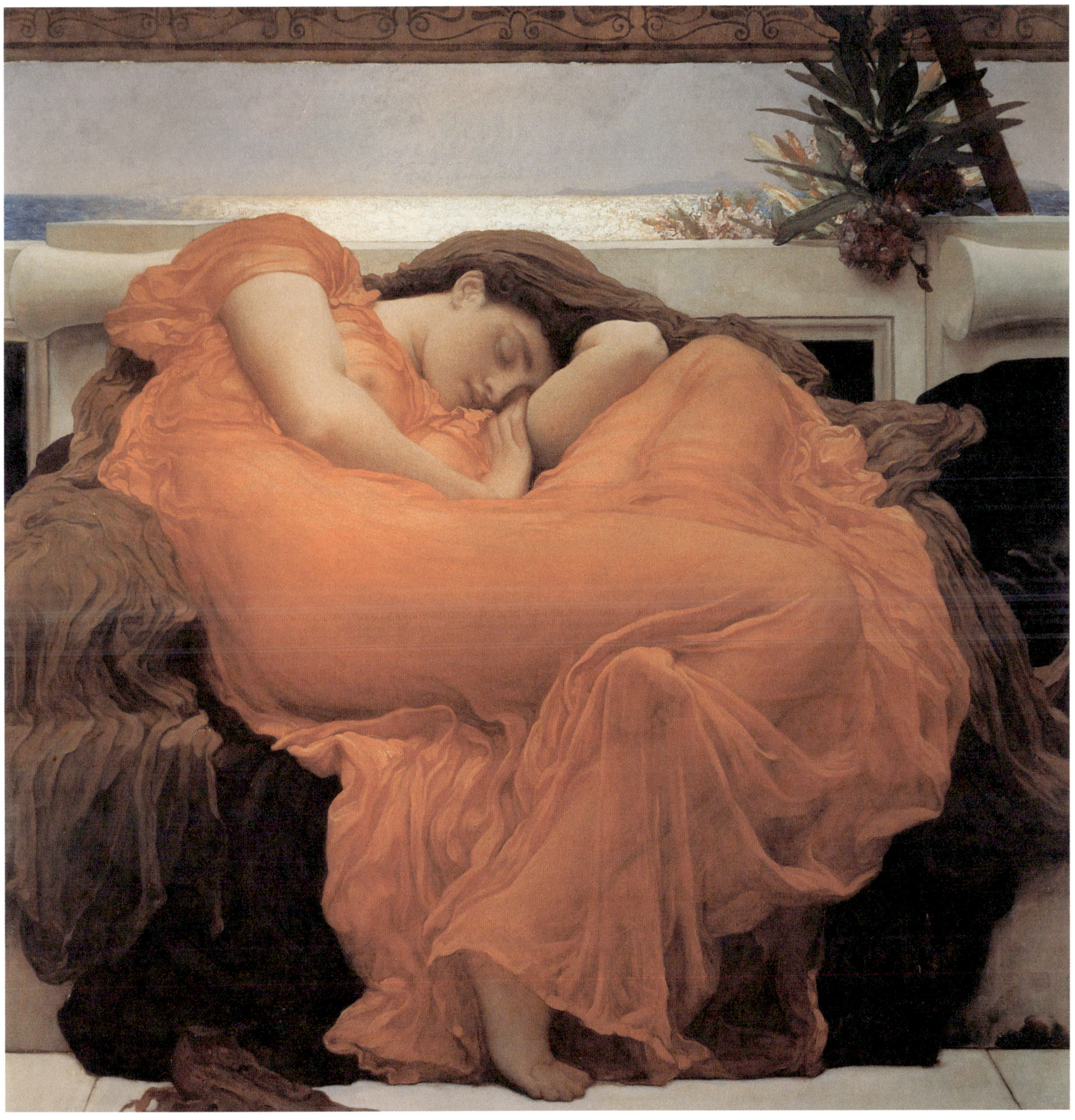

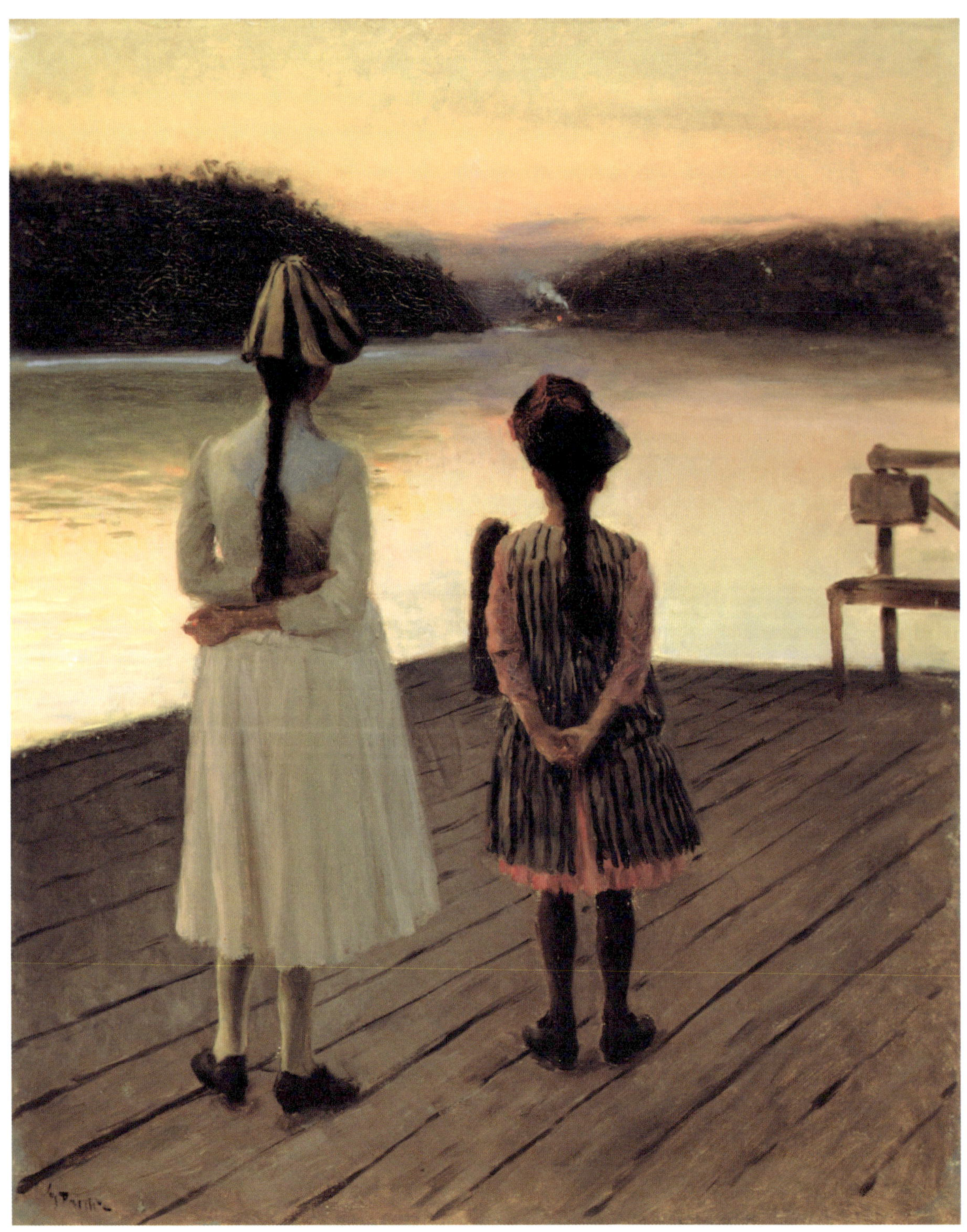

'When it was dark, you always carried the sun in your hand for me.'

Georg Vilhelm Pauli,
Pabryggan (The Asch Sisters), 1891–1892

'Write it on your heart
that every day is the best day in the year.
He is rich who owns the day, and no one owns the day
who allows it to be invaded with fret and anxiety.

Finish every day and be done with it.
You have done what you could.
Some blunders and absurdities, no doubt crept in.
Forget them as soon as you can, tomorrow is a new day;
begin it well and serenely, with too high a spirit
to be cumbered with your old nonsense.

This new day is too dear,
with its hopes and invitations,
to waste a moment on the yesterdays.'

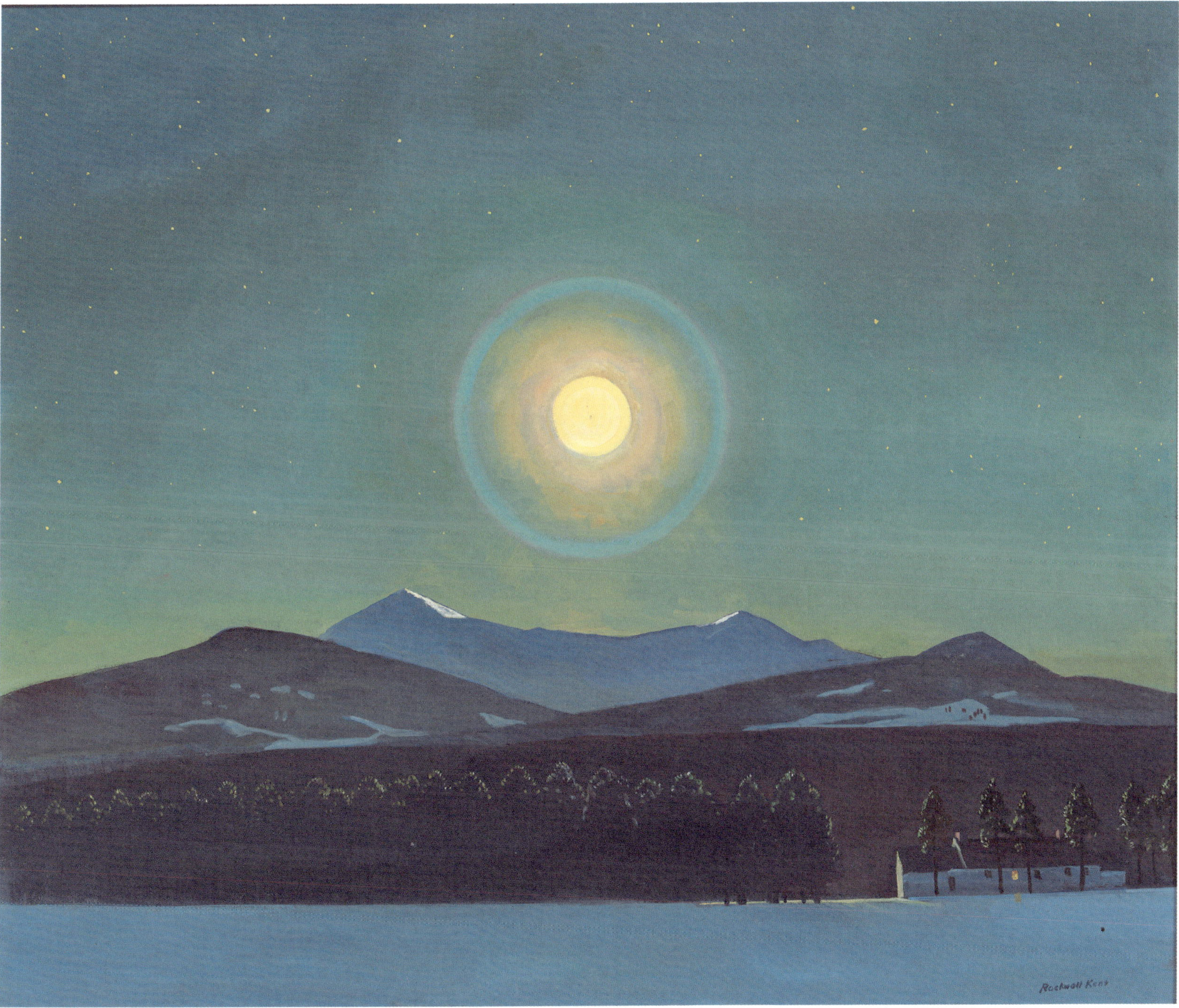
Rockwell Kent

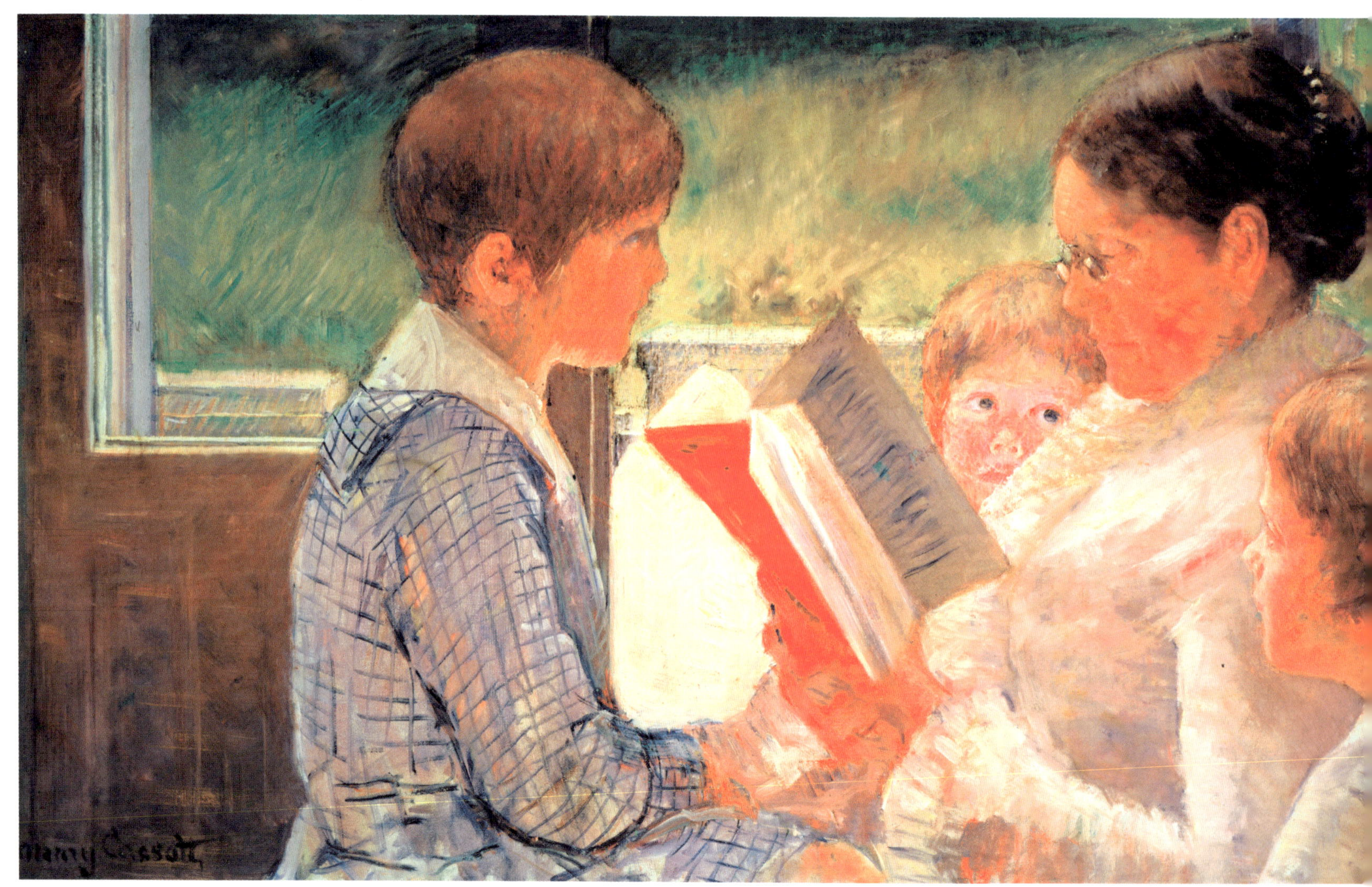

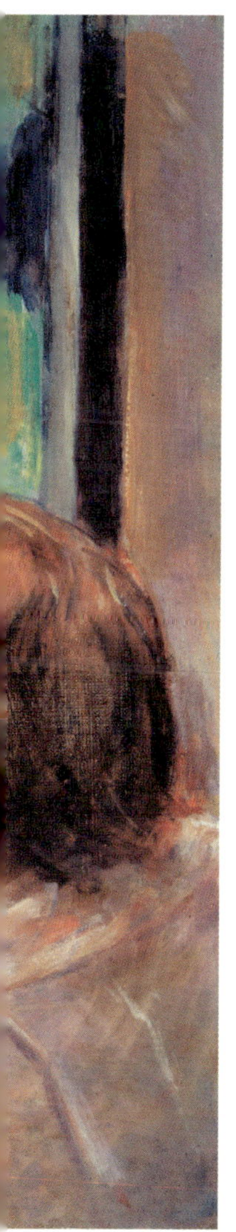

'A mother's happiness is like a beacon, lighting up the future but reflected also on the past in the guise of fond memories.'

Honoré de Balzac (1799–1850)

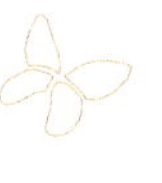

Mary Stevenson Cassatt,
Mrs Cassatt Reading to her Grandchildren, 1888

'Awake, my dear.
Be kind
to your sleeping heart.
Take it out
into the vast fields
of Light
And let it
breathe.'

Henri Martin,
The Nymphs in the Garden

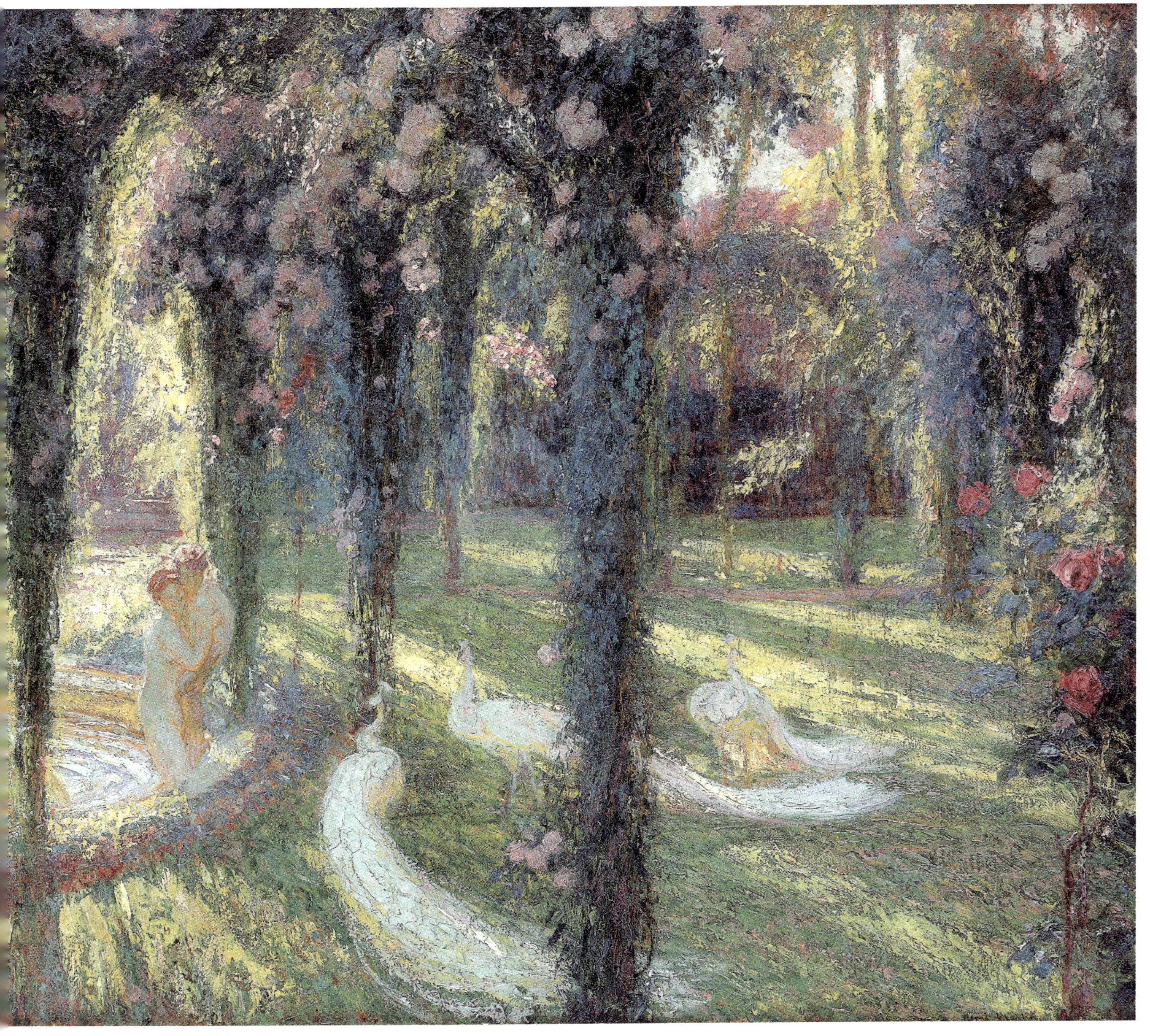

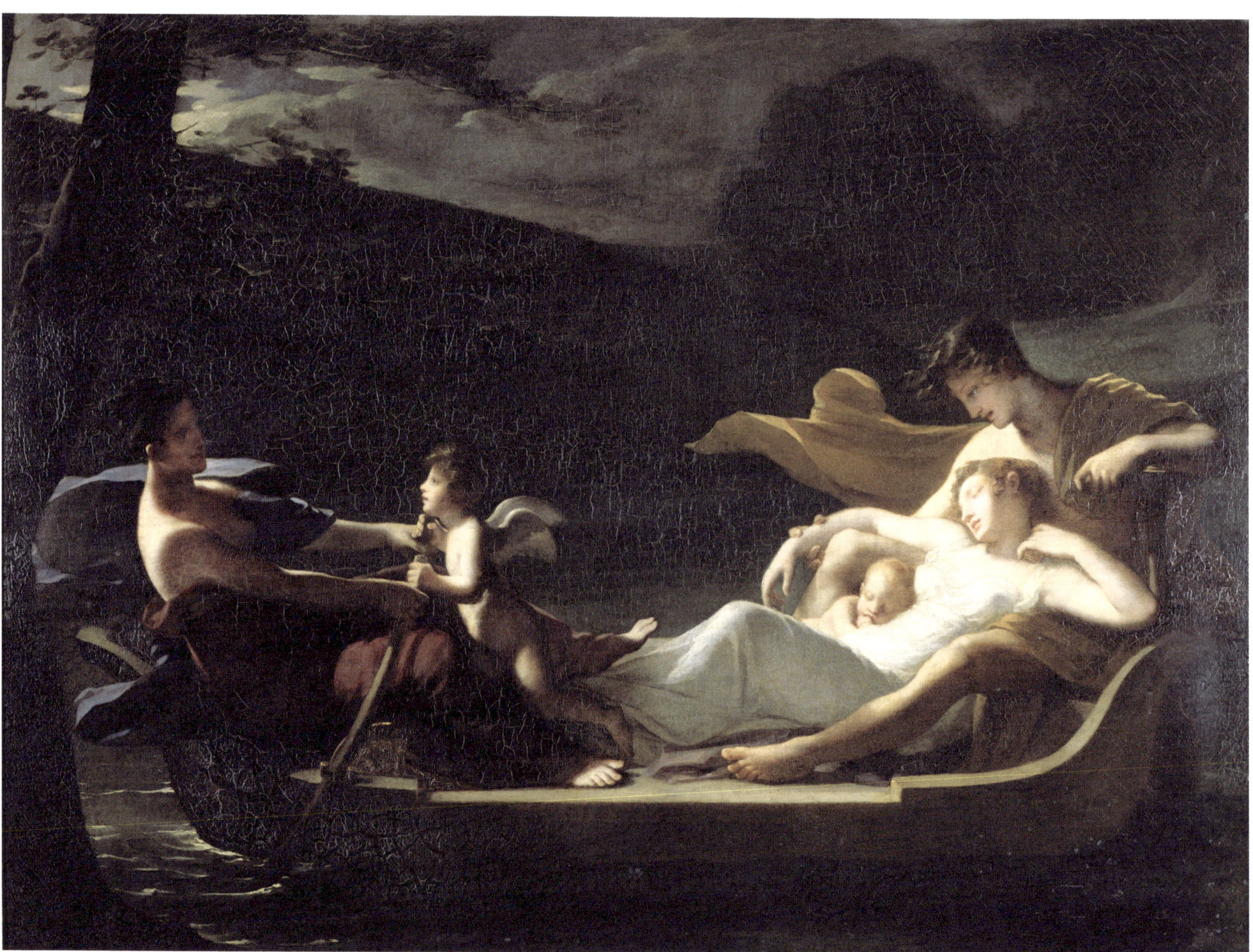

'In family life, love is the oil that eases friction,
the cement that binds closer together, and the
music that brings harmony.'

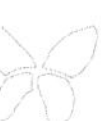

Constance Mayer,
The Dream of Happiness, 1819

'You are sublime; accept yourself
and delight in your beauty both
inside and out. Empower yourself
now; don't wait for tomorrow; you
will never be as gorgeous as you are
at this moment. Your body is both
your humble home and pleasure
dome; live in it fully and bask in the
glory of you!'

Lisa Azarmi, *Thoughts on Acceptance* (2022)

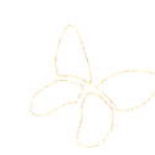

John William Waterhouse,
Hylas and the Nymphs, 1896

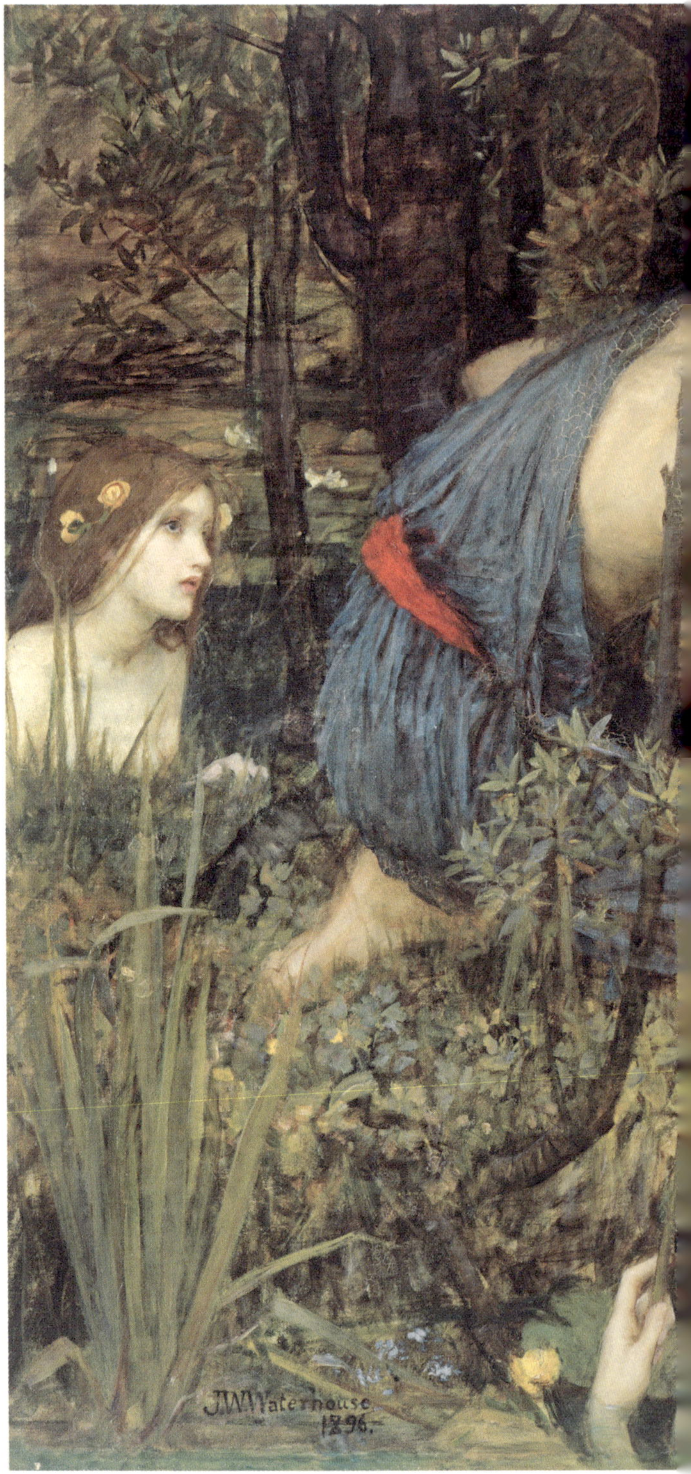

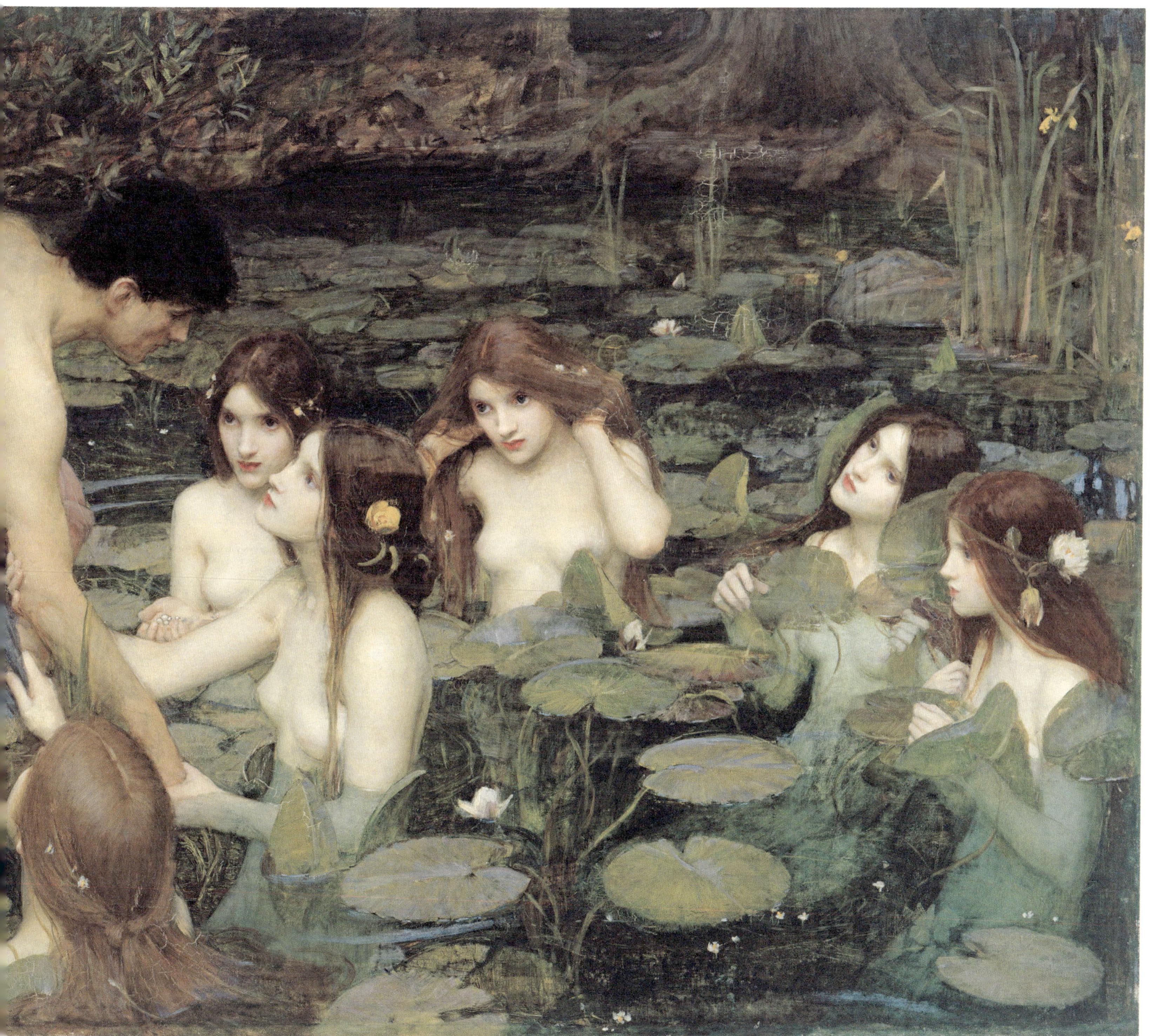

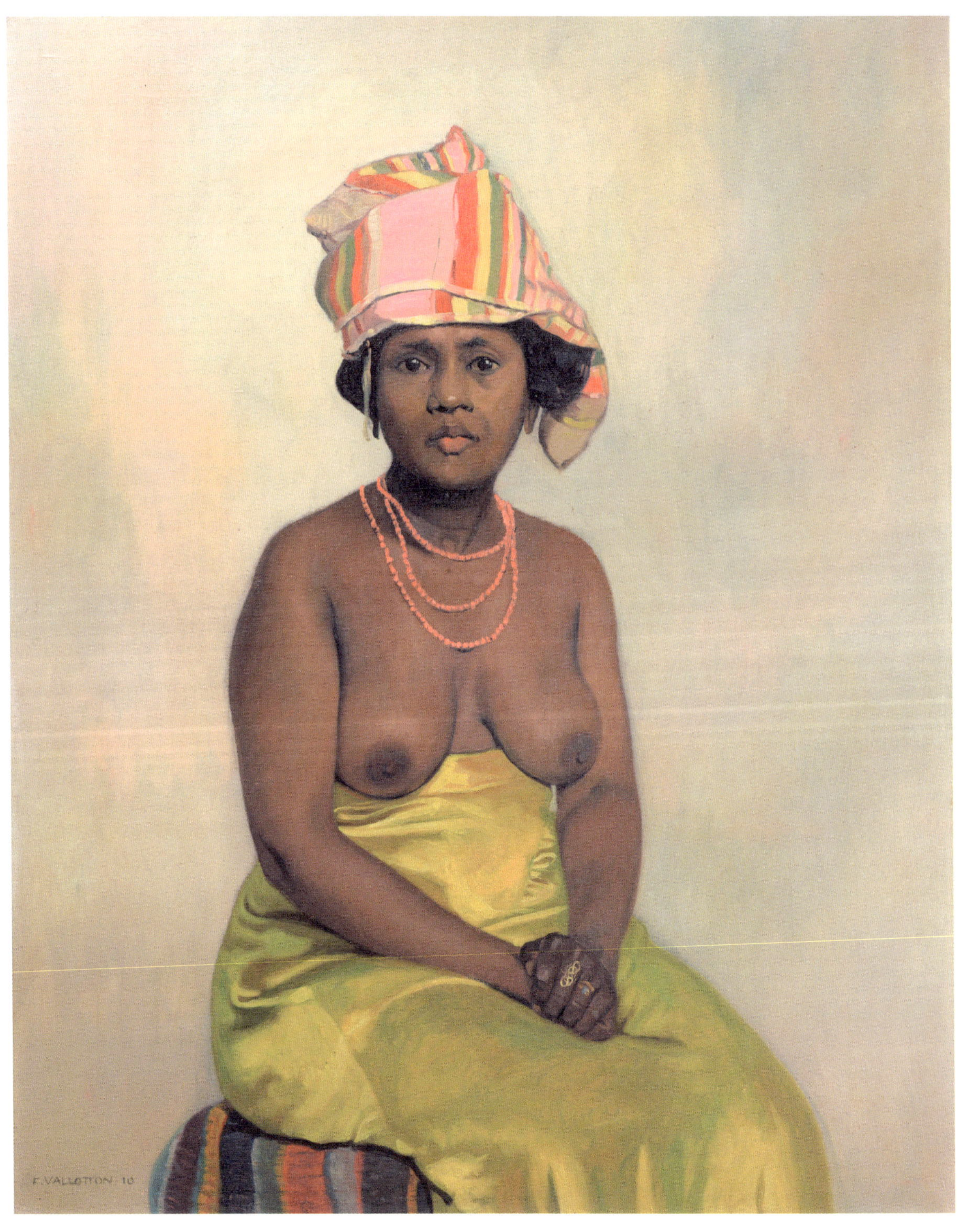
F. VALLOTTON 10

'Hold fast to dreams
For if dreams die
Life is a broken winged bird
That cannot fly.'

'I think of love, and you, and my heart
grows full and warm, and my breath
stands still … I can feel a sunshine
stealing into my soul and making it all
summer, and every thorn, a rose.'

Emily Dickinson, from *Letters of Emily Dickinson* (1894)

Herbert James Draper,
Pot Pourri, 1897

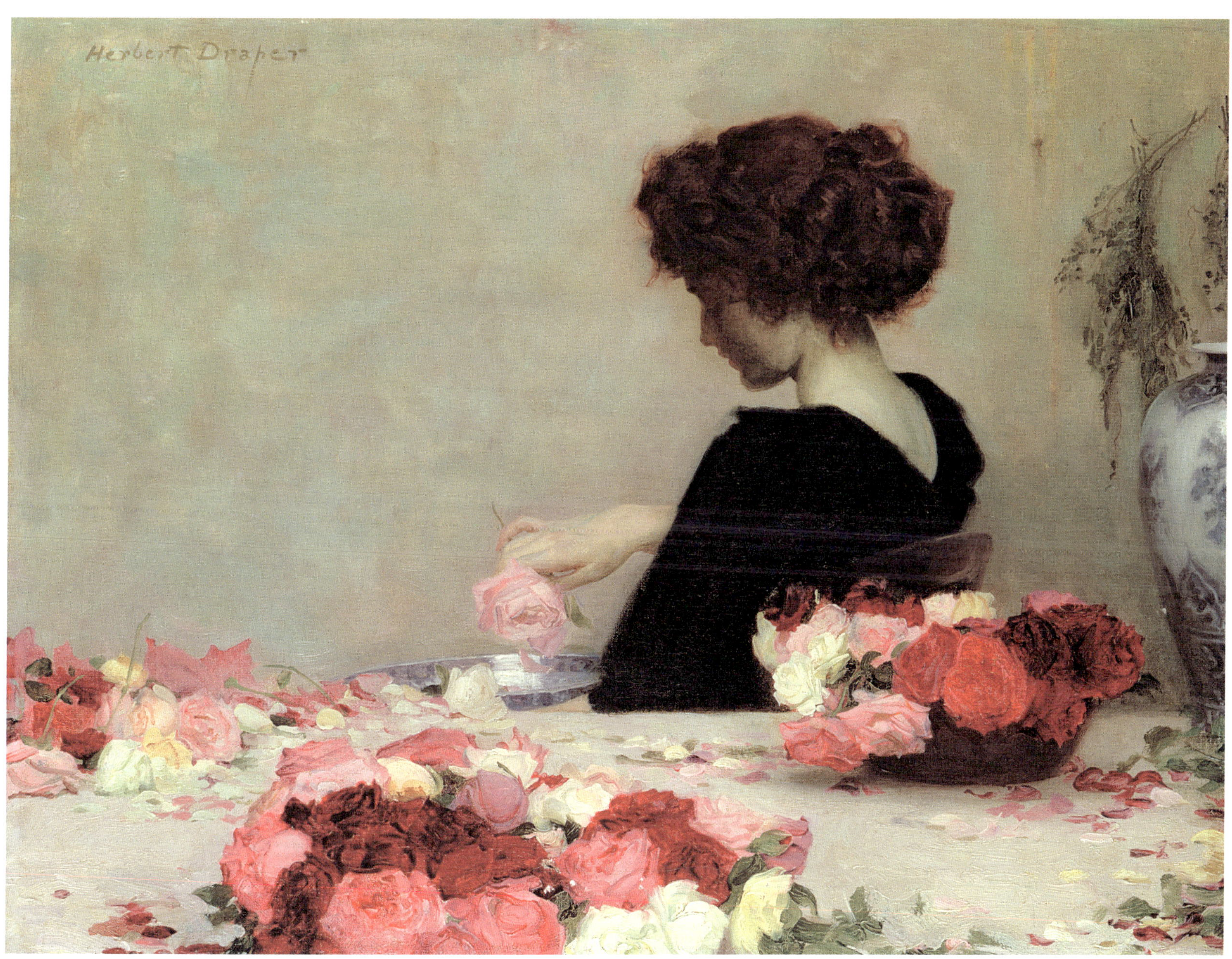
Herbert Draper

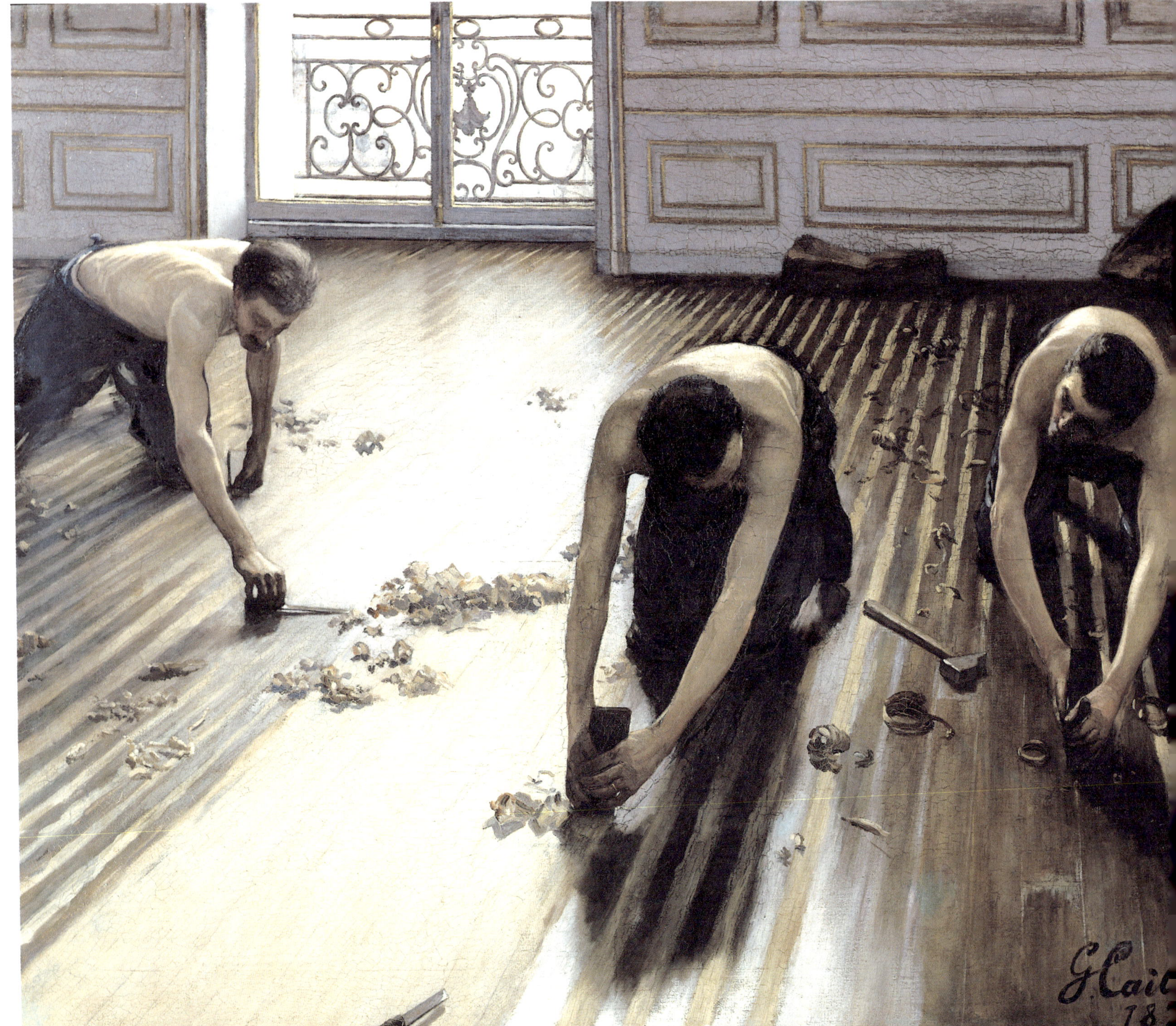

G Caill
187

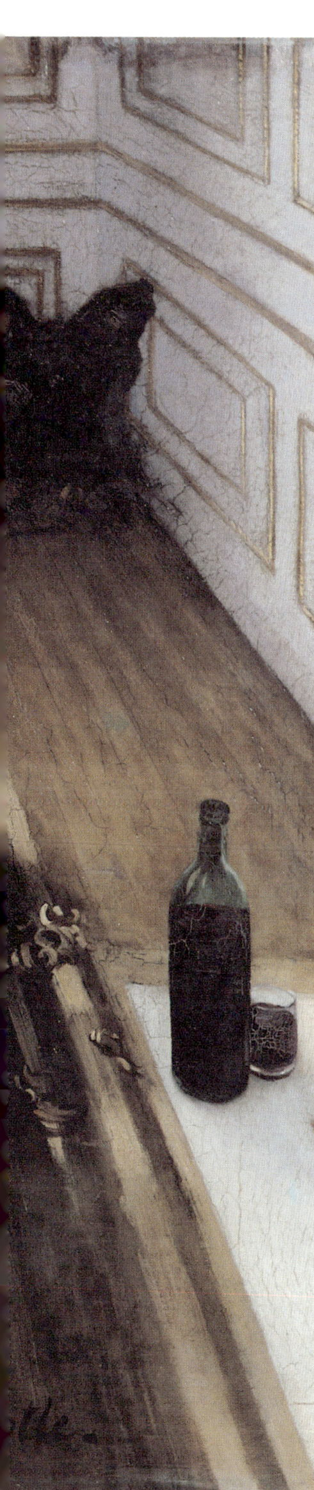

'Without labour, nothing prospers.'

Sophocles (c.496–c.406BCE)

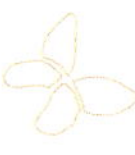

Gustave Caillebotte,
The Floor Scrapers, 1875

'Clouds come floating into my life, no
longer to carry rain or usher storm, but
to add colour to my sunset sky.'

Adrian Scott Stokes,
Sunset in a Wooded Landscape

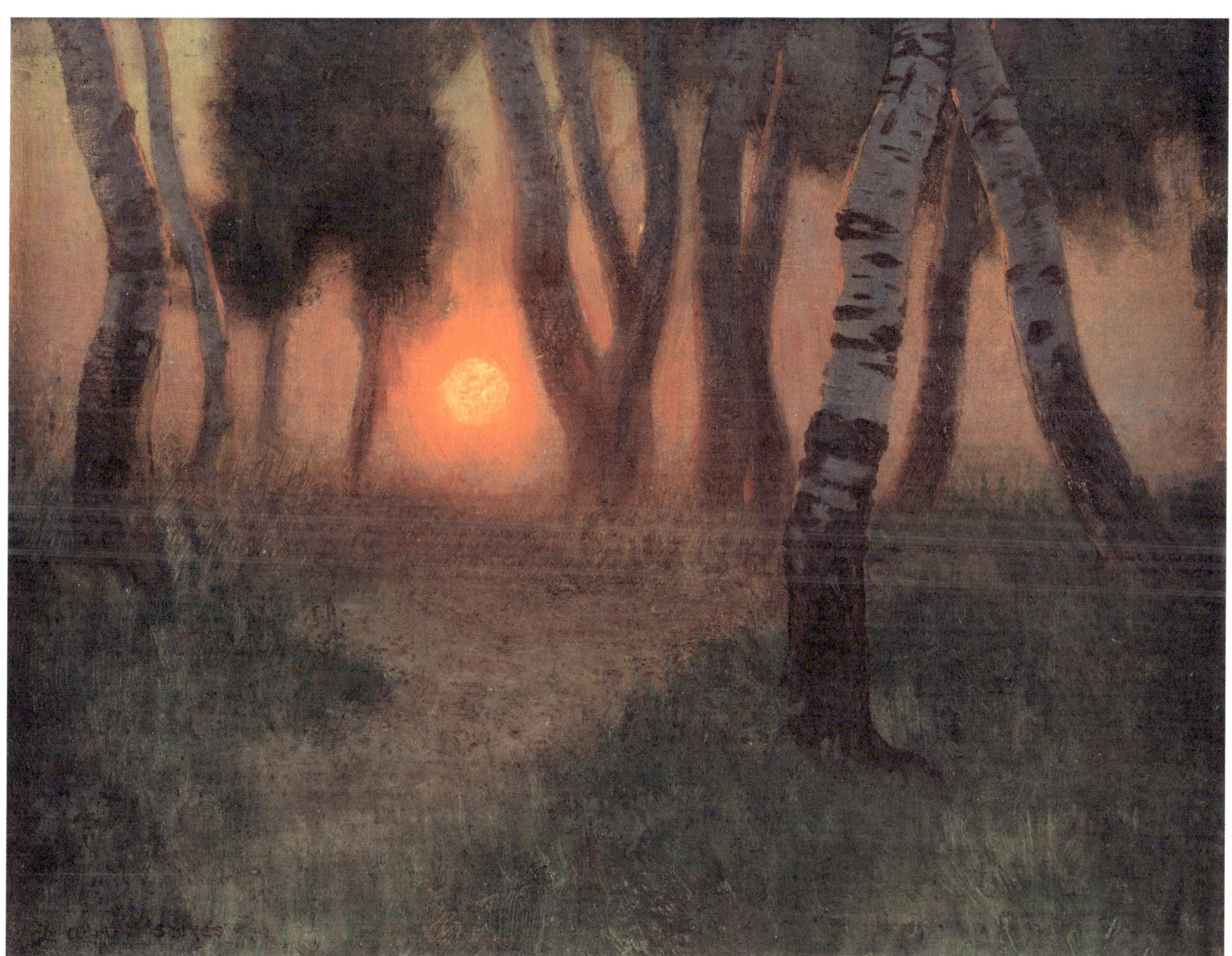

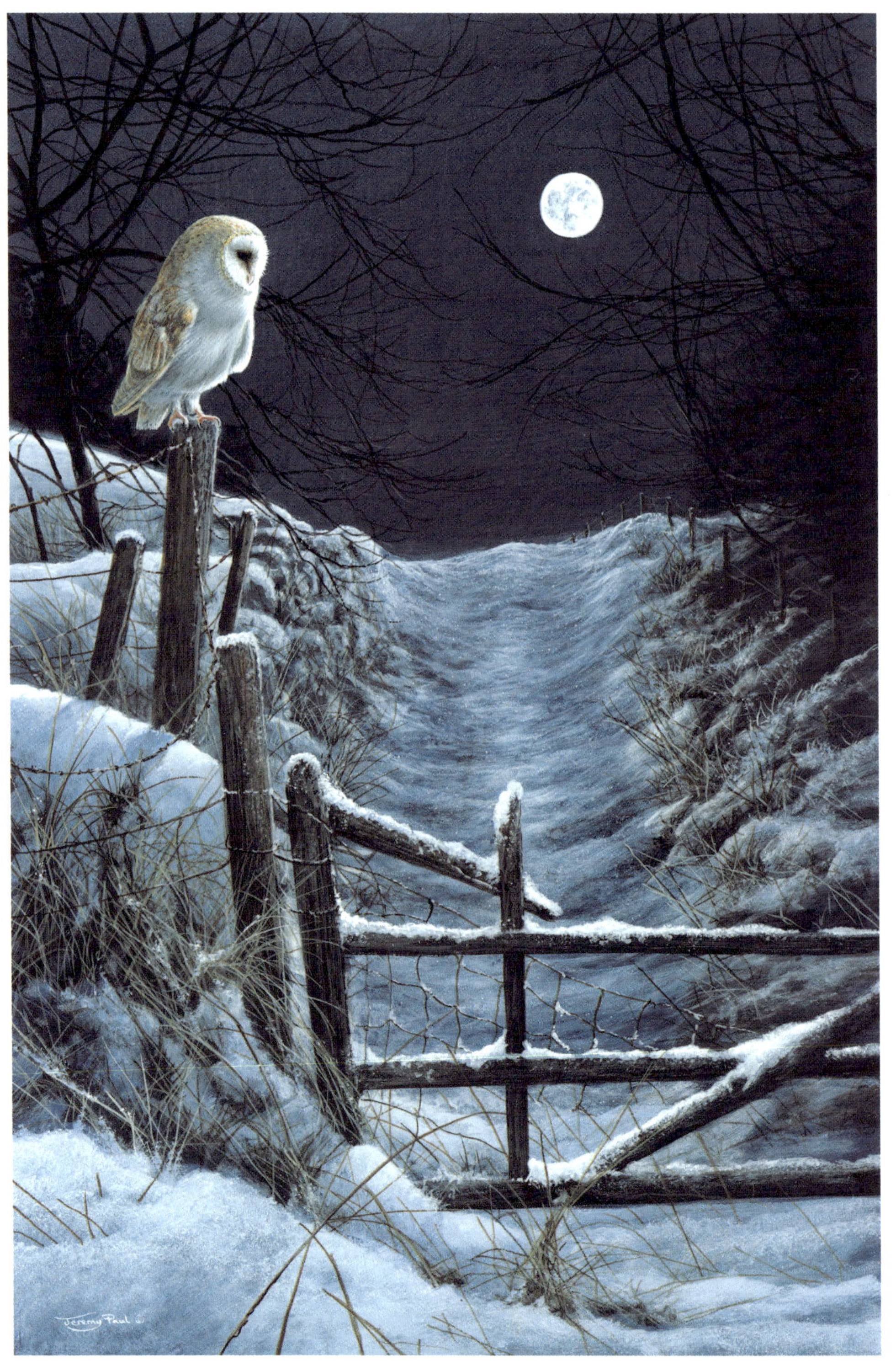

'Do not go gentle into that good night, Old age should burn and rave at close of day; Rage, rage against the dying of the light.'

Dylan Thomas, from *Do Not Go Gentle into that Good Night* (1947)

Jeremy Paul,
Moonlight – Barn Owl, 2013

Artist biographies

Abram Efimovich Arkhipov
1862–1930, Russia
Wanderers, Union of Russian Artists
Abram Efimovich Arkhipov was part of a group of artists
that appeared in the 1890s to replace the older generation
of 'peredvizhniki'; they were the primary creative force
in Russia between the 1870s and 1880s. Arkhipov often
painted the lives of Russian women. His realist paintings
were visceral, reflecting the harshness of social realism.
He counter-balanced this with lively paintings of peasant
women in rural Russia in vibrant traditional dresses and
national costumes. Like others in the Union of Russian
Artists, Arkhipov regularly painted en plein air and
painted scenes from the North of Russia.

Joaquin Sorolla y Bastida
1863–1923, Spain
Impressionism, Luminism
Joaquin Sorolla y Bastida was an energetic painter of
portraits, landscapes and monumental works of social
and historical themes; he captured the shimmering
luminosity of his homeland of Valencia, Spain.

Elisabeth Jerichau-Baumann
1819–1881, Poland/Denmark
Orientalism
Elisabeth Jerichau-Baumann travelled several times to
the Eastern Mediterranean and the Middle East. Being
a woman, she was able to gain access to the harems
of the Ottoman Empire and paint intimate scenes of
harem life. Her male contemporaries were forced to use
their imagination to paint such private scenes. Baumann
married art professor Jens Adolf Jerichau in 1846 and
they had nine children. Sadly, two died in infancy.
Several of their children became painters, and her
grandson J.A. Jerichau (1890–1916) was one of Denmark's
most talented modernist painters.

Jean Frédéric Bazille
1841–1870, France
Impressionism, en plein air
Jean Frédéric Bazille was a figure painter who mainly
painted in the open air, often placing the figure in the
landscape. He was inspired to paint by the works of
Eugène Delacroix, but his family only agreed to let him
study painting if he majored in medicine. After failing
his medical exams, he continued to paint full-time. His
close friends included Claude Monet, Alfred Sisley and
Édouard Manet. Bazille was generous with his wealth
and helped support his less fortunate associates by
giving them space in his studio and materials to use.

Sven Richard Bergh
1858–1919, Sweden
Naturalism, Swedish romantic nationalism
Sven Richard Bergh painted many landscapes and
portraits. He rejected Impressionism and plein-air painting
but spent some time at the artists' colony in France, Grez-
sur-Loing. In 1915, Bergh became the director of the Swedish
National Museum. He had an interest in psychology,
often incorporating it into his art, but the portraits of his
friends remain his most enduring paintings.

Paul-Albert Besnard
1849—1934, France
Academic, Impressionism
Paul-Albert Besnard was a student of the academic painter
Alexandre Cabanel. He won the Prix de Rome in 1874 and
was among the founders of the Société Nationale in 1890.
During the last thirty years of his life, he held significant
positions at the Académie de France in Rome, the École
des Beaux-Arts, the Académie française, the Académie
de Saint Luc and the Royal Academy. If you look closely
at the detail in his work, so much will reveal itself.

George Henry Boughton
1833—1905, Anglo-American
Painter, illustrator, writer
George Henry Boughton was born in Norfolk, England;
he was the son of a farmer. The family immigrated to the
United States in 1835, and he grew up in upstate New
York, where he began his career as a self-taught artist.
The Hudson River School of artists influenced him. In
1853, the American Art Union purchased one of his early
pictures, which financed six months of studying art in
England. Many of his portraits have a dream-like quality.
Boughton illustrated Nathaniel Hawthorne's *The Scarlet
Letter* and Henry Wadsworth's poems *Rip Van Winkle*
and *Sleepy Hollow*.

Amy Katherine Browning
1881—1978, Britain
Impressionism, en plein air
Amy Katherine Browning was one of eight children; her

parents encouraged her to paint. She was awarded a
scholarship to study at the Royal College of Art and was
tutored by Gerald Moira. She later went to Paris, where
she often painted en plein air. She was fascinated with
the complexities of painting sunlight. Browning went on
to teach at Camberwell, and Bromley and Beckenham
School of Art until the end of World War II. During the
war, she took in refugees and ran a Red Cross point.

Hans Ole Brasen
1849—1930, Denmark
Hans Ole Brasen was inspired to become an artist by
paintings of flowers his mother made as a young girl. He
later spent several summers in Sørup on Lake Esrom,
which became the luminous backdrop to many of his
paintings. His work is evocative and has a gentleness
about it. He won the Eckersberg Medal (an annual award
of the Royal Danish Academy of Fine Art) in 1894.

Gustave Caillebotte
1848—1894, France
Realism, Impressionism
Gustave Caillebotte graduated in law in 1868 and was
also an engineer. However, shortly after he graduated he
was drafted to fight in the Franco-Prussian War. Around
1874, Caillebotte met and befriended several artists
working outside the Académie des Beaux-Arts, including
Edgar Degas. Caillebotte made his debut in the second
Impressionist exhibition in 1876. His sizable allowance,
along with the inheritance he received after the death of
his parents, allowed him to paint without the pressure to

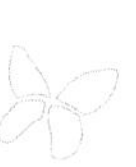

sell his work. It also allowed him to fund Impressionist exhibitions and support his fellow artists and friends by purchasing their works and even paying the rent for their studios. However, he was precise in his sponsorship; notably absent are works by Georges Seurat and Paul Gauguin. In 1890, he played a significant role in assisting Claude Monet in organising a public subscription and persuading the French state to purchase Édouard Manet's *Olympia* (1863).

Ramon Casas i Carbó
1866—1932, Spain
Modernism, Post Impressionism
Ramon Casas i Carbó was born in Barcelona to a wealthy Catalan family. Casas was a driven artist from a young age and abandoned his formal studies to become an apprentice in the studio of Joan Vicens. He later went to the Durand Academy in Paris, where he finished his formal training. Casas is best known for his sensitive portraits of women and for sketching and painting Barcelona, Paris and Madrid's intellectual, economic, and political elite. Casas was also an accomplished graphic designer; his posters and postcards helped to define modernism in Catalonia.

Mary Stevenson Cassatt
1844—1926, America
Impressionism, American Impressionism, Modernism, printmaking
Mary Stevenson Cassatt was born in Pennsylvania but spent much of her adult life in France, where she befriended Edgar Degas and Camille Pissarro and later exhibited with the Impressionists. She is best known for her studies of women and children in domestic environments. Cassatt was a feminist and advocate for women's rights, she never married and fought for equality in education. Later in life, Cassatt served as an advisor to several major art collectors and stipulated that they eventually donate their purchases to American art museums. She was awarded the Légion d'honneur in 1904 in recognition of her contribution to the arts.

Adriano Cecioni
1836—1886, Italy
Macchiaioli Group, caricaturist, critic, sculptor
Adriano Cecioni was part of the Macchiaioli, a group of Florentine painters who associated with the Barbizon school in France. Camille Corot and several other Barbizon members painted en plein air; this method later inspired the Impressionist painters. Cecioni liked to work outside, painting the world around him. He was interested in light, shade and colour.

Charles Courtney Curran
1861—1942, America
Impressionism
Charles Courtney Curran was a prolific painter who focused on women in landscapes, often bathed in sunlight. He attended art school in the US and later studied in Paris. Curran painted in the Impressionist style for his entire life, refusing to adapt his technique with the times. Curran and his wife were avid travellers, frequently

visiting Europe and even mainland China in 1936. The influences of his travels inspired his work in later life.

Elin Danielson-Gambogi
1861–1919, Finland
Realism
Elin Danielson-Gambogi was ten years old when her father, Karl Emil Danielson, committed suicide. Fortunately, she was supported and encouraged by her mother and brother, who was her long-term patron. Danielson-Gambogi was best known for her realist works and portraits. She was part of the first generation of Finnish women artists who received a professional art education, the so-called 'painter sisters' generation'. The group also included Helene Schjerfbeck (1862–1946), Helena Westermarck (1857–1938) and Maria Wiik (1853–1928).

Virginie Demont-Breton
1859–1935, France
Realism
Virginie Demont-Breton came from a family of distinguished painters and married the artist Adrien Demont in 1880. She served as President of the Union of Women Painters and Sculptors from 1895 to 1901. However, she resigned for a short period in 1892 due to a disagreement between her and the Union's community over what she saw as their unfair methods of voting. She also collaborated with Hélène Bertaux in a heroic effort to open the École des Beaux-Arts to women students, a goal achieved in 1897.

Herbert James Draper
1863–1920, Britain
Classicism
Herbert James Draper was a popular painter in the Victorian period. His allegorical works of Greek mythology are his most famous, but he was also known for his portraits. He beautifully captured pathos and drama.

Gustaf Fjaestad
1868–1948, Sweden
Rackstad Colony, craft, furniture design
Gustaf Fjaestad was an accomplished painter and craftsman and he assisted Bruno Liljefors at the Biological Museum in Stockholm. Fjaestad mainly painted scenes from nature and is particularly noted for his breathtaking winter landscapes. He also designed furniture for spaces, including the Thielska gallery. He co-founded the Rackstad Colony in 1898.

Jean-Hippolyte Flandrin
1809–1864, France
Neoclassical
Jean-Hippolyte Flandrin was the middle of three brothers, all painters. Hippolyte and Paul, his younger brother, settled in the studio of Jean Auguste Dominique Ingres, who became their tutor and friend for life. At first, Hippolyte struggled as a poor artist, but in 1832, he won the Prix de Rome. This prestigious scholarship meant that he was no longer limited by his poverty. Throughout his life, he painted several portraits and is also known for his monumental decorative paintings.

Frederick Carl Frieseke
1874—1939, America
Impressionism
Frederick Carl Frieseke spent most of his life as an
expatriate in France; he was an influential member of
the Giverny art colony. His work shows his fascination
with the effects of dappled sunlight. Most of his work
depicts the female form, nude or clothed, in harmony
with their surroundings.

Thomas Cooper Gotch
1854—1931, Britain
Pre-Raphaelite, Romanticism, plein air
Thomas Cooper Gotch created landscapes and portraits
using watercolours, oil and pastels. He founded the
Newlyn Industrial Classes and co-founded the Newlyn
Art Gallery, where he served on the committee for the
duration of his life. He married Caroline Burland Yates
and, with their daughter, Phyllis Marion Gotch, became
vital members of the Newlyn Art Colony. Can you feel
the warmth exuding from his painting?

Arthur Hacker
1858—1919, Britain
Classicism
Arthur Hacker was a versatile Victorian artist known
for his paintings of religious scenes, allegorical portraits,
landscapes and mythological subject matter. His work was
highly intricate, with complex narratives. In 1886, Hacker
helped to found the progressive New English Art Club.

Carl Vilhelm Holsøe
1863—1935, Denmark
Realism
Carl Vilhelm Holsøe studied at the Royal Academy in
Copenhagen, followed by the Kunstnernes Studieskoler
under Peder Severin Krøyer, the most highly esteemed
Danish artist of the time. Like his friend Vilhelm
Hammershøi, Holsøe is recognised for his atmospheric,
sparse interiors, which convey a sense of longing and
quiet, akin to Johannes Vermeer's Dutch masterpieces.

Harold Harvey
1874—1941, Britain
St Ives Modernist Movement, Impressionism,
Newlyn School
Harold Harvey, born in Penzance, Cornwall, moved to
Paris to attend the Académie Julian. On returning to
Cornwall, he immersed himself into en plein air painting;
his style became loose and free, sometimes verging on
the expressionist. Harvey was a vital member of the
Newlyn School and painted prolifically throughout
his life.

Martin Johnson Heade
1819—1904, America
Romanticism, realism
Martin Johnson Heade was a prolific painter known
for his romantic paintings of salt marsh landscapes,
seascapes, flora and fauna. Notice the exquisite detail on
the butterfly wing?

Edward Robert Hughes

1851–1914, Britain

Pre-Raphaelite, Aestheticism

Edward Robert Hughes was a painter of extraordinary imagination and skill; his subject matter has strong fantasy elements. Hughes was a vital member of the Pre-Raphaelite Brotherhood. He was also a studio assistant to Pre-Raphaelite Brotherhood founding member William Holman Hunt. Hunt suffered from glaucoma, and Hughes substantially contributed to several of Hunt's paintings.

John Atkinson Grimshaw

1836–1893, Britain

Aesthetic Movement

John Atkinson Grimshaw was a remarkably imaginative painter. His love for realism stemmed from a passion for photography, which would eventually lend itself to the creative process. Self-taught, he is known to have used a Camera obscura or lenses to project scenes onto canvas. Grimshaw demonstrated great skill with his use of colour, atmospheric lighting and shadow, and his ability to provoke strong emotional responses in the viewer. James McNeill Whistler, whom Grimshaw worked with in his Chelsea studios, stated, 'I considered myself the inventor of nocturnes until I saw Grimmy's moonlit pictures.'

Akseli Valdemar Gallen-Kallela

1865–1931, Finland

Romantic nationalism, Realism, Symbolism

Akseli Gallen-Kallela is best known for his illustrations of the *Kalevala*, the Finnish national epic. He captures the wild landscape, changing weather and seasons using a combination of strident and sensitive brushwork.

Hasui Kawase

1883–1957, Japan

Shin-hanga period, woodblock printing

Hasui Kawase was a significant landscape artist who specialised in printmaking. His work was inspired by his environment and is renowned for its serenity of mood and flawless composition. Born Bunjiro Kawase in Tokyo, Hasui Kawase was the son of a silk braid merchant. Unfortunately, his woodblocks and over 200 drawings were destroyed during an earthquake in 1923.

Rockwell Kent

1882–1971, America

Painting, printmaking, illustration, adventures

Rockwell Kent was best known as an artist and illustrator, although he had several other careers during his lifetime. His aunt Jo Holgate, an accomplished ceramicist, encouraged his creative ambitions. A transcendentalist and mystic in the tradition of Thoreau and Emerson, whose works he read, Kent found inspiration in the austerity and stark beauty of the wilderness. He said, 'I want the elemental, infinite thing; I want to paint the rhythm of eternity.' Kent rallied against fascism during World War II, and his political activism came to the fore in the latter part of the 1930s when he took part in several initiatives of the popular cultural front, including support for the Spanish Republic and the subsequent war against fascism. He was awarded the Lenin Peace Prize in 1967.

Dame Laura Knight

1877—1970, Britain

Impressionism, Newlyn School

Dame Laura Knight DBA, RA, RWS, was a prolific artist. She painted many subjects, from circus folk to designing a poster during World War II for the Women's Land Army. Laura (née Johnson) Knight met Harold Knight at art school; they became friends and married in 1903. In late 1907 the Knights moved to Newlyn, Cornwall before settling in the nearby village of Lamorna. Together with Lamorna Birch and Alfred Munnings, they became integral figures in the artist's colony known as the Newlyn School. In Newlyn, the Knights found themselves immersed in a vibrant group of artists, which appears to have allowed the more vivid and dynamic aspects of Laura's personality to come to the fore.

Peder Severin Krøyer

1851—1909, Norway

Realism, Impressionism

Peder Severin Krøyer (also referred to as P.S. Krøyer) was 14 years old when he enrolled at the Royal Academy of Fine Arts in Copenhagen. He was highly respected as a portrait painter and had many commissions. Krøyer helped Skagen grow as an artists' colony; he was fascinated with the town's life and portrayed the life of artists living there. He also painted many tranquil scenes of people walking along the beach and dining together. He was adept at capturing dreamy gardens, the evening atmosphere, and tranquil moonlit skies.

Sir John Lavery

1856—1941, Northern Ireland

Sir John Lavery RA, RSA, RHA, was best known for his society portraits and wartime depictions. His motivation to paint took him to Glasgow, where he tinted photographs to finance his art classes. There, Lavery befriended the artists known as the Glasgow Boys, with whom he shared an interest in subjects from modern life. He enjoyed great success after his move to London in 1896, where he combined his talents as a portrait painter with an interest in contemporary events. Lavery was knighted in 1918.

Henri Lebasque

1865—1937, France

Post-Impressionism, Fauvism

Henri Lebasque spent most of his career painting in the South of France with his friends Pierre Bonnard, Édouard Vuillard and Henri Matisse. His use of bold colours became more luminous and vibrant with time. Critics praised him for the intimacy of his subject matter and the joy in his use of paint. Lebasque was often referred to as 'the painter of joy and light' due to his ability to capture the shimmering scenes and lavish interiors of the French Riviera. He seamlessly transitioned between Post-Impressionism and Fauvism, simultaneously making bold and sensitive gestures with paint and colour. Look closely to see how expertly he captures that in his work.

Frederic Leighton
1830–1896, Britain
Pre-Raphaelite
Frederic Leighton, 1st Baron Leighton, PRA, known as
Sir Frederic Leighton, was a painter, draughtsman and
sculptor. His works depicted historical, biblical and
classical subject matter in an academic style. Leighton
travelled extensively around Europe, North Africa and
the Middle East. He designed the Arab Hall at Leighton
House, London, in 1877.

Frank Xavier Leyendecker
1876–1924, Germany
Illustrator, graphic artist, stained glass
Frank Xavier Leyendecker studied at the Académie
Julian in France before moving to Chicago with his
brother. He is known for his illustrations for posters,
magazines and advertisements. He also painted covers
for Street & Smith pulp magazines such as *People's
Favorite Magazine*, *The Popular Magazine*, and
Fawcett's pulp magazine *Battle Stories*. Unfortunately,
Leyendecker suffered from depression and poor health
from drug addiction.

Charles Sillem Lidderdale
1830–1895, Britain
Romantic
Charles Sillem Lidderdale exhibited 36 paintings at the
Royal Academy from 1856–1893 and demonstrated great
promise. His career was marred by eyesight trouble
which, after lengthy and skilful treatment by the oculist

Tirgolin Tweedy, yielded sufficiently to enable him to
continue his work. However, he was unable to continue
painting in watercolour.

Simon Maris
1873–1935, Netherlands
Hague School, Realism, Impressionism
Simon Maris was a student of his father, Willem Maris
and he studied at the Royal Academy of Fine Arts, The
Hague. In 1903, he travelled with his friend Piet Mondrian
and drew Mondrian's portrait in 1906. Maris enjoyed
painting portraits of women from around the world.

Henri Martin
1860–1943, France
Henri-Jean Guillaume 'Henri' Martin was elected to the
Académie des Beaux-Arts in 1917. He is known for his
early 1920s work on the walls of the Salle de l'Assemblée
générale, where the members of the Conseil d'État meet
in the Palais-Royal in Paris. His paintings are serene
and evocative, depicting the idyll of post-impressionist
landscapes.

Francesc Masriera
1842–1902, Spain
Orientalism, goldsmith
Francesc Masriera was born into a family of painters,
silversmiths and set designers. At thirteen, he
went to Geneva, where he studied enamelling and
painting. Masriera later travelled to London and Paris,

where he is thought to have worked in the studio of
Alexandre Cabanel.

Constance Mayer
1774—1821, France
Constance Mayer was a successful artist in her own
right, but, as was often the case with women artists
who were associated with better-known male artists,
there were claims that she produced only some of the
work attributed to her because of her long relationship
with Prud'hon. This confusion is mainly because the
two artists collaborated on several works: he sketched
the design, and she made the paintings. Many were
exhibited under her name, but when the works became
part of public collections, they were attributed to
Prud'hon. As pupil and tutor, their relationship was
complex. In many ways, they were more like peers.
When Prud'hon's wife died, Mayer expected that he
would marry her, but he did not. Prone to depression
throughout her life, Mayer committed suicide in 1821.
Prud'hon organised a retrospective of her works the
following year but was distressed by her death. They are
buried together in Paris's Père Lachaise Cemetery.

Amedeo Clemente Modigliani
1884—1920, Italy
Modernism, Surrealism
Amedeo Clemente Modigliani was an Italian painter and
sculptor who worked mainly in Paris. He is known for
his portraits and nudes of a modern style characterised
by the surreal elongation of faces, necks and figures. He
often painted the mother of his child, his muse and lover
Jeanne Hébuterne, depicting her with characteristically
hollow-looking eyes. Modigliani had a debauched lifestyle
and died tragically of tuberculosis at age thirty-four. The
day after Modigliani's death, Hébuterne was taken to her
parent's home, where inconsolable, she threw herself out
of a fifth-floor window, killing herself and her unborn child.

Claude Monet
1840—1926, France
Impressionism, Modern art
Claude Monet was the founder of Impressionist
painting and is credited for playing a significant role in
modernism. Monet attempted to paint scenes of ever-
changing light in nature in an attempt to capture the
fleeting moment. To achieve this, Monet would set his
easel up outside and paint en plein air. He'd often create
numerous paintings of the same image, most notably the
water lilies in his garden at Giverny.

Albert Joseph Moore
1841—1893, Britain
Pre-Raphaelite, Classical, Aestheticism
Albert Joseph Moore's early paintings were in the
Pre-Raphaelite style, but in the mid-1860s, with
inspiration taken from the Elgin Marbles, he turned to
classical subjects. A keen colourist of great sensitivity,
Moore often depicted women in a dream-like state,
bathed in beauty.

Evelyn De Morgan
1855—1919, Britain
Pre-Raphaelite Brotherhood, Symbolism, Aestheticism
Evelyn De Morgan, née Pickering, went against her gender
and upper-class upbringing to become one of the most
admirable artists of her generation. Her use of rich colour
exudes from the canvas and works beautifully with the
sweeping figures she often depicts. Messages of spirituality,
feminism, the de-glorification of war and the rejection of
consumerism make her work particularly relevant today.
In 1883, Evelyn met the Arts and Crafts ceramic designer
William De Morgan, whom she later married.

Berthe Morisot
1841—1895, France
Impressionism
Berthe Morisot was the first woman to join the
impressionists. She was part of the first exhibition where
the group called themselves 'impressionists' in 1877.
Women of this period did not go to bars or cafés alone,
therefore many of Morisot's subjects are in the home
or garden. Although successful in her lifetime, being a
female painter was still frowned upon and her work was
not fully appreciated until years later.

Alphonse Mucha
1860—1939, Czech Republic
Art Nouveau, illustration, graphic artist, decorative art
Alfons Maria Mucha, known as Alphonse Mucha, was a
Czech artist who lived in Paris during the Art Nouveau
period. His distinctive, highly decorative, flowing, and
organic style is evident in his work. Mucha worked on
allegoric themes depicting beautiful images of women in
many guises. His use of colour was sumptuous.

Edvard Munch
1863—1944, Norway
Expressionism, Symbolism
Edvard Munch focused much of his creative agenda
on the human condition, mortality, chronic illness,
sexual liberation, and religious aspiration. He seemingly
extracted emotion from the subject through some portal,
transcribing what he discovered onto canvas. His rich,
effervescent colour palette is evident in much of his work.

William Nicholson
1872—1949, Britain
Realism, woodcuts, printmaking, illustrator
Sir William Newzam Prior Nicholson was a painter
of still life and portraits. He was also a theatre
designer, illustrator and author of children's books. He
concentrated on woodblock, engraving and lithography
for his book design and illustration. He was the father
of sculptor Ben Nicholson and famously gave Winston
Churchill painting classes.

Maxfield Parrish
1870—1966, America
Illustrator
Maxfield Parrish was a prolific illustrator and artist. He
is noted for his distinctive saturated hues and idealised

neo-classical imagery. His career spanned fifty years and was wildly successful. The National Museum of American Illustration deemed his painting *Daybreak* (1922) the most successful art print of the 20th century.

Jeremy Paul

Born 1954, Britain
Realism
Jeremy Paul had a successful career in marine biology before becoming a professional wildlife painter. Drawn to wild and natural environments, he's travelled and worked extensively in Spain, Scotland, India, Africa, North America, Antarctica and the Arctic. His paintings celebrate the diverse majesty of the world's ecosystem and the beauty around us.

Georg Vilhelm Pauli

1855—1935, Sweden
Opponenterna Group, author
Georg Vilhelm Pauli was a Swedish painter known primarily for portraits and figures. He was also the author of numerous art-related books. Pauli was opposed to the teaching methods at the Royal Academy.

Paul Ranson

1864—1909, France
Les Nabis, Symbolism
Paul Ranson was a painter and writer and also performed and directed plays. Fascinated by theosophy, magic and the occult, his paintings often depicted scenes full of mythology, witchcraft and anti-clerical subjects. His colour palette was opulent, adding to the feel of mystery.

Pierre-Auguste Renoir

1841—1919, France
Impressionism, Modern Art
Pierre-Auguste Renoir celebrated beauty through his work, and especially feminine sensuality, it has been said that 'Renoir is the final representative of a tradition which runs directly from Rubens to Watteau.'

Ilya Yefimovich Repin

1844—1930, Ukraine
Ilya Yefimovich Repin learned his trade as an apprentice from an icon painter called Bunakov. In 1864, Repin went to the Academy of Fine Arts, St Petersburg, and in 1871 he won an academy scholarship that enabled him to visit France and Italy. In 1894, Repin became a professor of historical painting at the academy in St Petersburg. Look at the depth of skin tone he's captured in the portrait.

Briton Rivière

1840—1920, Britain
Watercolourist
Briton Rivière was a British artist of Huguenot descent. He exhibited various paintings at the Royal Academy and focused much of his life on animal paintings.

Georges Rochegrosse

1859—1938, France

Orientalism, Academic Art

Georges-Antoine-Marie Rochegrosse painted in the historic decorative style. Many of his paintings were epic in scale and subject matter. He revelled in detail, which enables the viewer to submerge into the picture.

Henri Rousseau

1844—1910, France

Post-Impressionism, Naïve, Primitive, Fauve, avant-garde

Henri J.F. Rousseau was also known as Le Douanier, the 'Customs Officer', due to his occupation as a tax collector before becoming a full-time artist at the age of forty-nine. Rousseau was often ridiculed throughout his life, but he went on to influence generations of avant-garde artists.

John Singer Sargent

1856—1925, America

Impressionism, American Renaissance

John Singer Sargent was born in Italy and died in London. He was the leading portrait painter of his generation. Later in life, he stopped taking commissions for society portraits and sought inspiration from his travels around Europe. Sargent made over nine hundred oil paintings, two thousand watercolours and countless drawings and sketches. Much of his early work represents the luxury of the Edwardian era and his later work is an homage to light. Sargent was a lifelong bachelor with a wide circle of influential friends. Scholars theorised he was a private, complex and passionate man whose homosexual identity was integral to shaping his art.

Dorothea Sharp

1874—1955, Britain

Impressionism

Dorothea Sharp had an impressionistic and loose style, giving her paintings an air of spontaneity. It is clear to see the impact and lasting effect that the work of Claude Monet had on her practice. In 1908, she became a member of the Society of Women Artists and was one of Britain's most influential female artists during the 20th century. She spent much of her career in Bosham and St Ives, Cornwall, where the changing light, sea and countryside played a significant role in her work.

Giuseppe Signorini

1857—1932, Italy

Orientalism

Giuseppe Signorini was a master of watercolour, specialising in North African and Near Eastern scenes. He popularised 'Islamic' themes during the 1880s, organising masquerades, festivals and parades. He was also an avid collector of Islamic objects, carpets and textiles.

Léon Spilliaert

1881—1946, Belgium

Symbolism, graphics

Léon Spilliaert was born in the coastal town of Ostend. He moved to Brussels at the age of twenty. Self-taught,

he developed an independent style and was inspired by poets and philosophers including Edgar Allan Poe and Friedrich Nietzsche. Spilliaert explored the relationship of the self with solitude; he often placed the subject in the nighttime, which created an eerie sense of being.

Harald Oskar Sohlberg

1869—1935, Norway

Neo-romanticism, Modernism, Symbolism, Realism

Harald Oskar Sohlberg sought inspiration from local scenes where he captured the ever-changing northern light. His unique colour pallet and tonal range impressed his contemporaries. His work captures an air of mystery and magic, tempting the viewer out beyond the horizon.

Catrin Welz-Stein

Germany

Digital art, illustration

Catrin Welz-Stein was born in Weinheim, Germany. In 2009 she started creating digital art by combining historical paintings, curiosities and fairytale illustrations into surreal and sensual images. Her work has magical and familiar qualities that lead the viewer deep into their imagination.

Adrian Scott Stokes

1854—1935, Britain

St Ives Group, Skagen Painters, author

Charles Adrian Scott Stokes was a prolific landscape painter concerned with atmospheric effects. Born in Southport, Lancashire, he became a cotton broker in Liverpool, where John Herbert RA noticed his artistic talent. The latter advised him to submit his drawings to the Royal Academy. He entered the Royal Academy Schools in 1872 and exhibited there from 1876. He won medals at the Paris Exhibition and Chicago World Fair in 1889 and became ARA in 1909 and RA in 1919. He became the first President of the St Ives Society of Arts and later the Vice President of the Royal Watercolour Society. He was also the author of *Landscape Painting* (1925).

Franz von Stuck

1863—1928, Germany

Symbolism, Art Nouveau

Franz von Stuck was a sculptor, printmaker, and architect. Stuck was best known for his paintings of ancient mythology and magical themes. He was awarded the Order of Merit of the Bavarian Crown and was henceforth known as Franz Ritter von Stuck.

Frits Thaulow

1847—1906, Norway

Impressionism

Frits Thaulow studied art in Denmark and Germany. In 1879, he travelled to Skagen, Denmark's northernmost town, and painted seascapes, landscapes and scenes of marine life. He was particularly interested in capturing the play of light on water. In 1892, he moved to Paris, where he met Auguste Rodin and Claude Monet, both artists with considerable influence. He enjoyed painting in small French towns as opposed to Paris, often seeking

out water in one form or another. Thaulow was inducted
into the French Legion of Honour for his artistic
accomplishments and received several other awards.

Henri de Toulouse-Lautrec

1864—1901, France

Post-Impressionism, Art Nouveau

Comte Henri Marie Raymond de Toulouse-Lautrec-
Monfa was an aristocratic-born painter, printmaker,
draughtsman, caricaturist and illustrator. His immersion
in Paris's colourful and theatrical life in the late
nineteenth century allowed him to produce a collection
of enticing and provocative images of bohemian Paris. He
broke both his legs around his adolescence and, due to
the rare condition pycnodysostosis, was very short as an
adult. He was an alcoholic and developed an affinity for
brothels and prostitutes, the subject matter for many of
his works.

Henry Scott Tuke

1858—1929, Britain

Newlyn School, Impressionism

Henry Scott Tuke was primarily a painter but also
a photographer and is best known for his paintings
of bathing scenes. During the 1880s, Tuke met Oscar
Wilde, John Addington Symonds, and many other poetic
luminaries. Tuke wrote a 'Sonnet to Youth', published
anonymously in *The Artist*, and also contributed an
essay to *The Studio*. Often painting in the open air, he
went against fashion, favouring immediate, strong brush
strokes rather than the more popular slick finish.

John William Waterhouse

1849—1917, Britain

Academic Style, Pre-Raphaelite

John William Waterhouse began working in the
Academic Style and later embraced the Pre-Raphaelite
Brotherhood's ethos. He is remembered for his intricate
detail and depiction of women from ancient Greek
Mythology, Arthurian Legend and poetry. Each of his
paintings brims with allegory and narrative.

James Thomas Watts

1853—1930, Britain

Pre Raphaelite, plein air

James Thomas Watts was deeply moved by the writings
of John Ruskin and the work of the Pre-Raphaelites.
His kinship with nature and fascination with portraying
realism in landscape painting resonates with Ruskinian
principles. He was seduced by the play of light in
woodland settings and painted en plein air at varying
times of the day, and he tried to capture the changing
seasons. He took his inspiration from North Wales,
Liverpool, and Lancashire landscapes.

Edwin Lord Weeks

1849—1903, America

Orientalism

Edwin Lord Weeks was a painter and explorer and avid
traveller. He was a pupil of Léon Bonnat and Jean-
Léon Gérôme in Paris. He made many voyages to the
East and Near East and focused on painting oriental
scenes. In 1895, he wrote and illustrated a book of travels,

From the Black Sea through Persia and India, and two years later, he published *Episodes of Mountaineering*. He was a member of the Légion d'honneur, an officer of the Order of Saint Michael, and a member of the Munich Secession.

Félix Édouard Vallotton
1865—1925, Switzerland/France
Les Nabis, printmaking, woodcuts, painting
Félix Édouard Vallotton was an essential figure in the development of the modern woodcut. He painted portraits, landscapes, nudes, still lifes and other subjects in an unemotional, realistic style. His vibrant use of colour defined his paintings. By contrast, his prints are characterised by broad masses of black and white with minimal detail. They include street scenes, bathers, portraits and a series of ten interiors titled 'Intimités' (Intimacies) that portray charged domestic encounters between men and women.

Jean-Édouard Vuillard
1868—1940, France
Les Nabis, Symbolism
Jean-Édouard Vuillard moved to Paris in 1877; he became a student at the École des Beaux-Arts in 1886, later moving to the Académie Julian, where he met Pierre Bonnard. Together with fellow artists Maurice Denis and Paul Sérusier, they founded Les Nabis in 1889. The Nabis focused on vibrant colour, pattern and distortion to emphasise psychological meanings beyond the appearance of ordinary subjects.

Hiroshi Yoshida
1876—1950, Japan
Woodblock prints, painting
Hiroshi Yoshida was a successful printmaker and won several prestigious awards. After the Great Kanto Earthquake of 1923, he travelled to the United States and Europe, painting and selling his work. When he returned to Japan in 1925, he started his workshop and focused on landscapes inspired by his travels abroad and in Japan. His work is a refreshing mix of Western aesthetics coupled with traditional Japanese techniques. Drawn to the tranquil moments of nature, his woodblock prints exude tranquillity, invite meditation and bring calm.

Paul Ranson,
Pommier aux Fruits Rouges, 1902

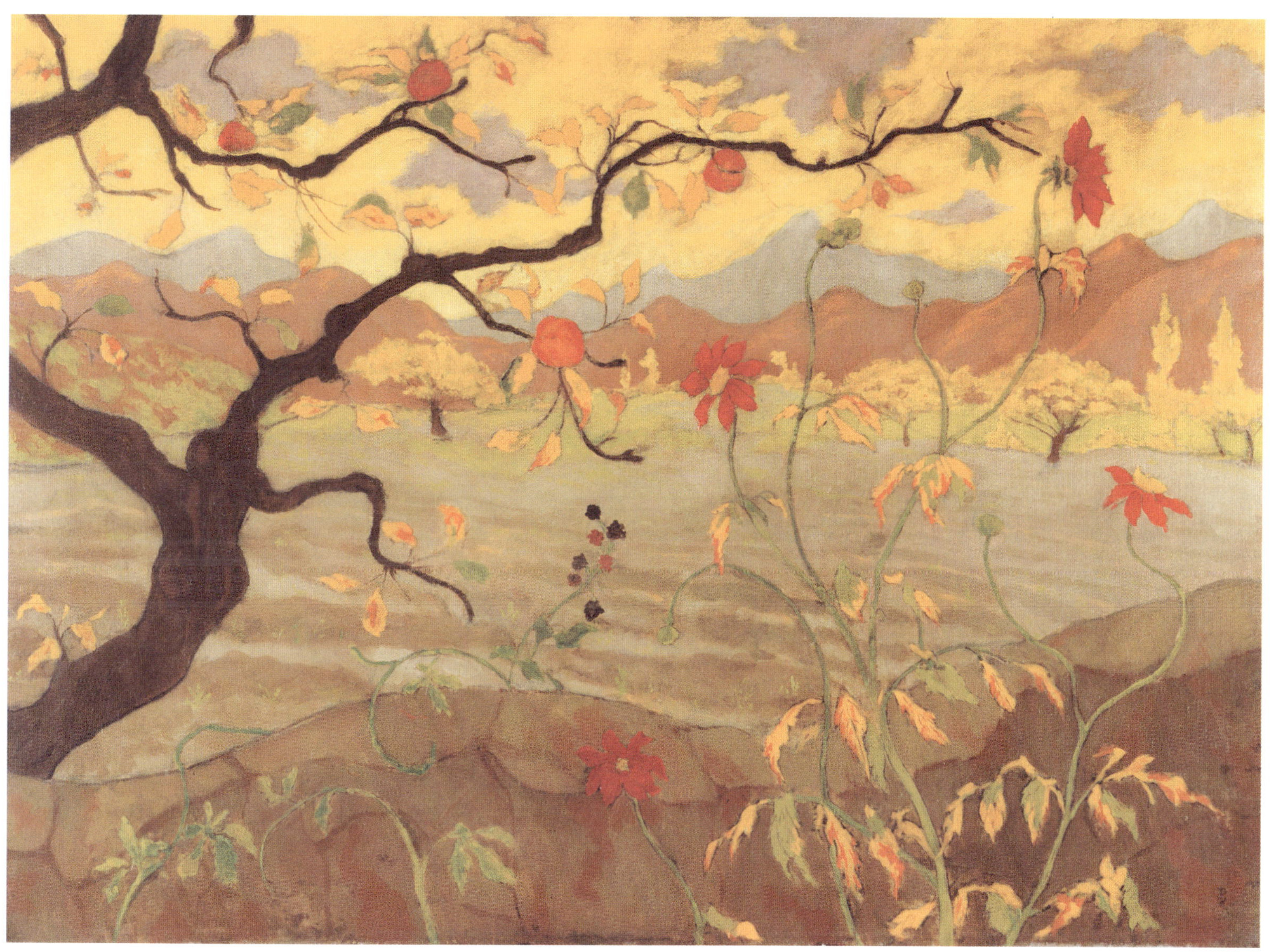

Index of artists

Index of writers

General index

Acknowledgements

Wendell Berry, from *The Peace of Wild Things*, Penguin, 2018. © Wendell Berry/Penguin Random House/Abner Stein Ltd.

Dale Carnegie, from *How to Win Friends and Influence People*, Vermilion, 1936. © Dale Carnegie, Penguin Random House Ltd.

Charles 'Charlie' Chaplin, from *My Autobiography*, Penguin Classics, 2003. © Charles Chaplin, Penguin Random House Ltd.

Masaru Emoto, from *The Secret Life of Water*, Scribner, 2003. © Masaru Emoto, Sunmark Publishing.

Aldous Huxley, from *Island*. Copyright © 1962 by Aldous Huxley. Reprinted by permission of Georges Borchardt, Inc., on behalf of the Estate of Aldous Huxley.

Langston Hughes, 'Dreams', from *The Collected Poems of Langston Hughes*, Alfred A. Knopf, 2002. Reprinted by kind permission of David Higham Associates Ltd.

Carl Jung, from *Modern Man in Search of a Soul*, Routledge Classics, 1933. Reproduced by permission of Taylor & Francis Group.

Dr Elisabeth Kübler-Ross, from *Death: The Final Stage of Growth*, 1974. Reproduced by permission of Elisabeth Kubler-Ross Family Limited Partnership.

Laurie Lee, *As I Walked Out One Midsummer Morning*, © The Estate of Laurie Lee, Penguin Random House.

Seán O'Casey, from *Red Roses for Me*, 1943. © The Estate of Sean O'Casey.

Arundhati Roy, from *The Cost of Living*, Vintage Canada, 1999.

Dylan Thomas, 'Do Not Go Gentle into that Good Night', from *The Collected Poems of Dylan Thomas*, Weidenfeld & Nicholson, 1947. Courtesy of The Dylan Thomas Trust.

Frank Lloyd Wright. © Frank Lloyd Wright Foundation.

B.T. Batsford is committed to respecting the intellectual property rights of others. We have therefore taken all reasonable efforts to ensure that the reproduction of all contents on these pages is done with the full consent of the copyright owners. If you are aware of unintentional omissions, please contact the company directly so that any necessary changes may be made for future editions.

Picture credits

'Beauty is truth, truth beauty,—that is all
Ye know on earth, and all ye need to know.'

John Keats, from *Ode on a Grecian Urn*, 1819

For my scrumptious children Oliver-Bizhan, Caspian,
Anousheh and Cosmos the wonder dog.

With huge thanks to Amelia Costley for her stellar design work, and to
Maryann Morris, Emilia Barclay, Piers Russell Cobb, John Honney, mum,
dad, my brother Giles and all my family, friends and Ravenous Butterflies
followers around the world — this is for you!

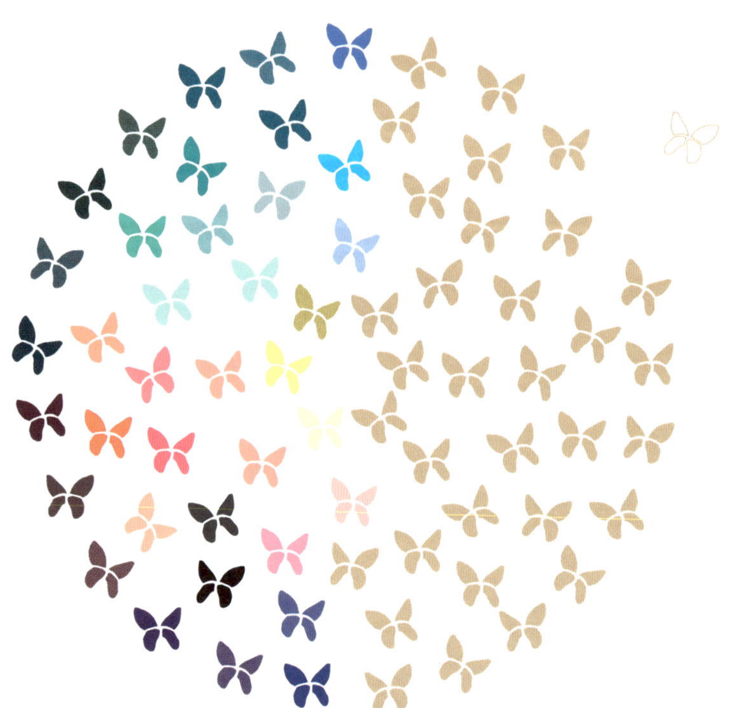